Air Power and National Security: India's Air Force Evolution, Growth and Future

Air Power and National Security:
India's Air Force Evolution, Growth and Future

Capt. (Retd.) Prem Singh

PRASHANT PUBLISHING HOUSE
DELHI-110094

Published by :
Prashant Publishing House
C-34, 28 Foota Road, Gali-3,
West Karwal Nagar, Delhi-110094
Phone : 011-22963970, Mob. : 9810396373
e-mail.: prashantpublishinghouse@gmail.com

Air Power and National Security: India's Air Force Evolution, Growth and Future

First Published 2017

ISBN 978-93-80565-2-55

PRINTED IN INDIA
Published by Mr. R.K. Jha M/s Prashant Publishing House and Published at H.S. Offset House Press, Delhi.

Contents

Preface

For democracies like India, Air power is uniquely suited to provide credible deterrence and play a major role in case of deterrence failure. There are numerous examples in IAF's history when application of air power for lethal or non-lethal effect has contributed immensely in altering the balance and ensuring speedy victory in condition, which would have otherwise precipitated into long drawn battles and even loss of territory. As IAF nears the completion of 81 years of its existence, it prepares to transform itself into a strategic air force with cutting edge technology and precise firepower.

The Royal Indian Air Force (RIAF) went into action shortly after independence in 1947. In a bid to gain control of the erstwhile principality of Jammu and Kashmir (J&K), Pathan tribesmen, armed and aided by Pakistan, poured into Kashmir . They went into a frenzy, killing, ransacking and pillaging as they advanced to Srinagar. Unable to turn the tide of the conflict, the Maharajah, who until then had vacillated over joining either India or Pakistan, appealed to the Indian government for assistance. Within hours of his signing the Instrument of Accession, the first Indian troops were airlifted to Srinagar . It was a remarkable achievement at such short notice.

In the process of transforming itself, IAF is witnessing a paradigm shift in operational planning and force level considerations. The approach has shifted from being 'platform-based' to being entirely 'capability based'. Effects based operational planning has replaced the strike packaging based on Over Target Requirements (OTR). Our operations are rapidly migrating to a network centric construct while the upcoming combat platforms will possess swing role capabilities.

The most obvious and significant opportunity is already before us i.e. the modernisation plan. Ideally, modernisation should be evolutionary and continuous. Yet, for a variety of reasons, the IAF has in the past modernised in spurts, often as a reaction to circumstances. Today, the IAF is in the throes of a most comprehensive modernisation—we can call it transformational, for it will change everything dramatically. Being based on long-term perspective plans, most of it is already crystallised. Yet, a lot remains to be determined; many new capabilities are still short of the decision stage. At this juncture, if we are able to synchronise these plans with national security objectives, we would really have utilised this opportunity well. From that arises another opportunity that must be seized and that is the formal enunciation of long-term national security objectives, strategies, as well as technology roadmap and indigenisation strategies.

The IAF today is in the process of a most comprehensive modernisation plan. Over the next few years, the force would induct more Su-30 MKI aircraft, the Light Combat Aircraft (LCA) and the Medium Multi Role Combat Aircraft (MMRCA). There are plans to augment the helicopter and transport fleets too. The IAF is also in the process of acquiring radars in various categories to meet the Air Defence requirements, accurate and advanced weapons, Network Centric Warfare systems, etc, to meet its assigned tasks.All the matter that has been given in public domain and we have just compiled it.

This book is all about the Indian Air Forces and their functions and operations.

—*Editor*

1

Introduction

The Indian Air Force is the air arm of the armed forces of India. Its primary responsibility is to secure and preserve peace within Indian airspace, and to conduct aerial warfare during a conflict. The Indian Air Force was officially established on October 8, 1932 as an auxiliary air force of the Indian Empire. In 1945, King George VI conferred the prefix*Royal* in recognition of its services during the World War II. After India achieved its independence from the United Kingdom in 1947, the Royal Indian Air Force served the Union of India and after India became a republic in 1950, the prefix was dropped.

Since independence the Air Force had been involved in several conflicts with neighbouring Pakistan and in 1962 with China. In 1961, the IAF played a crucial role during liberation of Goa and in 1971, during the Bangladesh liberation war. Apart from combat operations during war, the IAF is often called upon during natural disasters to provide relief to victims.

The President of India is Commander in Chief of the Air Force. Chief of the air staff, an Air Chief Marshal, is the commander of the Air Force. In 2002, for his service during the 1965 Indo-Pakistan war as Air Chief Marshal, Arjan Singh was given the honorary rank of Marshal of the Air Force. Officers holding this rank never retires and is the ceremonial chief of the Airforce. Approximately 170,000 men and women serve in the Air Force and with over 1,500 aircraft in active service, it is the world's fourth largest. Other than the officers and airmen, the IAF employs a large number of non-combat and civilian personnel for day to day affairs. Large number of aircraft in the Air Force's inventory are aging Soviet era MiGs and due to their ongoing decomissioning, the IAF fleet is shrinking. Therefore, in recent years, the IAF has undertaken an ambitious expansion and modernization program. With lengthy delays in the development of an indigenous replacement fighter, Indian launched the Multi-Role Combat Aircraft (MRCA) program. Under this program the IAF plans to induct 126 fighter jets at a cost of US$12 billion. India is increasingly projecting its power beyond South Asia. To assist its foreign policy, Government of India has authorized to increase the force level from 39.5 squadrons in present to 42 squadrons in 2022.

MISSION

Mission of the air force is defined by the Armed Forces Act of 1947, Constitution of India and the Air Force Act of 1950, in the aerial battlespace, as: *Defence of India and every part thereof including preparation for defence and all such acts as may be conducive in times of war to its prosecution and after its termination to effective demobilisation.* Moreover, the air force, along with the other branches of the armed forces, can assist local and state governments; if assistance is sought by such government during natural disasters and for maintaining internal security.

History

The Indian Air Force was established, as an auxiliary air force, when the Indian Air Force act was passed on October 8, 1932. On April 1, 1933, The IAF commissioned its first squadron, No.1 Squadron, with four Westland Wapiti biplanes and five Indian pilots. The Indian pilots were led by Flt Lt (later Air Vice Marshal) Cecil Bouchier. Until 1938, No. 1 Squadron remained the only squadron of the IAF even though two more flights were added. During the Second World War, the Air Force had grown to 7 squadrons in 1943 and to nine squadrons in 1945. In recognition of the crucial role played by the IAF, King George VI conferred it the prefix *Royal* in 1945.

After Indian independence in 1947, Royal Indian Air Force (RIAF) was bifurcated. Three of the ten operational squadrons and facilities located within the borders of Pakistan were transferred to Royal Pakistan Air Force. In 1947, when a conflict broke out over the control of erstwhile principality of Jammu & Kashmir, the Maharaja of the state decided to accede India in order to receive military help. The day after instrument of accession was signed, the RIAF was called upon to mobilize armed troops into the war-zone. This led to the eruption of full scale war between India and Pakistan without a formal declaration. During the war, the RIAF did not engage Pakistan Air Force in air-to-air combat; however, provided effective transport and close air support to the Indian troops. When India became a Republic in 1950, *Royal* title was dropped to become the Indian Air Force.

In 1960, when Belgium's 75-year colonial rule of the Congo ended abruptly, widespread violence and rebellion engulfed the nation. IAF aircraft arrived in Congo to support United Nations Operation in the Congo and started undertaking operational missions in November. The unit remained there until 1966, when the UN mission ended.

During the Sino-Indian War of 1962, India's military planners failed to deploy and effectively use the IAF against the invading Chinese forces. Three years after the Sino-Indian conflict, India went to war with Pakistan again over Kashmir. Learning from the experiences of the Sino-Indian war, India decided to use its air force extensively during the war. This was the first time the IAF actively engaged an enemy air force. However, instead of providing close air support to the Indian Army, the IAF carried out independent raid missions against Pakistani Air Force (PAF) bases. These bases were situated deep inside the Pakistani territory, making IAF fighters vulnerable to anti-aircraft fire. During the course of the conflict, the PAF enjoyed qualitative superiority over the IAF because most of the jets in IAF's fleet were of World War II-vintage. Despite this, the IAF was able to prevent the PAF from gaining air superiority over conflict zones. By the time the conflict had ended, Pakistan claimed to have shot down 113 IAF aircraft while the Indians claimed that 73 PAF aircraft were downed. More than 60% of IAF's air combat losses took place during the disastrous battles over Kalaikunda and Pathankot.

After the 1965 war, the IAF underwent a series of changes. In 1966, the Para Commandos regiment was created. With an intention of increasing its logistics supply and rescue operations ability, the IAF inducted 72 Avro 748s which were built by Hindustan Aeronautics (HAL) under license from Avro. India started to lay more stress on indigenous manufacture of fighter aircraft. A total of 147 HAL HF-24 Marut, designed by the famed German aerospace engineer Kurt Tank, were inducted into the air force. HAL also started working on a new improved version of the Folland Gnat, known as HAL Ajeet. During 1960s, the IAF also started inducting MiG-21 and Sukhoi Su-7 fighters which had a top speed of Mach 2. The induction of these advanced fighter jets was the beginning of close collaboration between India and the Soviet Union.

By late 1971, the intensification of the independence movement in erstwhile East Pakistan, war was inevitable. On November 22, 1971, 10 days before the start of a full-scale war, four Pakistani Air Force (PAF) F-86 Sabre jets attacked Indian and Mukti Bahini positions near the international border. Three of the 4 PAF Sabres were shot down by IAF's Folland Gnats. On December 3, India formally declared war against Pakistan following massive preemptive strikes by the PAF against Indian Air Force installations in Srinagar, Ambala, Sirsa, Halwara and Jodhpur. But the plan failed as the IAF had anticipated such a move and no major losses were suffered. The Indian Air Force was quick to respond to Pakistani air-strikes, following which the PAF carried out mostly defensive sorties. Within the first two weeks, the IAF had carried out almost 2,000 sorties over East Pakistan and also provided close air support to the advancing Indian Army. IAF also assisted the Indian Navy in its operations against the Pakistani Navy and Maritime Security Agency in the Bay of Bengal and Arabian Sea. On the western front, the IAF destroyed 29 Pakistani tanks, 40 APCs and a railway train during the famed battle of Longewala. The IAF pursued strategic bombing of West Pakistan by carring out raids on oil installations in Karachi, the Mangla Dam and a gas plant in Sindh. Similar strategy was also deployed in East Pakistan and as the IAF achieved complete air superiority on the eastern front, the ordnance factories, runways, and other vital areas of East Pakistan were severely damaged. By the time Pakistani forces surrendered, the IAF claimed that 94 PAF aircraft, including 54 F-86 Sabres. The IAF had flown over 6,000 sorties on both East and West fronts; including sorties by transport aircraft and helicopters. Towards the end of the war, IAF's transport planes dropped leaflets over Dhaka urging the Pakistani forces to surrender, demoralizing Pakistani troops in East Pakistan. The Indian Army too acknowledged the immense role which the IAF played towards a speedy, decisive and favorable end to the conflict.

In 1984, India launched Operation Meghdoot to capture the Siachen Glacier, in the contested Kashmir region. IAF's special helicopters, capable of flying in extremely thin air, airlifted hundreds of Indian troops to Siachen. Launched on April 13, 1984, this military operation was unique because of Siachen's inhospitable terrain and climate. The military action was successful, given the fact that under a previous agreement, neither Pakistan nor India had stationed any personnel in the area. The Indian forces, facing no odds, took control over most of the heights on the glacier.

On May 20, 1999, during Kargil conflict, the Indian Air Force was called in to provide close air support to the Indian Army. Due to Kashmir's high altitude and rigid terrain, the IAF initially expressed its reservations to deploy the slow-moving Mil Mi-8/17 helicopters which had a service ceiling of 10,000 feet. These concerns materialized when the Pakistani forces shot down an IAF Mi-8 helicopter and two fighter jets, MiG-21 and MiG-27, that had reportedly strayed into Pakistan's airspace. After the initial setbacks, the IAF deployed the Mirage 2000 which not only had better defence equipment compared to the MiGs, but also gave IAF the ability to carry out aerial raids at night. The Mirages successfully targeted enemy camps and logistic bases in Kargil and within days, their supply lines were severely disrupted. The IAF also deployed its radars and the MiG-29 fighter jets in vast numbers to keep check on Pakistani military movements across the border. The MiG-29s were also used extensively to provide fighter escort to the Mirage 2000. At the height of the conflict, the IAF conducting over forty sorties daily over the Kargil region. The IAF's operations in Kargil not only boosted the morale of the Indian Army, but also paved the way for the early recapture of Muntho Dhalo and Tiger Hill. By July 26, the Indian forces had successfully liberated Kargil from Pakistani forces and Islamist militants. On August 10, 1999, IAF MiG-21s intercepted a Pakistan Navy Breguet Atlantic which was flying over the disputed region of Sir Creek. The aircraft was shot down killing all 16 Pakistani Navy personnel on board. Indian experts believe that the Atlantic was on a *probing mission* to gather information on IAF air defence.

Since late 1990s, the Air Force is modernizing its fleet to counter challenges in the new century. The fleet size of the IAF has decreesed during this period due to the retirement of old aircraft. As new aircraft enter service and numbers recover, the IAF plans to have a fleet of 42 squadrons.

PARTITION OF INDIA (1947)

With the partition of the Indian sub-continent into two separate nations, the Union of India and the Dominion of Pakistan, the military forces were also partitioned. This gave a reduced Royal Indian Air Force and a new Royal Pakistan Air Force in 1947.

FIRST KASHMIR WAR 1947

In a bid to gain control of the erstwhile princely state of Jammu and Kashmir, Pathan tribesmen poured into Kashmir on 20 October 1947, aided by the Pakistani Army. Incapable of withstanding the armed assault in his province, the *Maharaja* of Kashmir, Hari Singh, asked India for help. The Government of India made its assistance conditional upon Kashmir's accession to India. The Instrument of accession was signed on 26 October 1947 and the next day Indian troops were airlifted into Srinagar. The agreement was later ratified by the British.

Taking off from Safdarjang, then known as *Willingdon Airfield*, the IAF landed Indian troops at Srinagar airfield at 09:30 hours IST on 27 October. This was the most instrumental action of the war as the troops saved the city from the invaders. Apart from the airlifting operations and supplying essential commodities to the ground troops, the Indian Air Force had no other major role to play in the conflict. On 31 December 1948, both nations agreed to a UN mediated cease-fire proposal marking the end of hostilities. A Line of Control has since separated Indian-held Kashmir from Pakistani-held Kashmir.

CONGO CRISIS (1961)

Belgium's 75-year colonial rule of the Democratic Republic of the Congo Congo ended abruptly on 30 June 1960. Unable to control the deteriorating situation in its former African colony, Belgium asked for UN assistance. In India, Prime Minister Jawaharlal Nehru was quick to respond to the initial appeal for help and sent IAF Canberra aircraft as a part of the UN-led mission in Congo.

SINO-INDIAN WAR (1962)

In 1962, border disputes escalated into full-scale war between India and China. Indian military and civilian leadership failed to organise and co-ordinate the air assaults efficiently and eventually the Indian Air Force was never used during the conflict apart from occasional supply missions.

SECOND KASHMIR WAR 1965

Three years after the Sino-Indian conflict, India went to war with Pakistan again over Kashmir. Learning from the experiences of the Sino-Indian war, India decided to use its air force extensively during the war. This was the first time the

IAF actively engaged an enemy air force. However, instead of providing close air support to the Indian Army, the IAF carried out independent raid missions against Pakistani Air Force (PAF) bases. These bases were situated deep inside the Pakistani territory, making IAF fighters vulnerable to anti-aircraft fire.

On 1 September 1965, the IAF fighters intervened in an on-going battle between Indian and Pakistani forces in Chhamb. However, it was inadequate in close air support role. Initially, IAF had sent the obsolete Vampires and later Mystères to stop Pakistani advance.

But after incidents of friendly fire, they were not called again for close air support. Two days later, IAF Folland Gnat fighters shot down a PAF F-86 Sabre over Chhamb area. The Gnats were effective against the F-86 and earned the nickname *Sabre Slayer*. According to one Western source, the Gnats accounted for at least 6 Sabre kills.

During the course of the conflict, the PAF enjoyed qualitative superiority over the IAF because most of the jets in IAF's fleet were of World War II-vintage. Despite this, the IAF was able to prevent the PAF from gaining air superiority over conflict zones. By the time the conflict had ended, Pakistan claimed to have shot down 113 IAF aircraft while the Indians claimed that 73 PAF aircraft were downed. More than 60% of IAF's air combat losses took place during the disastrous battles over Kalaikunda and Pathankot. However, the IAF lost most of its aircraft on ground and the attrition rate (losses per 100 sorties) of the IAF stood at 1.49 while PAF's attrition rate was 2.16, because the IAF has larger number of aircraft with higher number of take off and landing sorties.

BANGLADESH LIBERATION WAR 1971

After the 1965 War, the Indian Air Force went through an intense phase of modernisation and consolidation. With newly acquired HF-24, MiG-21 and Sukhoi Su-7BM (though the versions of these acquired between 1965 and 1971 did not have night-fight capability) aircraft, the IAF was able to measure up to the most powerful air forces in the world.

The professional standards, capability and flexibility were soon put to the test in December 1971 when India and Pakistan went to war over (then) East Pakistan. At the time, the IAF was under the command of Air Chief Marshal Pratap Chandra Lal. On 22 November, ten days before the start of a full-scale war, four PAF F-86 Sabre jets attacked Indian and Mukti Bahini positions near the Indo-Bangla border in the Battle of Garibpur. In what became the first ever Dogfight over East Pakistan skies (present day Bangladesh), three of the 4 PAF Sabreswere shot down by IAF Gnats, and hostilities commenced. 3 December saw the formal declaration of war following massive, but failed preemptive strikes by the Pakistan Air Force against Indian Air Force installations in the west.

The PAF targets were against Indian bases in Srinagar, Ambala, Sirsa, Halwara and Jodhpur on the lines of Operation Focus. But the plan failed miserably as Indians had anticipated such a move and no major losses were suffered. The Indian response over Pakistan skies however produced severe blows to the PAF.

Within the first two weeks, the IAF had carried out more than 4,000 sorties in East Pakistan and provided successful air cover for the advancing Indian army in East Pakistan. IAF also assisted the Indian Navy in sinking several Pakistani naval vessels in the Bay of Bengal. In the west, the airforce demolished scores of tanks and armoured vehicles in a single battle - the Battle of Longewala.

The IAF pursued strategic bombing by destroying oil installations in Karachi, the Mangla Dam and gas plant in Sindh. As the IAF achieved complete air superiority over the eastern wing of Pakistan within a few days, the ordnance factories, runways, and other vital areas in East Pakistan were severely crippled. In the end, the IAF played a pivotal role in the victory for the Allied Forces leading to the liberation of Bangladesh. In addition to the overall strategic victory, the IAF had also claimed 94 Pakistani aircraft destroyed, with some 45 of their own aircraft admitted lost. The IAF had however, flown over 7000 combat sorties on both East and West fronts and its overall sortie rate numbered over 15000. Comparatively the PAF was flowing fewer sorties (though PAF had qualitative advantage; its Mirage III fighter/bombers could fly at night, where no IAF fighter had that capability—the only aircraft in IAF with this capability was the Canberra bomber) by the day fearing loss of planes. Towards the end of the war, IAF's transport planes dropped leaflets over Dhaka urging the Pak forces to surrender; East Pakistani sources note that as the leaflets floated down, the morale of the Pakistani troops sunk.

OPERATION MEGHDOOT 1984

Operation Meghdoot was the name given to the preemptive strike launched by the Indian Military to capture most of the Siachen Glacier, in the disputed Kashmir region. Launched on 13 April 1984, this military operation was unique as it was the first assault launched in the world's highest battlefield. The military action was quite successful as Indian troops managed to gain two-thirds of the glacier with the rest remaining under Pakistani control.

OPERATION POOMALAI (1987)

Failing to negotiate an end to the Sri Lankan Civil War, India sent a convoy of unarmed ships to northern Sri Lanka to provide more than 1000 tonnes of humanitarian aid, but it was intercepted by the Sri Lankan Navy and sent back. Following this, the Indian Government decided to carry out an airdrop of the humanitarian supplies on the evening of 4 June 1987 designated Operation Poomalai (Tamil: Garland) or Eagle Mission 4 as a show of force to the Sri Lankan government, of symbolic support to the Tamil rebel and to preserve the credibility of the then Indian Prime Minister Rajiv Gandhi. Five An-32s of the Paratroop Training School in Agra, escorted by five Mirage 2000s of the No. 7 Squadron were to carry out the supply drop. The message was conveyed to the Sri Lankan Ambassador to New Delhi that Indian Air Force would be flying a mission at 1600 Hours to drop supplies over Jaffna. The ambassador was told that the aircraft were expected to complete their mission unhindered and any opposition by the Sri Lankan Air Force 'would be met by force' by the escorting Mirage 2000s. The air drop was a success and the IAF was unopposed by the Sri Lankan forces. Sri Lanka accused India of "blatant violation of sovereignty". India insisted that it was acting only on humanitarian grounds.

OPERATION PAWAN (1987)

The IAF supported the Indian Peace Keeping Force (IPKF) in northern and eastern Sri Lanka. About 70,000 sorties were flown by the IAF's transport and helicopter force in support of nearly 100,000 troops and paramilitary forces without a single aircraft lost or mission aborted. IAF An-32s maintained a continuous air link between air bases in South India and Northern Sri Lanka transporting men, equipment, rations and evacuating casualties. Mi-8s supported the ground forces and also provided air transportation to the Sri Lankan civil administration during the elections. Mi-25s of No. 125 H.U. were utilised to provide suppressive fire against militant strong points and to interdict coastal and clandestine riverine traffic.

AIR WEAPONS

Surface to Air Missiles

- Isayev SA-3 Goa: The Indian Air Force is considering upgrading its Pechora SA-3 missiles with Polish help whilst it waits for the Akash. According to Janes Missiles and Rockets (December 2005), the IAF would like to conduct the Newa-SCM upgrade package upgrade to 20 S-125M Pechora-CC systems, using primarily the Tatra 8x8 chassis, which is licence-built in India. Installation on specially adapted heavy equipment trailers or Tatra 8x8 vehicles was studied at the request of the Indian Air Force. It incorporates a new ZNO-X digital transmitter/receiver block developed by the Przemyslowy Instytut Telekomunikacji (PIT) to replace the original magnetron-based hardware. The unit uses digital technology, including digital frequency synthesis, and has automatic built-in test facilities. While the ZNO-X is an expensive upgrade, it significantly improves system performance. Most of the upgrade work would be done in India, although the core elements of the upgrade would be delivered from Poland.Pechora SAM will be phased out by 2012.

- SA-5 Gammon
- SA-8 Gecko
- SA-10 Grumble
- SA-16 Gimlet - MANPAD

Air to Air Missiles

- Vympel AA-8 Aphid
- Matra Magic 2
- AA-7 Apex
- Matra Super 530
- Vympel AA-10 Alamo
- Vympel AA-11 Archer
- Vympel AA-12 Adder

Air to Surface Missiles

- Zvezda AS-10 Karen
- Aerospatiale AS-30L
- Hawker-Matra Martel Missile
- Kolomna AT-6 Spiral
- Molniya AS-14 Kedge
- Zvezda AS-17 Krypton
- BAe Sea Eagle
- Raduga AS-18 Kazoo

Future Aircraft

- Medium Multi-role Combat Aircraft

The IAF plans to rise the strength of its combat fleet to 42 squadrons by 2022. The Air Force will reach the peak of strength with the induction of the planned Su-30 MKIs, Jaguars, Medium

Multi-role Combat Aircraft (M-MRCA), Fifth Generation Fighter Aircraft (FGFA), the Light Combat Aircraft (LCA) and medium combat aircraft (MCA).

The Indian Air Force operates around 250 MiG-21 aircraft. Due to metal fatigue and outdated equipment, many MiG-21s used in training have crashed over the past six years, killing over 50 IAF pilots. Also, they are nearing the end of their service life having been in the IAF for many decades and are being decommissioned at an increasing pace. The IAF initially planned to replace the MiG-21 fleet with indigenously-built HAL Tejas aircraft by 2006. However, the target could not be met due to developmental delays and a US sanction, following the Pokhran-II nuclear tests, which blocked the delivery of GE F404 engines - a crucial component of the LCA.

The Indian Air Force has a requirement for combat aircraft to replace the MiG-21 in service. The Mirage-2000 were considered as a replacement. However, Dassault announced that it has shut down the assembly line of the Mirage-2000. Hence the IAF included the Mig-35, Gripen and F-16 in its itinerary of consideration. This was the first time in the IAF's history that an American aircraft was being considered. Later the number of manufacturers was widened to include heavy-weight aircraft like the F/A-18 Super Hornet, the Eurofighter Typhoon, and Dassault Rafale. In an interview, the then Air Chief of the IAF M. Shahindra Pal Tyagi admitted to allowing heavy-weight aircraft to compete, "to allow more competition".

The limited series production of the indigenous LCA Tejas aircraft is ongoing at Hindustan Aeronautics Limited. The aircraft is supposed to get full operational clearance by December 2010, as the Tejas' development has been accelerated. It is believed that the MRCA's procurement may take a much longer time than Tejas' induction in the IAF, and its subsequent mass production. The air force has issued an Intent (RoI) for procurement of MRCA (Multi Role Combat Aircraft). The following aircraft are participating: Russian MiG-35, French Rafale, European Eurofighter Typhoon, Swedish Gripen and the US F-16IN. Besides the F-16s, the US has also offered the sale of F/A-18E/F Super Hornet combat aircraft. IAF pilots and technicians are familiar with earlier aircraft from MiG and Dassault and would need minimal retraining. Infrastructural and logistical support for maintenance and spares would also be easier for these aircraft compared to the unfamiliar Gripens, F-16s and F/A-18s.

Apart from the 126 multi-role combat aircraft (with an option for another 74 aircraft), 110 Su-30MKI air superiority fighters (out of the 230 Su-30MKI fighters ordered at cost of 8.4 billion US$, 120 are already in service with the IAF), 220 Light Combat Aircraft, 47 Jaguar combat aircraft, 4 Tu-22M3 bombers, the Indian Air Force has signed contracts for 66 BAE Hawk Mk.132 trainers (deliveries in the pipeline), 80+ combat helicopters, 3 new Long Range UAVs, 8 mid-air refuelling planes, 225+ HJT-36 Sitara Intermediate Jet Trainer aircraft and some additional medium-range transport aircraft. The Indian Air Force planned to upgrade its fleet of MiG-29 aircraft in 2007. India awarded Russia a $965 mn contract to upgrade its multi-role MiG-29 warplanes, on Monday March 10, 2008. The two post-Cold War allies signed the deal on Saturday March 8, 2008 to extend the life of India's fleet of 70 MiG-29 jets another 15 years from their current 25 years. Russia will re-arm the twin-engined MiG-29s with air-to-air missiles, modern bombs, increased fuel capacity and the latest avionics, the contract said.

- Hawk AJT: Deliveries of the first order of 66 Hawk 132 Advanced Jet Trainers began in November, 2007 with induction in February, 2008. An order for 57 (40 for IAF and 17 for Indian Navy) more was placed in 2008. The Hawk, along with the HJT-36, will serve the IAF's future fighter training needs.
- C-130J Hercules: Indian Air force signed a deal to acquire 6 C-130J Super Hercules in early 2008 for US$1.06 billion. Lockheed Martin will deliver the planes on 2011.
- Light Helicopters: A tender for supply of 317 light helicopters will be floated by Ministry of Defence combining the requirements of Indian Air force (125)

and Indian Army (197). The Navy is too likely to join this tender. The requirements of Indian Navy being 50–60 Helicopters and this is likely to increase the tender to 367. Unnamed Defence Ministry official stated that Letters of interest have been sent to Kamov, Bell, Augusta Westland and Eurocopter. Last week, Bell withdrew from the race, citing differences in offset clause with the Government of India. HAL has also recently joined the race with its Light Observation Helicopter (LOH). Although it is still on the drawing board, HAL officials seem to be confident to deliver in time.

- Medium Lift Helicopters: During Russian President Dmitry Medvedev's visit to India in December 2008, the two countries inked a deal for the supply of 80 Mi-17V-5 (also known as Mi-171) medium lift helicopters at a cost of US$1.2 billion. The two countries had earlier negotiated a price of $650 million, but early in 2008 Russia asked for a revision of the contract price. Russia is expected to deliver the Mi-171 to the IAF in 2010. The deal also envisages a US$405 million "offset" obligation by Russia. The new choppers, which have an 18,000 ft operational ceiling, will replace 50 Mi-8s currently in service with the IAF, some of which are over 35 years old, and boost IAF's capability to support high-altitude posts in Siachen and Ladakh sectors. The helicopter will come with the circuitry and hard points to carry weapons.
- Heavy Lift Helicopters: Indian Air Force has circulated the Request for Information for Heavy Lift Helicopters to the vendors. For this contract, the bidders could include Boeing's CH-47 Chinook, Sikorsky and Russian MI's. Indian Air Force has the requirement of 6 such helicopters. This information was provided by Chief of Air Staff Air Chief Marshal F H Major on February 6, 2008.
- VIP Helicopters: Indian Air force had floated a tender in 2006 for supply of 12 VIP Helicopters and 4 Medium

Lift Helicopters to replace Mi-8 Helicopters of VIP Squadron. IAF concluded the trials of competing helicopters, Augusta Westland EH-101 and Sikorsky S-92 in the period of January 14—19, 2008.The government is on the verge of clearing a US$300 million deal to purchase 12 advanced VIP helicopters from Italian armament major Augusta Westland EH-101. Owned by Finmeccanica, the Italian firm had fielded the EH101 — whose variant, US101, serves the US President — to compete for the Indian tender floated some two years ago. Based on the contract schedule, the first helicopter is likely to join the air force fleet around 2011.

- Attack Helicopters: Indian Air Force has plans to induct two more squadrons (22) of Attack Helicopters, capable of operating in high altitudes. The new purchase would give the force capability to operate helicopter gunships in both day and night as also in high altitude areas like Siachen, Jammu and Kashmir and North-East. It would give an option to armed forces as it can be deployed in fighting militants in insurgency-prone areas. The US aviation giant Boeing's world best seller AH-64A Apache helicopters, Russian Kamov and MI series and European consortium EADS would be bidding for the IAF's order, which could run up to more than a billion US dollars. A request for proposals has been issued to seven companies for the supply of 22 attack helicopters for the Indian Air Force. The new helicopters will replace IAF's aging fleet of Mi-35 helicopters. The contract is estimated to be worth US$500 million. The deal is expected to be finalized within two years and supply completed over the next three years. The qualitative requirements are as follows: twin engine, high maneuverability, anti-armor capability, all weather capability and all terrain capability. The helicopters are likely to be equipped with an electronic warfare and self protection suite developed by EADS and India's Defence Avionics Research Establishment. Competing for the order will be: Boeing AH-64D Apache Longbow, Eurocopter Tiger,

AgustaWestland AW129, Bell AH-1Z SuperCobra, Kamov Ka-50, Mil Mi-28, and HAL's Light Combat Helicopter. Boeing said in October, 2008 that it won't bid for a contract to supply 22 helicopters due to time constraints. HAL's Light Combat Aircraft, which is still underdevelopment, is expected to take to the air sometime this year. However the government had canceled the tender, as only 3 of the top 5 companies participated in the entire process & none could match the qualitative requirements of the IAF. The Indian Defence Ministry has said that soon a new tender will be floated for the same.

Under Development

- HAL Tejas: The IAF will also buy 220 indigenously-built HAL Tejas Light Combat Aircraft. It has already ordered a total of 28 Tejas aircraft. Weaponization is underway as an LCA Tejas successfully test-fired a Russian R-73 close-combat air-to-air missile off the coast of Goa in October, 2007. These aircraft are expected to enter service in 2010.As on February 3, 2009, LCA has completed 1011 Test Flights successfully using these prototypes: TD1-233, TD2-298, PV1-182, PV2-107, PV3-120, LSP1-33, and LSP2-38.
- Medium Combat Aircraft: India is also planning to develop a fifth generation aircraft called Medium Combat Aircraft or MCA. Development(HAL & ADA) work on the MCA is awaiting government approval and design phase is in its early stages. The Medium Combat Aircraft (MCA) is a twin-engined 5th generation stealth mutlirole fighter being developed by India. It will complement the HAL Tejas and the Sukhoi Su-30MKI in the Indian Air Force. The main purpose of this aircraft is to replace the aging SEPECAT Jaguar & MiG-27. Design work on the MCA has been started.
- Fifth Generation Fighter Aircraft : In 2001, the Ministry of Defence signed a deal with Russia to jointly develop and fund the FGFA/PAK FA, Perspektivnyi Aviatsionnyi

Kompleks Frontovoi Aviatsyi (*Future Air Complex for Tactical Air Forces*) program. The program was initiated to develop a fifth generation fighter aircraft to fill a role similar to that of Lockheed Martin's F-22 Raptor in all aspects. Initially, Mikoyan-Gurevich's Project 1.44 was expected to get the contract. However, Sukhoi Aviation Corporation came up with a more cost-effective aircraft and won. Design work has commenced on Sukhoi's experimental Su-47 Berkut aircraft. PAK FA proves to be a very ambitious program and the estimated costs for developing the aircraft vary between US$15–20 billion. However, it was announced in August, 2007 by Russian Air Force Commander Alexander Zelin that the development stage of the PAK FA project is complete without any Indian involvement and an Indo-Russian pact on building a fifth-generation fighter has only recently been agreed. The new project may effectively result in the development of an export version of the Russian PAK FA or very closely based on the PAK FA's final article. An official project name had not been assigned to this possible Indo-Russian fifth-generation fighter aircraft development programme as of November, 2007. Sukhoi has already started construction of a prototype which is expected to feature super maneuverability, super cruise, stealth and precision in destroying ground and sea targets. Flight tests of the fighter are due to begin as early as 2009, and the aircraft may go into production by 2015. The Sukhoi and HAL will sign a formal contract to jointly develop the fighter at the beginning of 2009, the head of the United Aircraft Corporation said on Friday, December 5, 2008. "We are planning to conclude the contract at the beginning of next year," Alexei Fedorov said. According to the latest reports FGFA will have its first flight by 2015 or before 2015.

- HAL HJT-36 Sitara: The HAL HJT-36 Intermediate Jet Trainer carried out its maiden test flight in 2003 and is all set to enter service within the next 5 years. HAL recently signed a deal with Russian company Saturn DDB for supply of a specially designed engine for the trainer.

- Multirole Transport Aircraft: India's Hindustan Aeronautics (HAL) and Russia's United Aircraft Corporation (UAC) will form a joint-venture in mid-2009 for the development of a Multirole Transport Aircraft, which will replace the IAF's ageing fleet of Antonov An-32s. Both HAL and UAC will invest US$300 million each on the program.
- HAL Light Combat Helicopter: Hindustan Aeronautics Ltd is developing an Attack Helicopter for the IAF based on HAL Dhruv. It is being designed to fit into an anti-infantry and anti-armour role and will be capable to operate from altitudes an 6,500 metre. HAL selected the M621 cannon incorporated in a Nexter THL 20 turret for the gun armament of the helicopter. The helicopter will have a glass cockpit with multifunction displays, a target acquisition and designation system with FLIR, Laser rangefinder and laser designator. Weapons will be aimed with a helmet mounted sight and there will be an electronic warfare suite with radar warning receiver, laser warning receiver and a missile approach warning system. First flight of HAL LCH (Light Combat Helicopter) is expected in 2009.
- Airawat (AEW&C): India has also revived the Airavat Project, which was India's first attempt in developing an indigenous AEW aircraft. According to various sources, Centre for Airborne Systems (CABS), is coordinating the Rs.1,800-crore effort to develop an indigenous airborne early warning and control system (AEW&CS), scheduled to be completed by 2012.The AEW&CS will comprise of an indigenous radar and control system mounted on a Brazilian Embraer EMB-145 regional jet. Under a $210 million deal signed with Brazilian aviation company Embraer in summer 2008, Embraer will supply India 3 EMB-145s with the system

mounted on them. The CABS is looking for an experienced partner who will be responsible for integrating the Active Array Antenna Unit (AAAU), other antennas, trans receiver modules and various sub systems being developed by Indian defence laboratories onto the three Brazil manufactured EMB-145. It has sent a request for proposal to six vendors - Israel's Elta, the European consortium EADS, France's Thales, Sweden's SAAB Erikson and the United State's Raytheon and Northrop Grumman. The vendors have time till the third week of January 2009 to submit their proposals. The first EMB-145 is scheduled to be delivered in 2011 and the complete system will be flight tested by the DRDO along with the Indian air force from 2012.

Aerospace Command

The IAF is setting up an aerospace command. This command will have space technology including satellites available to them. This command is said to be utilised by all the three services of the Indian armed forces and also for civilian purposes by ISRO.

A specialized surveillance satellite for the IAF will be operational by the end of 2010. The satellite will enable the IAF to carry out precise strikes against targets like terrorist training camps. The Satellite has been named RISAT 2 and will use an Israeli Synthetic Aperture Radar mounted on a ISRO developed satellite bus and will be launched on a fast track basis in the aftermath of the 2008 Mumbai attacks in place of the civilian RISAT 1.

Surface to Air Missile Systems

- Trishul (Trident): Development of Trishul is complete. It has met the IAF requirements during its various developmental flight trials. DRDO is presently in dialogue with IAF for possible induction. Frontier India reports that Indian Air force is considering to induct small quantity to meet partial requirement of LLQRM (Low Level Quick Reaction Missile) System. However it is not known if IAF has placed a formal order of Trishul SAM System.

- SPYDER (*S*urface-to-air *PY*thon and *DER*by): Indian Air force plans to acquire 18 Spyder SAM Systems at a cost of Rs. 1800 crore (approx. $395.4 million). A typical squadron consists of 1 Mobile Command and Control Unit and 4 Mobile Firing Units with missiles, each with their own built-in power supplies. SPYDER will reportedly replace India's Russian-made OSA-AKM (SA-8 Gecko) and ZRK-BD Strela-10M (SA-13 Gopher) SAM systems. If the deal is approved RAFAEL would be the prime contractor, and Israel Aircraft Industries the major subcontractor. But recently Defence Ministry has ordered a probe into the deal following allegations of illegal influencing of the purchase process. Central Vigilance Commission is reviewing the deal. It was reported in February, 2008 that Rafael is to sign Production Transfer Program (PTP) agreement with Tata Power for maintenance and production of the SAM System. Cabinet Committee on Security (CCS) cleared the deal in January 2008. It was reported on August 18, 2008 that the Defence Acquisitions Council had approved the deal for 18 SpyDer systems at a cost of Rs. 1800 crore. On December 14, the Government of India informed the upper house that India has signed a deal with Rafeal for the supply of 18 SPYDER missile system.
- Maitri LLQRM (Low Level Quick Reaction Missile): DRDO is in talks with MBDA to develop Maitri LLQRM for Army, Air force and Navy. Sources said that DRDL is preparing feasibility report and is awaiting formal clearance from defence ministry.
- Akash: Indian Air force has approved the induction of Akash Missile System and had initiated the process of inducting the system. Akash has successfully demonstrated its performance through number of flight tests. DRDO and IAF jointly began a ten day intensive trial of Akash on December 13, 2007 aimed at making

IAF familiar with the system. Defence News reports that IAF has already ordered two units (squadrons) of Akash which are likely to be inducted by 2009.

Surface to Surface Missiles

- Prithvi II: 250 km Prithvi-II Ballistic Missile is under IAF service which could be used to target airfields, command and control centres etc.

Air to Surface Missiles

- DRDO- NPO Mashinostroeyenia Brahmos- Air launched version under Development.

INDIAN AIR FORCE

The Indian Air Force is the air arm of the Indian armed forces. Its primary responsibility is to secure Indian airspace and to conduct aerial warfare during a conflict. It was officially established on 8 October 1932 as an auxiliary air force of the British Raj and the prefix *Royal* was added in 1945 in recognition of its services during World War II.

After India achieved independence from the United Kingdom in 1947, the Royal Indian Air Force served the Dominion of India, with the prefix being dropped when India became a republic in 1950. The Indian Air Force plays a crucial role in securing Indian airspace and also in India's power projection in South Asia and Indian Ocean.

Therefore, modernizing and expanding the Indian Air Force is a top priority for the Indian government. Over the years, the IAF has grown from a tactical force to one with transoceanic reach. The strategic reach emerges from induction of Force Multipliers like Flight Refueling Aircraft (FRA), Unmanned Aerial Vehicle (UAV) and credible strategic lift capabilities.

Aircraft

Historically, the IAF has generally relied on Soviet, British, Israeli and French military craft and technology to support its growth. IAF's primary air superiority fighter with the additional capability to conduct air-ground (strike) missions is Sukhoi Su-30MKI. The IAF have placed an order for a total of 272 Su-30MKIs of which 170 are in service as of 2013. The Mikoyan MiG-29 is a dedicated air superiority fighter and constitutes a second line of defence after the Sukhoi Su-30MKI. At present, 66 MiG-29s are in service, all of which are being upgraded to the MiG-29UPG standard.

The Dassault Mirage 2000 is the primary multirole fighter in service and the IAF operates 49 Mirage 2000Hs which are being upgraded to the Mirage 2000-5 MK2 standard. As part of the upgrade, the aircraft will also be equipped with MBDA's MICA family of medium range missiles. For giving the IAF fighters an edge in anti-ship and land attack roles, smaller version of BrahMos missile is being developed to be integrated in Sukhoi Su-30MKI and is expected to be delivered to IAF by 2015.

In the aerial refueling (tanker) role, the IAF operates six Ilyushin Il-78MKIs. For strategic military transport operations the IAF uses the Ilyushin Il-76, and has placed orders for 10 Boeing C-17 Globemaster III, four of which were delivered by November 2013. The C-130J Super-Hercules planes of the IAF is used by special forces for combined Army-Air Force operations. There are six C-130Js in service and six more are planned to be procured. The Antonov An-32 serves as medium transport aircraft in the IAF.

As an airborne early warning system, the IAF operates the Israeli EL/W-2090 Phalcon AEW&C. A total of three such systems are in service, with possible orders for two more. The Airborne Early Warning and Control System (AEWACS) is a project of India's DRDO to develop an AEW&C system for the Indian Air Force. The DRDO AEWACS program aims to deliver three radar-equipped surveillance aircraft to the Indian Air Force. The aircraft platform selected was the Embraer ERJ 145. Three ERJ 145 were procured from Embraer at a cost of US $ 300 Million, including the contracted modifications to the airframe. Probable delivery date for the first batch of three is 2015.

Network-centric Warfare

The Indian Air Force (IAF) got a boost towards becoming a truly network centric air force with launching Air Force Network (AFNET), a reliable and robust digital information grid that enables accurate and faster response to enemy threats, in 2010.

The modern, state-of-the-art AFNET is a fully secure communication network, providing IAF critical link among its command and control centre, sensors such as the Airborne Early Warning and Control Systems and shooters like the fighter aircraft and missile squadrons. Integrated Air Command and Control System (IACCS), an automated command and control system for Air Defence (AD) operations will ride the AFNet backbone integrating all ground-based and airborne sensors, AD weapon systems and C2 nodes.

Subsequent integration with other services networks and civil radars will provide an integrated Air Situation Picture to operators to carry out Air Defence role. AFNet will prove to be an effective force multiplier for intelligence analysis, mission planning and control, post-mission feedback and related activities like maintenance, logistics and administration. A comprehensive design with multi-layer security precautions for "Defence in Depth" have been planned by incorporating encryption technologies, Intrusion Prevention Systems to ensure the resistance of the IT system against information manipulation and eavesdropping.

In October, 2013, IAF launched its own stand-alone Rs 300 crore cellular network through which secure video calling and other information exchange facilities will be provided. The IAF also plans to issue around one hundred thousand mobile handsets to its personnel of the rank of Sergeants and above to connect and provide secure 'end-point' connectivity to the air warriors deployed across the country. The captive network has been named 'Air Force Cellular'. While Phase I of the project will ensure mobile connectivity to all air warriors in the National Capital Region, its Phase II will cover the rest of the bases.

Future Developments

The Medium Multi-Role Combat Aircraft (MMRCA) competition, also known as the MRCA tender, was a competition to supply 126 multi-role combat aircraft to the Indian Air Force (IAF). The Defence Ministry has allocated ~ US$13 billion for the purchase of these aircraft, making it India's single largest defence deal. The MRCA tender was floated with the idea of filling the gap between its future Light Combat Aircraft and its in-service Sukhoi Su-30MKI air superiority fighter. On 31 January 2012, it was announced that Dassault Rafale won the competition due to its lower life-cycle cost. The Indian Air Force (IAF) is also in the final stages of acquiring 22 Apache Longbow gunships, armed with Hellfire and Stinger missiles in a $1.2 billion contract and 15 heavy-lift Boeing CH Chinook helicopters. The IAF has initiated the process for acquisition of additional Mi-17 IV helicopters, heavy lift helicopters, Advanced Light Helicopter and Light Combat Helicopters. Among trainer aircraft, the Hawk Advanced Jet Trainer has been inducted and the Intermediate Jet Trainer (IJT) would be acquired in the near future.

In recent times, India has also manufactured its own aircraft such as the HAL Tejas, a 4th generation fighter, and the HAL Dhruv, a multi-role helicopter, which has been exported to several countries, including Israel, Burma, Nepal and Ecuador. An weaponized version of Dhruv is called HAL Rudra, which is armed with high-velocity M621 20 mm cannon, long-range 70 mm rockets (8 km), air-to-air missiles (Mistral-II). and MAWS (missile approach warning system). Combat in Kargil highlighted the requirement of an attack helicopter specially made for such high altitude operations.

The HAL Light Combat Helicopter (LCH) is a multirole combat helicopter being developed in India by Hindustan Aeronautics Limited (HAL) for use by the Indian Air Force and the Indian Army. The LCH is being designed to fit into an anti-infantry and anti-armour role and will be able to operate at high altitudes. LCH will be fitted with indigenous anti-tank missileHelina.

India also maintains UAV squadrons (primarily Searcher-II and Heron from Israel) which can be used to carry out ground and aerial surveillance. India is also testing its own long range BVR air to air missile named Astra and also building a Medium Altitude Long Endurance Unmanned Aerial Vehicle (UAV) called Rustom.

India is also in an ambitious collaboration program with Russia to build fifth-generation fighter aircraft, called HAL/ Tejas FGFA which will be based on Russian PAK-FA fighter. Earlier in 2013, the two sides completed the preliminary design of the FGFA and are now negotiating a detailed design contract. Although there is no reliable information about the PAK FA and FGFA specifications yet, it is known from interviews with people in the Russian Air Force that it will be stealthy, have the ability to supercruise, be outfitted with the next generation of air-to-air, air-to-surface, and air-to-ship missiles, and incorporate an AESA radar.

Co-development and co-production of Multi-role Transport Aircraft (MTA), jointly by Russian partners and HAL, is being launched to meet the requirement of Russian and Indian Air Forces. The aircraft will be designed for the roles of a 15-20 ton Cargo / Troop transport, Para trooping / Airdrop of supplies including Low Altitude Parachute Extraction System (LAPES) capability. It will be configured such that all types of cargo can be transported and the aircraft would be capable of operating from semi prepared runways. The MTA is expected to replace the Indian Air Force's aging fleet of Antonov An-32 transport aircraft. The aircraft is expected to conduct its first flight by 2017, and to enter service by 2018.

To protect IAF assets on the ground, there has been search for short-range surface-to-air missile and in that regard, Maitri missile project is a next-generation quick-reaction Surface-to-Air Missile (QRSAM) with a lethal hundred per cent kill probability under development. It is a short-range (15 km, 9.3 mi) surface-to-air point defence missile system. The $6 billion worth of SR-SAM project is a co-development joint venture between India and France and would be developed by MBDA of France and DRDO from the Indian side. It is believed to be a blend of the French MICA and DRDO Trishul.

INDIAN ARMY ALONE CANNOT MEET THE TWIN THREATS OF PAKISTAN AND CHINA

After half a century, the Indian Army (IA) is once again radically increasing its numbers. Both times it was to cater for threat from China. After the 1962 rout, six new divisions were raised; two infantry and four mountain divisions, and the Officer Training Academy in Madras were established. Now, between 2009 and 2011, the IA raised two mountain divisions and the third artillery division, and a new Officers Training Academy has been set up in Gaya. A corps headquarters and two more mountain divisions will be raised in the 12th defence plan (2012 to 2017). Huge amounts will be spent on building infrastructure, accommodation, equipment and ammunition storage facilities against China. And by the 14th defence plan (2022 to 2027), the IA hopes to have its first air assault division; 54 mountain division has been earmarked for this role. The once-again threat from China provokes two pertinent questions: What happened to post-1962 preparedness? And, is India bracing itself enough this time to dissuade adversaries from military adventurism, and fight a successful war, if needed?

For 14 years after the ignominious 1962 debacle, India had no relations with China. After the Chinese unilateral troops' withdrawal from Indian territories, a 320km Line of Actual Control (LAC) came up in Ladakh where the IA had given a reasonable account of itself. The eastern sector, called McMahon Line, where the IA performed abysmally, remained a 'frontier' rather than a 'border.' The word 'frontier' denotes the limit of a nation's political and military influence, while 'border' is defined as the territorial limit of national sovereignty. While diplomatic relations were restored with China in 1976, domestic political upheavals delayed the initiation of a military build-up against China until 1980 when Prime Minister Indira Gandhi returned to power. In 1980, the army chief, General K.V. Krishna Rao presented a strategic military plan called Operation Falcon to the Prime Minister which she accepted. Repudiating Nehru's 'forward policy,' in a step-by-step approach over 15 years, the army's planned heavy deployment on the Chinese front where forward build-up would keep pace with infrastructure development along with viable lines of communications. Arunachal Pradesh, north Sikkim and trans-Ladakh range were to get special attention, and the Prime Minister made it clear that in a future conflict with China, Tawang should not fall. Recalling his deliberations with Mrs Gandhi, General Rao in a detailed interaction with FORCE in August 2005 confirmed that the Prime Minister took great interest in the army's initiative. Issues like would China get provoked by India's military preparedness and start a conflict and the possibility of it using nuclear weapons were discussed threadbare. The plan could well be called a top-down approach. Keeping with times, the plan did not cater for a two-front war, and was an amalgamation of first and second generation warfare with the Indian Air Force (IAF) in a tactical support role. The first generation warfare reflected the tactics of line and column, while the second generation relied on massed firepower. The concepts of air-land battle and active defence had yet not been borrowed from the United States; a mere co-ordination rather than jointness between the IA and the IAF was the need of the hour.

In a show of goodwill, India under Prime Ministers Rajiv Gandhi and P.V. Narasimha Rao abandoned Operation Falcon in 1988, just when China focussed on its neglected west and commenced furtive military infrastructure build-up in Tibet Autonomous Region (TAR) against India. New Delhi's decision was taken without consulting the IA, which was informed that the external affairs ministry would engage China by diplomacy. The Indian defence forces were told to instead concentrate on Pakistan. All lessons of the 1962 conflict were forgotten and it was business as usual. India signed the 1993 and 1996 agreements with China; both worked to India's military disadvantage. The first re-named the entire disputed border as the LAC which by definition meant it could be altered by military force, and the second ensured that no division and high formation army exercises would be held close to LAC. Even for a brigade exercise involving 3,000 troops, India will be required to inform China well in advance.

Meanwhile, the Peoples Liberation Army's (PLA) military plans were unfolding quietly. After India's 1998 nuclear tests, the PLA started pushing LAC inside India by its aggressive patrolling, and whenever India objected, the concerned pockets were added to the increasing list of 'disputed areas' by China. Giving the high altitude and harsh climatic conditions on TAR, the PLA did not intend to station troops close to the LAC and hence it had little need to conduct exercises in location. It instead concentrated on building Rapid Reaction Forces (RRF), 30 divisions of which, in Indian estimate, can be brought from nearby Chengdu and Lanzhou military regions to TAR in one season against India. Excellent border management and mind-boggling infrastructure on TAR would support the PLA divisions to fight a war on Indian territories. In comparison, India lacks RRF capabilities, and is building defences along the LAC to keep its troops perched on high altitudes holding ground. The IA started feeling the heat of PLA's regular transgressions by the turn of the century. In March 2001, Prime Minister A.B. Vajpayee allocated funds and cleared construction of 73 strategic roads on the Chinese border to be completed in a decade. Nothing much happened on the ground. In December 2011, defence minister A.K. Antony informed the Parliament that 13 out of 73 strategic roads had been built and massive allocations have been made for infrastructure construction to include bunkers and storage facilities.

Today, the IA, the fourth largest in the world after the US, Russian and Chinese, is already 13,00,000 strong. It has 37 divisions, five force headquarters for counter-insurgency operations (each equivalent of a division), 10 independent brigades (over three divisions), higher field formations' headquarters, and various combat support arms elements. Of these, 12 divisions and three independent brigades are pitted against China, the rest are meant for Pakistan. According to the IA, it no longer thinks in terms of threats from Pakistan and China, but has chiselled a larger role for itself under the rubric of transformation. It is transforming from a threat-based to a capability-based force to meet challenges of the entire spectrum of war below the nuclear threshold. From conventional to sub-conventional war (terrorism), capabilities to secure island territories, out-of-area (intervention) capabilities to protect India's interests and provide assistance to friendly neighbours, including humanitarian help and disaster relief, and participation in UN operations. The driver for the transformational thinking is not the government, but IA's own assessment that it needs to absorb the technology revolution underway in the world, and given India's rising economy, it should possess capabilities to meet the nation's strategic reach aspirations.

Considering that threats from Pakistan and China have increased and not diminished, isn't transformation oxymoronic? Not at all, says a general associated with IA's perspective planning. The government has kept the defence forces on the fringes of national security policy-making. Neither understands one another. But as the force with boots on ground, the IA has to be prepared for all contingencies, was the firm reply. Notwithstanding denial, one can easily detect IA's rivalry with the other two defence services. While being the largest of the three defence forces, in terms of numbers and capital expenditure, the risen profile of the IAF and the Indian Navy (IN) may have spurred the IA to seek its own transformation. In the larger sense, if the three defence services had been united, the Chiefs of Staff Committee (COSC), which was declared ineffective by the Group of Ministers' report in February 2002, would have worked better. So well, that they would not have missed opportunities to be part of national security policy-making.

The first came in the Fifties. On 25 March 1955, Prime Minister Jawaharlal Nehru announced in Parliament the change of the designation of the Commander-in-Chief of the three defence services to Chiefs of Staff. He added that his government was going into the matter of integration of the defence ministry and the three services headquarters. The Prime Minister intended to be fair. While dismissing the need for a military advisor to the Prime Minister of independent India, he desired the defence forces to be part of national security policy-making. The defence services failed to hold the Prime Minister to his promise missing the point that integration of defence services with the defence ministry would position them as the more knowledgeable partner able to influence policy-making. Nehru was persuaded by the wily bureaucracy in 1961 to designate the three service headquarters as 'Attached offices of the Department of Defence' under the Government of India 'Allocation of Business Rules.'

The next opportunity had to wait for the subcontinent's security status quo to get altered with the 1998 nuclear tests by India and Pakistan. Within a year, after the 1999 Kargil conflict, the K. Subrahmanyam headed 'Kargil Review Committee Report' noted that:

'India's is perhaps the only major democracy where the armed forces headquarters are outside the apex government structure. The Chiefs of Staff have assumed the role of operational commanders of their respective forces rather than that of Chiefs of Staff to the Prime Minister or defence minister. They simultaneously discharge the roles of operational commanders and national security planners/managers, especially in relation to future equipment and force postures.'

Following the Report, the Arun Singh-led task force on 'Defence Management' recommended the creation of the Chief of Defence Staff (CDS), and integration of defence services headquarters with the defence ministry. Both suggestions were watered down before acceptance by Group of Ministers report announced by the Deputy Prime Minister, L.K. Advani in February 2002. Instead of the CDS, Advani suggested a step-by-step approach; while holding out the promise of the CDS, a Vice-CDS was formed, which was subsequently re-named as the Chairman of Integrated Staff to Chairman (CISC), Chiefs of Staff Committee (COSC). The three services' headquarters were cosmetically re-designated as 'Integrated Headquarters of Ministry of Defence', without actual integration.

While all this was happening, what did the defence services do? It is an open secret that the Indian Air Force (IAF) opposes the CDS. Unlike the tactical air force that it was, since the arrival of Su-30 aircraft, it talks about strategic reach. Moving away as a support service to the IA, the IAF is building capabilities for effect-based operations. This implies an emphasis on offensive counter-air operations, which would by its effect assist land operations. The IAF fears that a CDS from the IA may seek to curtail its offensive posture. While it is debatable if this would happen, the argument was welcomed by the bureaucracy worried by the Arun Singh committee recommendation of the CDS becoming the Military Advisor to the defence minister. In 2010, the matter was finally settled, when the bureaucracy amended the 'Allocation of Business Rules', with the defence secretary made responsible for the 'Defence of India and every part thereof'. Ironically, the three service chiefs in 2011 in turns (not together) deposed before the Naresh Chandra task force set up by the government to review the decade old GOM report. The three service chiefs sought a formal say for themselves, individually, in security policy-making. Shouldn't they have approached the Prime Minister together years ago to seek integration of the services headquarters with the defence ministry? If they could do so for the Sixth Pay Commission, surely this issue that has implications at the strategic, operational and tactical levels deserved fuller attention. Unfortunately, the intense rivalry between the services has played into the hands of the bureaucracy.

Learning from Past

Armies, it is said, prepare for the last war. The IA seems to be no exception. Since 1990, when Pakistan-supported proxy war started in Jammu and Kashmir, senior army commanders have been conscious that unlike the 1971 war, little preparatory time would be available next time around. A trigger in J&K

could easily escalate into a full-fledged war, and the IA would have to fight with whatever wherewithal it has. Another truism became evident after the 1998 nuclear tests by India and Pakistan: the next conflict, if it is to achieve meaningful military aims, would have to be short, swift and intense; anything between seven to 10 days, after that a mix of enormous international and nuclear weapons spectre would loom large. During the 1971 war, the army chief, General Sam Manekshaw had sought six months of preparatory time for war from Prime Minister Indira Gandhi. The military posture against Pakistan was: strategic defence with operational level offence(s). It was appreciated that after three to four weeks, military results would start showing in favour of India being the larger force. This military thinking has been drastically altered by three factors: nuclear weapons, ballistic missiles, and Pakistan Army's ability to use irregulars (terrorists) as its first line of offense. A going back to 1971 is nothing short of suicidal.

Yet, in all recent conflicts, the IA does not seem to have grasped the realities. During the 1999 Kargil conflict (Operation Vijay), the IA was caught completely off-guard. Overnight, flights were sent to Russia and Israel to procure stores and ammunition; the artillery was moved from various theatres, creating operational gaps in the event of an escalated all-out war, to reinforce firepower in Kargil; guns were employed in direct firing role, a near impossibility in case of a total war; and the army chief admitted major equipment shortcomings by saying: "We will fight with whatever we have." All this happened when the Pakistan military did not even join the war; its Mujahids, and the then paramilitary force (Northern Light infantry) did the fighting.

The next crisis, Operation Parakram, when the two armies stood facing one another for 10 months, from 18 December 2001 to 16 October 2002, was no better. The IA took 22 days for its build-up of offensive (strike) forces, and according to the government, 800 lives were lost/debilitated during preparatory phase. There are two other frightening little-known facts about this crisis. Insiders have confirmed to FORCE that once mobilisation for war was ordered, the then Northern army commander (responsible for J&K, the supposed trigger for a full-fledged war), Lt. General R.K. Nanavaty told the army chief, General S. Padmanabhan, that he needed preparatory time as troops lacked essential stocks of ammunition, stores and spares. The IA ineptness got covered up by disingenuous political naivety. It was believed that international pressure, especially from the US, during the IA's preparatory phase, dissuaded the Vajpayee government from going to war with Pakistan. The truth is devastating. The then US National Security Advisor (NSA), Condoleezza Rice has confirmed in her recent memoir: No Higher Honour, that it was the other way round. The US had resigned to a war between India and Pakistan, when India's NSA, Brajesh Mishra, who was doubling up as the Prime Minister's principal secretary, frantically called her for help. "I cannot contain the war lobby here without some help," he said.

This led US President George Bush to speak with Pakistani President General Pervez Musharraf to persuade him to make the statement that his soil would not be allowed to be used by terrorists; the fig leaf for India to not start war. Mishra had indicated that Musharraf was forced to make the statement because of India's successful coercive diplomacy. The then President, APJ Abdul Kalam told Parliament on 17 February 2003 that: "After the December 13 (2001) attack on our Parliament by Pakistan-based terrorists, we were constrained to deploy our troops along the international border. This decision achieved its purpose by showing both our firmness and our self-restraint in dealing with our hostile neighbour."

Put into perspective, mobilising the IA was a knee-jerk reaction of the Vajpayee government in the vain hope that Pakistan would get coerced. He did not consult its own army before ordering mobilisation. After the de-mobilisation, the army chief, General Padmanabhan said on 9 November 2002: "Whenever there is a situation calling for the army's help, the latter's role should be clearly defined to avoid confusion." Here was a government which instead of coercing got coerced, and the army chief who ordered his command to mobilise for war without knowing what he was supposed to do. If travesty of national security could not be imagined further, one had to only wait for 26/11 attacks in Mumbai to happen.

FORCE has the politico-military inside view of 26/11 from one of the three service chiefs at the time. For first three days as Pakistan-sent terrorists were creating mayhem in Mumbai, the government in New Delhi seemed in a tailspin; the political leadership did not contact the military leadership, and the three defence services did not deem it necessary to consult one another. After 72 hours, the National Security Advisor, M.K. Narayanan called the three chiefs for a meeting with Prime Minister Manmohan Singh, in which the intelligence agencies were not present. By then, it was clear that Pakistan was behind the dastardly act.

The mood in the room was tense and all agreed that Pakistan should not get away with its audacious move. When asked, the army chief, General Deepak Kapoor suggested artillery fire and raids by Special Forces across the Line of Control. The chief of air staff, Air Chief Marshal F.H. Major recommended punitive air strikes inside Pakistan Occupied Kashmir to hit terrorist camps and visible infrastructure, to which the army chief added that it would certainly lead to a full-scale war. There was disagreement over whether the Pakistan Army would escalate matters if the IAF conducted a few punitive sorties across the LC. The army chief felt that had the IAF crossed the LC during the 1999 Kargil conflict, the Pakistan military would have joined the conflict. The navy chief, Admiral Sureesh Mehta kept his counsel; he was neither asked much nor did he offer advice. Strangely, nuclear weapons were not discussed or even remotely mentioned especially when Pakistan has an undeclared nuclear weapons policy which has led to the speculation that it may use weapons early in a war. Maximum time was spent on debating the most inane issue meant for researchers: Pakistan's motives behind 26/11 attacks. The overarching sense was to explore retaliatory options which would not lead to war. As none existed, the meeting broke with the Prime Minister telling the service chiefs to prepare for war. However, the army chief was unequivocally told by the NSA to not recall personnel from leave or move any formations forward till further orders as it would alert Pakistan. The next day, the defence minister A.K. Antony held his meeting attended by service chiefs and senior ministry bureaucrats. The single point agenda was the need to procure critical war equipment for the three services on fast-track basis.

The service chiefs heard nothing from the Prime Minister's Office for a week, after which NSA informed them that India would not go to war with Pakistan. The inevitable two conclusions of the single meeting between the Prime Minister and his service chiefs on 26/11 are: Neither wanted war and all hoped that the crisis blow over quickly, and none wanted to talk about nuclear weapons; probably there are too many unresolved issues. The services sought to utilise the crisis to make up for its critical equipment, something they never seem to do during peacetime. Few nations would have let 164 people die in vain as India did after 26/11 attacks without retribution for the aggressor. The killings which worried the world of a possible war were a non-event for India and its defence forces.

2

Power of Indian Air Force in Indo-Pak Wars

INDO-PAKISTANI AIR WAR OF 1965

The Indo-Pakistani War of 1965 saw the Indian and Pakistani Air Forces engaged in large-scale aerial combat against each other for the first time since the Partition in 1947. The war took place during the course of September 1965 and saw both air forces conduct defensive and offensive operations over Indian and Pakistani airspace. Both countries made contradictory claims regarding the number of losses that they suffered and the number of planes that they claimed to have shot down. Indian losses have been placed at between 59 and 110, while Pakistani losses were between 18 and 43.

Background

The war began in early August 1965 and initially the fighting was confined mainly to the ground. Later, however, as the war progressed, the war took on another dimension as the two sides began air operations against each other. Although the two forces had previously taken part in the First Kashmir War which had occurred shortly after Partition, that engagement had been limited in scale compared to the 1965 conflict and the air operations that both sides had undertaken were limited and largely confined to interdiction and other strategic purposes such as re-supply and troop transport operations. Although there had been one incident where Indian fighter aircraft intercepted a Pakistani transport, there had been no significant air-to-air combat. During the 1965 conflict, however, the PAF flew a total 2,364 sorties while the IAF flew 3,937 sorties.

All out War erupted between India and Pakistan, and during the vicious 17 day conflict PAF flew defensive CAPs over its own bases, offensive counter air missions against Indian airfields, and close-support and interdiction sorties, causing significant damage.

Main Battle

The aerial phase of the war began on 1 September 1965 when the Indian Air Force (IAF) responded to an urgent call for air strikes against the Pakistani Army, which had launched an attack known as Operation Grand Slam. The IAF's 45 Sqn was tasked to carry out Close air Support missions in support of Indian troops. The squadron had recently been moved from Pune to Pathankot, after a merger of No 220 Sqn into it, under the command of Sqn. Ldr. S.K. "Marshal" Dhar. Three missions of four aircraft each were tasked, with the first wave taking off at 1719 hours. These strafed Pakistani positions and attacked Pakistani tanks and ground targets, though a lot of damage from "friendly fire" was also reported later on. The Indian aircraft were intercepted by two Pakistan Air Force (PAF) F-86 Sabres, flown by S/L Sarfraz Rafiqui of No 5 Sqn and F/L Imtiaz Bhatti of No 15 Sqn. In the ensuing dogfight four IAF Vampires were lost, one from the first wave and three from the second. After this, the IAF immediately withdrew about 130 Vampires, together with over 50 Ouragons, from front-line service.

On 2 September, both sides flew in support of their ground forces, however no major aerial engagement was observed.

The next day witnessed an aerial combat of two Sabres of No 11 Squadron and four Gnats of No 27 Sqn from Akhnur. The Sabres were augmented by an F-104. In the course of action, one Sabre was severely damaged, though its pilot managed to land safely. Later on, one of the Gnats landed at Pasrur Airfield, resulting in the capture of the aircraft. On 4 September, an F-86 Sabre was lost. The PAF claimed the cause to be friendly ground fire while the IAF claimed to have shot it down.

Rafiqui was shot down over Halwara on 6 September, while Bhatti ended the war with 34 combat missions to his credit, the maximum combat missions flown by any pilot during the war.

During the conflict, the Pakistani F-86 Sabre Flying Ace, Muhammad Mahmood Alam shot down seven Indian aircraft including claims of two as 'probable'. Five Hawker Hunter aircraft were shot down in one minute, of which four were brought down in 30 seconds.

On September 6, the Indian Army crossed the border at Lahore to relieve pressure on the Chamb Jaurian sector. On the evening of the same day, the PAF responded with attacks on Indian airfields at Pathankot, Adampur and Halwara. The attack on Pathankot was successful, while the attacks on Adampur and Halwara were failures. The IAF lost almost ten aircraft on the ground at Pathankot. The Adampur strike turned back before even reaching Adampur while at Halwara two of the three attacking raiders were shot down for the loss of two Indian Hunters in air combat. Both the Indian pilots survived as they ejected over their base, whereas the intruding Pakistani pilots were killed in action. This included the ace Squadron Leader Sarfaraz Rafiqui who had shot down two Vampires on 1 September. Before being shot down, Rafiqui is credited with shooting down the first of the Hunters. He was later posthumously awarded the Sitara-e-Jurat for the Chamb action and the Hilal-i-Jurat for the Halwara action.

On 7 September 1965 the PAF parachuted 135 Special Services Group (SSG) para commandos at three Indian airfields (Halwara, Pathankot and Adampur). The daring attempt proved to be an "unmitigated disaster". Only ten commandos were able to return to Pakistan, the rest were taken as prisoners of war (including one of the Commanders of the operations, Major Khalid Butt). At Halwara and Adampur these troops landed in residential areas where the villagers caught and handed them over to police.

Also on 7 September the IAF mounted 33 sorties against the heavily guarded PAF airfield complex at Sargodha. The IAF lost two Mysteres and three Hunters due to the defence mounted by the PAF's local squadrons. One of the Indian Hunter pilots, who ejected near Sargodha, was made POW and released after the war. One of the crippled Mysteres flying solo got involved in a dogfight with an F-104 Starfighter and each somehow shot the other down; the Pakistani pilot safely ejected, while the Indian pilot, Squadron Leader Ajamada B. Devayya, was killed. Squadron Leader Devayya was awarded the Maha Vir Chakra for his bravery 23 years later, after his feat was revealed by an author appointed by the PAF to write its official history of the 1965 war.

The seventh of September also marked the day when the PAF attacked IAF airfields in the Eastern Sector. During the PAF's raid on Kalaikunda, Indian pilot Flight Lieutenant A T Cooke engaged four Pakistani Sabres, shooting down one while flying at tree-top height and making another a write off in the process.

The war lessened in intensity after 8 September, with occasional clashes between the IAF and the PAF. Both air forces now changed their doctrine from air interdictions to ground attack and concentrated their efforts on knocking out soft skin targets and supply lines, such as wagons carrying ammunition; and armoured vehicles. During the conflict IAFEnglish Electric Canberras raided a few of the Pakistani bases. On 10 September one Mystere was downed by anti-aircraft fire in Pakistan but the pilot ejected safely.

On September 13 one PAF F-86 Sabre was downed while attacking a train near Gurdaspur and the pilot was killed. In another encounter the same day between PAF Sabres from Sargodha and IAF Gnats from No. 2 Squadron, an Indian Gnat was shot down by a PAF F-86 Sabre flown by Flt Lt Yusaf Ali Khan although the Indian pilot managed to eject safely. The other Gnat was engaged and damaged in air combat by Flt

Lt Imtiaz Bhatti. The experienced pilot somehow managed to return to base, where according to All India Radio the Gnat's pilot later died of wounds sustained during the combat. He was said to have brought his damaged aircraft back to base and to have died during landing. His funeral was attended by the Indian President. Yusaf Ali Khan was credited with a kill whereas, Imtiaz Bhatti was credited with damaging the IAF Gnat despite the later confirmation that the pilot died of wounds and the Gnat crashed during its landing attempt.

Later in the night of 13/14 September, Indian Canberras undertook the deepest penetration of Pakistani airspace of the war, attacking Pakistani bases around Peshawar and Kohat. Rather than bombing the Peshawer runway, however, IAF bombers mistook the mall road in Peshawer as the runway and dropped their bombs there instead. The PAF admits that the IAF came very close to annihilating its entire fleet of B-57 bombers.

The Canberras were intercepted by a Pakistani F-104 near Lahore but they managed to evade the Starfighter and return home safely. They also had an encounter with F-86 Sabres, one of which fired at the Canberras, which sustained some damage. A Pakistani F-86 Sabre also crashed while conducting an evasive maneuvere in an attempt to escape pursuit, from an escorting Gnat as it tried to defend the Canberra bombers; the PAF pilot was killed. The Gnat pilot, W/C Singh, was later credited with an aerial victory for this incident near Amritsar. Later, one Pakistani B-57 was shot down by anti-aircraft fire over Adampur, although both of its crew managed to eject safely and remained POWs.

On 15 September the PAF employed a number of its Lockheed C-130 Hercules transport aircraft as bombers, which proved unsuccessful; two of them were shot down by the IAF. The following day, one IAF Hunter and a PAF F-86 Sabre were shot down over Halwara. The IAF pilot was killed in the encounter, although the Pakistani pilot ejected and spent the rest of the war as a POW. A Pakistani Cessna was also shot down that day, as well as an Auster observation aircraft. On

18 September a Sabre was shot down by a Gnat over Amritsar; the matter was reported by the Collector, who had witnessed the entire dogfight. The same day a Pakistani Sabre shot down a civilian Indian aircraft even after the civilian plane indicated its identity, the PAF pilot assuming it to be a reconnaissance mission. Years later, the PAF pilot wrote a letter to the Indian pilot's daughter to apologize for shooting down the aircraft. The aircraft had been carrying the then Gujarat Chief Minister Balwant Rai and his family.

On 19 September a Gnat and two Sabres were downed over Chawinda. One of the Sabres that were shot down was credited to Squadron Leader Denzil Keelor, the brother of Trevor Keelor, who was credited with the first Indian aerial victory of the war. The following day, another two Hunters and an F-86 Sabre were lost over Kasur, Pakistan.

At one stage the IAF was operating 200 air missions simultaneously. IAF Folland Gnats of Nos 9 and 23 squadrons played a significant role in major air battles.

On 21 September IAF Canberras carried out a daring daylight strike into Pakistan against the radar complex in Badin. The raid proved to be successful. Under the command of Wing Commander Peter Wilson, six Canberras from No. 16 Squadron took off from Agra, over 1,000 km from Bladin and proceeded towards the radar complex at low level. About 80 miles (130 km) short of the target, one Canberra climbed to an altitude of 10,000 feet in order to act as a decoy, before returning to base. The other five Canberras continued on towards the target. The flight then separated and four of the aircraft approached the target in two sections, each two minutes apart, at low level; before climbing to 7,000 feet from where they carried out bombing runs, dropping approximately 10,000 lbs of explosives. Wilson then approached from the south at an altitude of just 30 feet firing a salvo of 68mm rockets at the radar dome.

On the same day a PAF F-104 intercepted a Canberra bomber on its way back from Sargodha and shot it down, while one Hunter pilot who was the son of Chief of the Indian Army was shot down by anti-aircraft fire; he ejected and was taken POW. The ceasefire was declared on the night of September 22, 1965.

Outcome

There are conflicting claims by either side on this issue. Pakistani sources suggest that Indian losses were in the range of 59–110 and Pakistani losses were around 18–43. Recent works have, however, attempted to move beyond the raw statistics of the number of losses each side incurred, arguing that in terms of aircraft lost to sorties flown, the Indian Air Force's attrition rate (1.5%) was lower than the Pakistani attrition rate (1.82%). Arguably this indicates that had the war continued, the PAF would have found it increasingly difficult to sustain operations at the same level. Nevertheless, a similar argument can be made about the IAF also, although it did have a significant size advantage that might have proved telling if the war had been prolonged.

Another factor which makes it difficult to determine the outcome of the 1965 air war is the issue of aircraft lost in the air in air-to-air combat or to ground fire as opposed to aircraft lost on the ground due to bombing. Indian sources claimed that a large number of Indian aircraft losses occurred on the ground during the attacks on Kalaikkunda and Pathankot—up to 60 per cent by some accounts

Learning the Lessons

Much of the lessons of the 1965 war lead India to refine tactics which proved decisive in the 1971 war. Pakistani forces failed to take account of the extent to which they had relied on two factors which the IAF could not take for granted-complete ground based defensive radar coverage and an adequate supply of air-to-air missiles. Much effort was expended in India to remedy these deficiencies before 1971.

With Soviet aid, India established a modern early warning radar system, including the recently introduced 'Fansong-E' low-level radar, linked with SA-2 'Guideline' surface-to-air missiles and a large number of AA guns. By December 1971 the IAF comprised a total of 36 squadrons (of which 10 were deployed in the Bengal sector) with some 650 combat aircraft.

Moreover, the 1965 war resulted in the USA imposing a 10 year arms embargo on both sides. This had no effect, on India, which had always looked to Britain, France and even Russia for arms, but was disastrous for Pakistan, which was forced to acquire 90 obsolete second hand Sabre via Iran, a mere 28 Mirage IIIs from France and 74 maintenance intensive Shenyang F-6s. It was unable to replace losses among its (already weak) force of B-57s, or to acquire a modern interceptor in realistic numbers.

THE INDIAN AIR FORCE IN THE KARGIL WAR

"Aviators have traditionally been a haughty breed. They are used to spending solitary hours with their machines, aloof, on top of the world, far removed from its mundane troubles. Everything that seemed important on terra firma becomes so much smaller. In the cockpit, few things can humble this pride. The mountains can. When you fly at the roof of the world and still have the impassive peaks of the mighty Himalayas look down on you at Flight Level 200, your perspective changes. The experience of air warfare in mountains teaches stern lessons. The aviator must respect the mountains."

An Indian Air Force Mirage 2000 pilot who flew in the Kargil War

The Indian Air Force (IAF) is the world's fourth-largest air service, operating more than 1,300 aircraft out of some 60 bases nationwide. It also is one of the world's oldest continuously functioning air forces, with roots going back to October 8, 1932, when it was established by Great Britain's Royal Air Force as an auxiliary of the Indian Empire during the time of the British Raj. Until the early 1990s, it was principally a support entity for the Indian Army.

Today, it has acquired independent strategic missions, most notably including those of nuclear deterrence and retaliation, and it is a diversified fighting force with manifest ambitions toward global reach and status. It also is a full-spectrum combat air arm with a precision conventional strike capability, fielding not only fourth-generation multirole fighters, but also force-extending tankers, a recently acquired airborne warning and control system capability, intertheater airlifters, unmanned aerial vehicles equipped with multispectral sensors for longdwell strategic and tactical reconnaissance, and the beginnings of a military space surveillance capability.

The field of strategic regard in which this maturing force most centrally figures now extends from the east coast of Africa to Sumatra and the entire Indian Ocean operating area. Like few other air arms around the world, the IAF operates over the most diverse range of geographic areas, from the Siachen glacier in the north to the deserts, jungles, and oceans that surround India's periphery. A former air officer commanding-in-chief (AOC-in-C) of the IAF's Western Air Command well captured the IAF leadership's now oft-expressed characterization of the steadily modernizing service when he wrote in 2009 of the IAF's "growing aspirations to transform itself from a mere subcontinental tactical force to an intercontinental strategic aerospace power in conformity with other leading air forces in the world."

India's principal external challengers—and hence the IAF's main objects of strategic and operational concern—are China and Pakistan, in that order.

China is generally regarded by the Indian defence community as posing a more downstream source of potential trouble, whereas Pakistan is deemed both a longer-term *and* a here-and-now threat to the country's security. Because both India and its two leading rivals all possess well-stocked inventories of readily available nuclear weapons, most planners in New Delhi assess the likelihood of an all-out war on the subcontinent as being quite low. The uppermost concern of the IAF leadership with respect to combat readiness today entails operating decisively at a conventional level against either rival when all sides in any conflict will be within immediate reach of a nuclear response option. Given this omnipresent risk of escalation, most Indian threat assessors believe that any future combat engagement with either China or Pakistan will, in all likelihood, be sharp and intense but also brief and for limited stakes.

In this regard, an official IAF publication released in 2007 frankly acknowledged the "likely short duration" of any war that India may have to contend with in the near-term future. The most probable prospect, according to retired IAF Air Commodore Jasjit Singh, is for "prolonged periods of peace with spurts of armed violence of great variety."

In a thoughtful enumeration of the diverse conflict possibilities that could confront Indian security planners in the next decade, a retired IAF air marshal in 2007 listed as being among the most plausible of those possibilities an extended border war with China, with little likelihood of nuclear weapons use; a shorter and more intense war with Pakistan entailing a very real chance of nuclear use—unlike India, Pakistan has never proclaimed a nuclear no-first-use policy; a simultaneous war with China and Pakistan operating in collusion; and a prolonged lower-intensity war in Kashmir against both Pakistani regular forces and indigenous Kashmiri insurgents.

An instructive preview of this last type of conflict scenario can be seen in the Kargil War that unfolded in the high mountains of Indian-controlled Kashmir in May, June, and July 1999. That intense border clash for limited but important stakes, which ensued for seventy-four days at a cost of more than a thousand casualties on each side, was overshadowed by NATO's higher-profile air war for Kosovo that occurred thousands of miles away in the Balkans at roughly the same time. In large part because of that more attention-getting distraction, the Kargil War remains only dimly appreciated by most Western defence experts—and barely at all by students and practitioners of airpower.

Western defence professionals have much to gain from a closer inquiry into this little-known chapter in the history of air warfare.

Nevertheless, it was a milestone event in Indian military history and one that represents a telling prototype of India's most likely type of future combat challenge in the immediate years ahead. No less important, it offers both an exemplary case study in the uses of airpower in joint warfare and a particularly revealing testament to the special difficulties of modern air employment in high mountain conditions. The Kargil experience is key to a proper understanding of India's emerging air posture because it constitutes the one instance of recent Indian exposure to high-intensity warfare that provides insights into the IAF's capabilities, limitations, relations with its sister services, and interactions with India's civilian leadership.

The conflict was also emblematic of one type of border skirmish between India and Pakistan, and perhaps also between India and China, that could recur in the next decade in light of the inhibiting effect of the nuclear overhang on more protracted and higher-stakes tests of strength. As retired Air Commodore Singh reflected on the experience six years after its successful conclusion for India, the conflict was "a typical example of a limited war in a nuclear weapons environment." For all these reasons, Western defence professionals have much to gain from a closer inquiry into this little-known chapter in the history of air warfare.

KARGIL AND TODAY'S THREATS

This leaves us with the still-unanswered question as to whether the Kargil experience offers an instructive prototype for the most probable near-term threats that may face the IAF along India's borders with Pakistan and China in the decade ahead.

Without question, the unusually demanding challenges presented by Operation Safed Sagar made for a sobering wake-up call for the IAF, which evidently had not given much thought to such a scenario and had not trained routinely at such elevations until it was forced to do so by operational necessity. Not long after the fighting ended, Indian defence experts began contemplating such limited engagements in time and scale as the most likely wave of the future with respect to any provocations of that sort that might arise anew along the volatile LoC running through Kashmir.

In that regard, Air Commodore Singh voiced the opinion of many when he called Kargil "a template for limited war and future options if war becomes inevitable."

The unusually demanding challenges presented by Operation Safed Sagar made for a sobering wake-up call for the IAF, which evidently had not given much thought to such a scenario and had not trained routinely at such elevations until it was forced to do so by operational necessity.

Viewed in hindsight, the Kargil War is replete with insights into the dynamics of deterrence in the Indo-Pakistani relationship. Especially important in this regard, Pakistan's military leaders miscalculated badly in their apparent belief that the international community would press immediately for a cease-fire in Kashmir out of concern over a possible escalation of the fighting to the nuclear level, with the net result that Pakistan would be left with an easily acquired new slice of terrain on the Indian side of the LoC.

In addition, General Malik later suggested that those who concocted the incursion gambit had erroneously convinced themselves that a stable deterrent relationship between India and Pakistan at the nuclear level would enable a Pakistani conventional offensive into Kashmir with virtual impunity. That analysis was based on the putative premise that India would not counter the provocation with an all-out conventional response that would risk either escalation or ending in a costly stalemate.

Since the Vajpayee government scrupulously kept its combat operations confined to Indian controlled Kashmir, the international community had no compelling reason to intervene.

In the end, both of those likely Pakistani assumptions proved unfounded. The nuclear balance between the two countries did *not* deter a determined Indian conventional response, and the successful reaction that India ultimately mounted on the Kargil heights fell well short of being all-out in scale. Furthermore, since the Vajpayee government scrupulously kept its combat operations confined to Indian-controlled Kashmir, the international community had no compelling reason to intervene.

As a result, a remote but high-intensity and high-stakes showdown was allowed to run on for more than two months, something the Pakistan Army's leaders all but certainly did not anticipate when they first conjured up their incursion plan.

Indeed, in the view of a retired Indian Army major general, Pakistan's military leaders "had not thought beyond the first week or 10 days" in their approach to planning the confrontation. They also, the general suggested, all but surely did not bargain on the combat involvement of Indian airpower. An informed and insightful former Pakistan Army brigadier later well characterized the introduction of IAF fighters into the conflict on May 26 as an effective asymmetric vertical escalation that Pakistan could not match without running unbearable risks of a larger and more consequential confrontation.

The Kargil experience also suggested that if China and Pakistan came to appreciate that India possessed an overwhelming conventional force preponderance in the region, that presence could act as a deterrent against such provocations in the future. Such a realization ultimately led to a new Indian declaratory policy toward that end that was enunciated in January 2000 by India's then minister of defence, George Fernandes. At a seminar in New Delhi that month, Fernandes observed that in precipitating the Kargil War, Pakistan "had not absorbed the real meaning of nuclearization—that it can deter *only* the use of nuclear weapons, but not all and any war." The overarching teaching of the war experience, he added, was that nuclear weapons had not rendered war in the region obsolete or made "covert war by proxy ... the only option." A no less important teaching, Fernandes said, was that "conventional war remained feasible, but with definite limitations [now] if escalation across the nuclear threshold was to be avoided." The Kargil experience suggested that if China and Pakistan came to appreciate that India possessed an overwhelming conventional force preponderance in the region, that presence could act as a deterrent against such provocations in the future.

A related question of note here concerns the extent to which the IAF's role in helping to enable India's successful outcome in Operation Vijay may offer a central ingredient of *conventional* deterrence against future such provocations. In this regard, a reflective IAF warrior/scholar suggested that the IAF's "never done before" high-elevation interdiction operations during the Kargil fighting contributed significantly to the achievement of the government's ultimate strategic goal of evicting Pakistan's forces from the positions that they had occupied. He further observed that its telling strikes against enemy troop emplacements and supply dumps "created a strategic effect" by forcing Pakistan's leadership to reassess its strategy of conducting an open-ended proxy war against India. This airman added that those operations "also silenced critics within India who [previously had] felt that airpower was essentially escalatory in nature."

Without a doubt, the air balance throughout the Kargil War stood markedly in India's favour, with an overall fighter force ratio of 750 to 350. With respect to the most cutting-edge fighters then fielded by the two sides, Pakistan's inventory of just 26 U.S.-provided F-16As was greatly outmatched numerically, and perhaps qualitatively as well, by the IAF's 145 highest-performance aircraft (70 MiG-29s, 45 Mirage 2000Hs, and 30 Su-30s). Air Commodore Singh suggested that this advantage in India's favour "clearly deterred Pakistan from using its air force to come to the rescue of its soldiers, whose large numbers were being killed by the Indian Army and Air Force [and were] being denied critically needed supplies like ammunition, rations, and reinforcements."

Yet at the same time, prudent Indian defence planners will likely find themselves shortchanged in their preparations for the full spectrum of possible challenges to their country's security in years to come if they draw undue comfort from the happy ending of the Kargil experience and accept that conflict as their *only* planning baseline for hedging against future contingencies along the LoC. Much like NATO's air war for Kosovo that unfolded in the Balkans at roughly the same time, the Kargil War was a poor test of India's air warfare capability. The IAF's fighter pilots were consigned to do what they could rather than what they might have done in a less restricted engagement in which they would not have been bound by such operating constraints. Moreover, like NATO's roughly concurrent Operation Allied Force against Serbia, the enemy had the initiative throughout most of the Kargil War, and both the nature of the operational challenge the IAF faced in the Kargil heights and the targeting requirements that ensued from that challenge necessarily dictated an unconventional and suboptimal use of India's increasingly capable air weapon.

Prudent Indian defence planners will likely find themselves shortchanged in their preparations for the full spectrum of possible challenges to their country's security in years to come if they draw undue comfort from the happy ending of the Kargil experience and accept that conflict as their only planning baseline for hedging against future contingencies along the Line of Control.

A decade after Operation Safed Sagar's successful conclusion, Air Marshal Patney observed that "Pakistan had a reasonably good air force but elected not to use it or was wary of the consequences of its use.... [It] handed over air dominance to India without a fight. Had Pakistan offered [aerial] combat ... the pattern of air activity would have been very different. We would have had to fight for air dominance, even if it was at the cost of other air operations of the war." That suggests that a bolder Pakistani risk calculus, or even an inadvertent escalation dynamic emanating from misjudgment on either side, could have resulted in a higher-intensity showdown over the same initial stakes. That escalated conflict, in turn, would have demanded a far more robust and sustainable Indian conventional force posture than that which prevailed well enough over Pakistan in 1999. Ultimately, one can only speculate as to what kept a major aerial clash between the IAF and PAF from occurring at any time during the Kargil fighting. However, it is clear that a recurring border challenge along the LoC in years yet to come could end up presenting a more demanding test of the IAF's strength than the Kargil conflict that would require a more exacting approach to airpower employment.

Insofar as India's clear preeminence in the bilateral air balance contributed materially to its success in 1999, the IAF should have every incentive henceforth to sustain a no-less-pronounced combat edge over Pakistan in its future force development. It should also have strong motivations to maintain at least a local preponderance of air capability along India's border with China.

For students of air warfare, the IAF's combat experience during the 1999 Kargil War reaffirmed a number of abiding characteristics of modern air arms around the world today. It showed, for example, that innovation and adaptability under the stress of confining rules of engagement—in this case the Vajpayee government's strict injunction that the IAF not cross the LoC under any circumstances—is a generic hallmark of modern airmanship. It further showed that professionalism in such operationally crucial matters as campaign planning, presentation of forces, accommodation of new and unique tactical challenges (in this instance the need to engage hard-to-see targets in unprecedentedly high-elevation Himalayan battlespace), and effectively underwriting the needs of a joint force commander is scarcely a monopoly of more familiar Western air arms. It demonstrated yet again how the effective application of air-delivered firepower, particularly if unmatched by the opposing side, can shorten and facilitate the outcome of an engagement that might otherwise have persisted indefinitely.

And when it comes to still-needed improvements in the joint arena, it showed that an absence of transparency in cross-service communication, to say nothing of interdependence in campaign planning, is by no means a malaise unique to the

United States and its allies. On this important count, an informed Indian assessment of useful teachings to be drawn from the Kargil experience underscored the post-campaign "revelations about the quarreling between the air force and army chiefs over the use of airpower in Kargil" and concluded that "the problem is clearly not a minor one. At least one lesson ... of Kargil appears not to have been sufficiently well learned—the high cost of bureaucratic politics." The issue is still controversial, and many observers of India's military organization and defence decisionmaking arrangements, both in India and worldwide, have argued for some time that a major step toward ameliorating that high cost, at least at the margins, would be to create the position of chief of the Defence Staff. The job of the new chief would be to oversee and adjudicate interservice differences when it comes to the apportionment of military roles and resources, as has long been the practice in the United States (with its chairman of the Joint Chiefs of Staff) and in most other developed Western countries.

PRELUDE TO A SHOWDOWN

Flare-ups along the border between Pakistan and India have a long history, going back as far as 1947 when British rule of the subcontinent ended and the former British Indian Empire was subdivided into the newly independent Union of India and the Dominion of Pakistan. That development prompted Pakistan to launch a guerilla incursion into Kashmir in an attempt to establish control over the contested region. The Indian Army and the IAF countered in force by entering Kashmir and driving the Pakistani-sponsored irregulars out of all but a small portion of the high mountain state.

The seeds of the Kargil conflict were first planted in March and April 1999. Then, determined units of the Pakistan Army crossed the Line of Control (LoC) into the Indian portion of contested Kashmir in the remote and rugged Himalayan heights overlooking Kargil between the Kashmir Valley and the Ladakh plateau. The LoC running through Jammu and Kashmir that separates the Indian-held and Pakistani-controlled portions of the disputed territory is a long-standing product of the third Indo-Pakistani war that created Bangladesh. It bisects some of the most forbidding terrain to be found anywhere in the world, with most of the main ridgelines being offshoots of K2, the world's second-highest mountain.

While preparations were under way for an upcoming meeting of India's and Pakistan's prime ministers in Lahore, Pakistan, senior leaders in the Pakistan Army, led by the chief of the Army Staff, General Pervez Musharraf, and the chief of the General Staff, Lieutenant General Mohammed Aziz, were conducting initial reconnaissance and laying the logistical groundwork for the impending operation. The most likely aim of the planned gambit, apart from seeking to internationalize the Kashmir issue in Indo-Pakistani relations, was to take control of India's sole line of communication to troops on the Siachen glacier by obstructing the use of the key two-lane national highway NH1A in Ladakh running from Srinagar through Kargil to Leh. It provided access to the IAF's airfield at Thoise on the axis to Siachen.

The incursion's planners took full advantage of the relaxed atmosphere that had come to prevail in New Delhi after the visit of Prime Minister Atal Vajpayee to Pakistan to help promulgate the Lahore Declaration, which was signed by Vajpayee and his Pakistani counterpart, Nawaz Sharif, on February 21. With it, the governments of both countries swore their commitment to the vision of peace and stability embodied in the United Nations charter. The Pakistan Army leaders chose to exploit the nascent, and ultimately short-lived, feeling of goodwill that had emanated from that declaration in a way that might irreversibly change the status quo along the LoC to Pakistan's advantage.

Because of the capricious weather that predominates in the area, the Indian Army during the harshest winter months that immediately preceded the Kargil crisis vacated its most inhospitable forward outposts—typically at elevations of 14,000 to 18,000 feet—that were normally manned on India's side of the LoC throughout the remainder of the year. Since substantial gaps existed in India's defences in the segment of Kashmir that lay on both sides of the LoC, a segment featuring very few trails leading off from the main roadways, the Pakistani planners thought the vacated outposts made prime targets for seizure. Adding further to the attractiveness of the planned gambit, the outposts were situated on easily defended high ground that Indian troops would have to attack from below in order to try to recapture them. A clever mix of regular combat troops and local civilian porters would infiltrate the area and present the Indian government with a fait accompli in Kashmir.

Pakistan's military leaders were all but surely emboldened by their country's acquisition of a nuclear weapons delivery capability within the preceding year. They may also have been encouraged by a derivative belief that the awareness of that capability in key leadership circles in New Delhi would more than offset any conventional military advantage India enjoyed in the region. And even if the operation were to be detected by India while it was still in progress, the incursion's planners likely judged that the Indian Army's reaction to it would be slow and limited at best. Most important, they probably took it as a foregone conclusion that were India to seek to conventionalize the ensuing conflict, pressure from the international community would quickly intervene and force the Vajpayee government to cease combat operations within a week, thus leaving Pakistan "comfortably in possession of gains it would make by infiltration," in the words of retired Indian Army Major General G. D. Bakshi.

Ultimately, in what turned out to be a phased infiltration in uniquely challenging mountain terrain, Pakistani troops moving by foot and helicopter occupied roughly 130 outposts on India's side of the LoC before the intruders were first detected by local shepherds on May 3. At least eighteen artillery batteries, most of them from across the LoC in Pakistani-controlled territory, were said to have supported the operation. Indian sources later reported that the occupying force numbered from 1,500 to 2,000 combatants, with perhaps four to five times that many troops mobilized to help supply the most forward elements on the Indian side of the LoC. The occupying troop contingent consisted mainly of elements of the local Pakistan Army Northern Light Infantry (NLI) and members of Pakistan's elite Special Services Group, with many outfitted in civilian garb so as to appear as indigenous Kashmiri mujahideen. The intruders were well armed, well trained in mountain warfare, and accustomed to operating at high elevations.

India's security principals and other informed experts have freely admitted that the Pakistan Army achieved "complete strategic and tactical surprise" in its execution of the incursion, owing to its having relied on inplace NLI formations rather than moving in a heavier troop contingent that would have generated a larger deployment signature. The incursion's organizers further sought plausible deniability of any culpability for their aggressive action through the use of a shrewd deception measure. They generated indigenous militant Islamist radio traffic within Pakistani-occupied Kashmir to convince Indian signals intelligence monitors that the incursion was insurgent activity over which Pakistan had no control. Finally, the intruders took special care to move only at times that would allow them to avoid detection by periodic Indian winter air surveillance operations.

As the Indian Army units that had manned the temporarily vacated outposts began returning to their stations during the first week of May, they slowly discovered the full extent of the occupation of those positions by Pakistani troops. The Indian Army's 121st Infantry Brigade assigned to monitor the LoC above Kargil launched a succession of probing patrols on May 5 that confirmed the infiltration. The full scale of the intrusions was validated on May 8 by IAF pilots in Cheetah light helicopters as they flew surveillance sorties along the Tololing ridge in the Dras subsector of the Kargil region.

It took more than a week in all for the Indian Army to take stock of its challenge at hand and to develop the beginnings of a course of action to drive the invaders out. Even then, the army's local commanders grossly underestimated and, accordingly, misreported the full magnitude of the situation they were facing. As late as May 19, Lieutenant General Krishan Pal, the commander of 15 Corps that represented the Indian Army's main fighting presence in Kashmir, was said to have been "blissfully oblivious [of] the deathly situation." At a key Unified Headquarters meeting in Srinagar to discuss next steps for addressing the situation, he predicted that in the coming showdown, the incursion "would be defeated locally." Other reporting up the line by the Indian Army offered soothing assurances that "the infiltration will be vacated in 48 hours." Clearly, local ground commanders in Kargil and Srinagar did not appreciate the full gravity of the Pakistani challenge at the start of the gathering crisis.

Once they understood more fully what had transpired along the LoC, the army's leaders finally responded by moving five infantry divisions, five independent brigades, and 44 battalions from the Kashmir Valley to the Kargil sector, ultimately mobilizing some 200,000 Indian troops in all. Most of this buildup occurred during the three weeks between the initial detection of the incursion and the eventual start on May 26 of a major joint counteroffensive codenamed Operation Vijay (meaning "victory" in Hindi). The avowed objectives were to drive out the intruding forces and to restore the LoC to its previous status. The response was almost certainly more determined than anything the Pakistan Army leaders had anticipated.

ENLISTING THE IAF'S INVOLVEMENT

After several early firefights with the entrenched Pakistanis that occasioned numerous Indian fatalities in an unsuccessful bid to recapture the closest of the occupied positions, the Indian Army approached the IAF on May 11 and asked it to help turn the tide through a commitment of armed helicopters to support the embattled ground troops. Conflicting views persist to this day regarding what happened over the ensuing two weeks after that initial army entreaty with respect to when and how the IAF should become involved in the conduct of India's looming counteroffensive.

One view maintains that the IAF initiated combat operations over Kargil only "reluctantly" and sought "to avoid involvement in the conflict altogether, claiming inexperience in mountain warfare and unfamiliarity with the terrain, as well as the risk associated with the heightened SAM [surface-to-air-missile] threat in the mountains." That view holds that the IAF committed itself to the fight only after an insistent demand for such involvement from the Indian Army leadership. This interpretation drew much of its claim to veracity from an assessment by an Indian civilian defence writer that appeared shortly after the war ended. The writer alleged that once the extent of the Pakistani intrusions was discovered, the IAF at first "sidestepped requests by the army to attack the infiltrators" and agreed to lend its support to the ongoing fighting only after its leadership "was presented with a *fait accompli* and pressed [presumably by higher government authority] into making attacks on May 26."

In truth, the IAF began conducting initial reconnaissance sorties over the Kargil heights as early as May 10, less than a week after the presence of the enemy incursion was first confirmed by Indian Army patrols. It also began deploying additional aircraft into the Kashmir Valley in enough numbers to support any likely combat tasking, established a rudimentary air defence control arrangement there because there were no groundbased radars in the area, and began extensive practice of air-to-ground weapons deliveries by both fighters and attack helicopters at Himalayan target elevations. On May 12, an IAF helicopter was fired upon near the most forward-based Pakistani positions overlooking Kargil and landed uneventfully with a damaged rotor. That hostile act prompted Air Headquarters to place Western Air Command, the IAF unit responsible for the Jammu and Kashmir sectors, on heightened alert and to establish quick-reaction aircraft launch facilities at the IAF's northernmost operating locations at Air Force Stations Srinagar and Avantipur.

The next day, IAF Jaguar fighters conducted tactical reconnaissance sorties in the Kargil area to gather prospective target information using their onboard long-range oblique photography systems, and a forward direction center for the tactical control of combat aircraft was established at the IAF's highest-elevation airfield at Air Force Station Leh.

Concurrently, Canberra PR57 and MiG25R reconnaissance aircraft were pressed into service over Kargil, and electronic intelligence missions began to be flown regularly by the IAF in the vicinity of the detected intrusion and beyond. Finally, on May 14, Air Headquarters activated the IAF's air operations center for Jammu and Kashmir and mobilized its fielded forces in that sector for a possible all-out air counteroffensive. At the same time, in close conjunction with their 15 Corps counterparts, Western Air Command planners developed a tailored concept of operations for kinetic air employment in the Kargil heights that included target-selection procedures, force deconfliction and other safety criteria, and an arrangement for conducting and communicating prompt battle damage assessment. From the very start, the IAF expected that it would be engaged in earnest against the intruders just as soon as it and the army leadership could agree on a final course of action. As the AOC-in-C of the IAF's Western Air Command at the time, Air Marshal Vinod Patney, later affirmed, "we were ready for a full-fledged war and had been for some days before May 25, 1999, when government clearance [to commit the IAF to combat] was received."

In an effort to set the record straight once and for all, since-retired Air Chief Marshal Anil Tipnis, who was chief of the Air Staff at the time of the incursion and who later oversaw the IAF's response, offered a detailed reconstruction in October 2006 of his own recollections regarding the sequence of events during the high command's initial deliberations about the Kargil crisis. As Tipnis recalled, on May 10, a full week after the incursion was first detected and the Indian Army had attempted an initial armed response on its own, his vice chief, Air Marshal Prithvi Singh Brar, informed him of a report passed up the line that morning by the IAF's assistant chief of staff for intelligence that the army "may be in some sort of difficulties in the Kargil area." Queried by Tipnis as to the nature of the rumoured difficulties, the vice chief replied that he was not sure but that "there reportedly was unusual artillery firing."

Tipnis learned later that day that the ground force organization responsible for the Kargil sector, Northern Army Command, had communicated nothing of its ongoing operations to its assigned provider of air support in case of hostilities along the LoC, the IAF's Western Air Command. The next day, Tipnis's vice chief told him that his army counterpart had indicated that the army "could handle the situation." Tipnis further learned that Northern Army Command had asked the local air officer commanding (AOC) for Jammu and Kashmir to provide immediate fire support by Mi-25 and Mi-35 helicopter gunships and armed Mi-17 helicopters to "evict a few 'intruders' who had stepped across the LoC in the Kargil sector." The AOC replied that the high terrain over which the requested support was to be provided lay above the effective operating envelope of the helicopters. He added that if the army genuinely needed significant air support for its operations, it would need to convey that requirement to higher headquarters for detailed consideration and approval.

In the meantime, Tipnis's vice chief again pulsed his army counterpart as to whether Northern Army Command really needed help from the IAF. As Tipnis recalled, the army vice "had expressed the army's ability to manage, but was upset that AOC Jammu and Kashmir had not acceded to Headquarters Northern Command's fire-support demand." At that, Tipnis recalled, "there was no doubt in my mind that the situation was desperate." Because committing airpower in close proximity to the LoC could dangerously escalate the conflict, Tipnis insisted that the army "needed political clearance" before the IAF could provide the requested fire support. He also ruled out any employment of IAF armed helicopters because they would be "sitting ducks" for enemy infrared surface-to-air-missile fire. Fixed-wing fighters, he said, would be essential for mission effectiveness, and the IAF "reserved the prerogative to give fire support in the manner it considered most suitable." To this, the army vice chief responded that "the army was capable of throwing back the intruders on its own" but, as Tipnis recalled, that doing so would take time and that air support from the IAF would hasten the process. The army vice continued to insist that such support be provided solely in the form of armed helicopters.

Facing this continued impasse in his dealing with the army, Tipnis called a meeting of his most senior subordinates at Air Headquarters on May 15 to review the known events as they had played out thus far. After being briefed on the situation, the air chief issued this assessment and direction:

I observed that the ground situation was grave. Army required air force help to evict the intruders. Army Headquarters was reluctant, possibly because it was embarrassed to have allowed the present situation to develop, to reveal the full gravity of the situation to the Ministry of Defence. Thus it was not amenable to Air Headquarters' position to seek government approval for use of airpower offensively.

Tipnis then reiterated his determination that despite the army's continued insistence on the use of helicopters in a fire-support role, such use would continue to be denied by the IAF because the helicopters "would be vulnerable in the extreme."

The following day, Tipnis met with the army vice chief at the latter's request (the army chief, General Ved Malik, was out of the country on official travel). The army vice chief once again pressed his request for immediate support by armed helicopters.

Air Marshal Patney proposed that Tipnis call a Chiefs of Staff Committee meeting to seek high-level closure once and for all on the IAF's involvement in the coming counteroffensive. In the meeting, Tipnis reiterated the need for prior government approval for any introduction of Indian airpower into the looming fight, since the chance that such a commitment could trigger a major escalation of the fighting was, in his view, very high.

As for the manner in which the army had responded to the crisis in its assessment and conduct up to that point, Tipnis recalled that there had been a *total lack of army-air force joint staff work. When the army found itself in difficulties, information/intelligence had not been communicated by Army Headquarters in any systematic manner to Air Headquarters. There had been no call for a joint briefing, leave alone joint planning, both at the service and command headquarters; just repeated requests for armed helicopter support.... There had been no joint deliberations at any level.*

On May 23, General Malik, having since returned to New Delhi, summoned Tipnis and the chief of the Naval Staff, Admiral Sushil Kumar, to his office. As Tipnis recalled,

His main thrust was that we needed to put up a united front to the CCS [Cabinet Committee on Security].... Ved said the air force had to join in as the army was in a difficult position. I told him that there was no doubt of that and the air force was very keen to join in, my only reservation being in respect of the use of helicopters—they would be too vulnerable.

After going back and forth with Tipnis on the helicopter issue, General Malik retorted, "If that's the way you want it, I will go it alone." Tipnis eventually gave in "against [his] better judgment" out of a desire "to save army-air force relations."

The next day, the Chiefs of Staff Committee met and adopted a unanimous stance regarding what should be done with respect to the intrusion. In the end, it took the incontrovertible evidence of the reconnaissance imagery provided by the IAF and by other sources for the army chief to realize the full extent of the problem and to agree to take the issue to the prime minister.

During a pivotal May 25 meeting of the Cabinet Committee on Security (whose members were the prime minister, defence minister, home minister, finance minister, and external affairs minister) chaired by Prime Minister Vajpayee, General Malik explained the seriousness of the situation in the Kargil sector and the need for the IAF "to step in without delay."

At that, Vajpayee reportedly said: "OK, get started tomorrow at dawn." Tipnis then asked the prime minister for permission to cross the LoC while attacking enemy targets on India's side of the LoC. To that, Vajpayee responded adamantly: "No. No crossing the LoC."

With that binding rule of engagement firmly stipulated by the civilian leadership, the die was finally cast for full-scale IAF involvement in the counteroffensive. Later the same day, Tipnis paid an incognito visit to the IAF's main operating base in Kashmir at Srinagar for an on-scene assessment of the situation. While there, he personally assured the commander of 15 Corps that his troops taking fire would receive all needed air support.

To be sure, Tipnis's seemingly conclusive firsthand recollection in no way closed the books on the interservice contretemps over the delay in getting the IAF engaged in the campaign.

On the contrary, while not contesting the basic facts as outlined by the air chief, a former Indian Army vice chief lambasted Tipnis for, among other things, having refused to honour Northern Army Command's request for immediate on-call attack helicopter support, having voiced allegedly baseless concern over the chance that the introduction of airpower could result in escalation, and having delayed IAF involvement in the fighting until political approval by the Cabinet Committee on Security was first sought and granted. The former army vice chief went on to author an even more outspoken litany of similar complaints in 2009, which prompted, in close succession, a point-by-point rebuttal by a retired IAF air marshal; a riposte against that rebuttal from the former army vice chief; and a more authoritative rebuttal from another retired air marshal who had been the AOC for Jammu and Kashmir during the lead-up to and conduct of the Kargil operation. Despite the testy interservice back and forth both at the outset of planning for the campaign and later, the IAF was fully prepared for the looming conflict. It had been busy almost from the first day of the incursion's discovery marshaling its assets and positioning them to show how India's air arm might make an effective difference in the gathering confrontation.

DIFFICULTIES AFFECTING THE PROVISION OF CLOSE AIR SUPPORT

Just three weeks before the commencement of Operation Safed Sagar, Western Air Command had concluded a three-week-long annual exercise during which it had flown some 5,000 training sorties involving upward of 300 aircraft that included simulated attacks against targets in the Himalayas. Nevertheless, the IAF experienced a slow start in the Kargil campaign and rode a steep learning curve at first as its pilots and planners gradually adapted to unfamiliar operating conditions and steadily improved their performance over time. As a former IAF air marshal frankly conceded on this score, the service "took some time before honing the [needed] skills and becoming effective" in a high mountain combat setting that no air force had ever experienced before. Until that happened, the PAF's director of operations during the Kargil crisis was on firm ground in remarking retrospectively that "the results achieved by the IAF in the first two days were dismal." In a similar vein, some Indian Army field commanders later complained that for the campaign's first three weeks, the effectiveness of the IAF's effort to provide close air support for their troops was "near negligible."

The IAF experienced a slow start in the Kargil campaign and rode a steep learning curve at first as its pilots and planners gradually adapted to unfamiliar operating conditions and steadily improved their performance over time.

There are two compelling reasons why the attempted delivery of effective close air support was so problematic for the IAF throughout most of the Kargil fighting. First, the enemy targets that presented themselves in the Kargil heights were nothing like the more conventional target array that fighter aircraft typically engage when providing support to ground combat operations. As one IAF airman later pointed out, the target complex did not consist of troop concentrations, command posts, and logistical supply lines, but rather "near-invisible humans well dug into hideouts ... on various hilltops and slopes," where "only their tents and earthwork structures were identifiable" from the air when not masked by the natural camouflage that was provided by "the ubiquitous black and white colour combination of the terrain." By this account, the largest target struck by the IAF during Operation Safed Sagar, the enemy's supply camp at Muntho Dhalo, "would normally have been the smallest target considered for the use of airpower during a normal allout war."

To make matters worse, the IAF, which was well familiar with the use of forward air controllers in support of friendly troops in close contact with enemy forces, was unable to employ ground-based terminal attack controllers for its close air support missions during the Kargil counteroffensive. Such use was precluded because the enemy's shooter positions were generally remote, most close air support–related targets were small and either naturally or artificially camouflaged, and the required minimum safe distance from the target ruled out a clear view of the target from the ground and any practical way of designating it accurately. The depicts two typical enemy target arrays situated along high Himalayan ridgelines, well captures the IAF's visual target acquisition problem throughout the Kargil War.

Second, IAF operations were hampered from the very start by multiple constraints on their freedom of action. To begin with, because of their high gross weight when fully fuelled and armed, the IAF's heavy Mi-25 and Mi-35 Hind attack helicopters were unable to operate at the high mountain elevations where most of the fighting took place. Accordingly, they were not used at any time during the Kargil campaign. In addition, prohibited from crossing the LoC, fast-moving fighters were driven to employ target attack tactics using ingress and egress headings that were not optimal or, in many instances, even safe.

By way of example, in the case of a fighter aircraft flying inside a mountain valley with high ridgelines on either side, a turn into a wrong valley that ends up being a box canyon can result in disaster for the pilot if he has insufficient lateral maneuvering room or available power to clear vertical obstructions. Likewise, successfully servicing targets situated on steep mountain slopes requires cross-valley attacks in which the establishment of a direct line of sight between the attacking aircraft and the target occurs late in the pilot's setup for weapon release because of intervening ridgelines. When one adds to such complicating factors an unusually small target size, the result all too often is a delayed or failed visual target acquisition or, depending on the terrain layout, an abnormally steep dive angle for weapon delivery. Since altitude loss during dive recoveries is substantially greater at high mountain elevations than during strike operations conducted closer to sea level, such abnormal dive angles allow little target tracking time before a recovery from the dive must be initiated. All of these complicating factors invariably make errors more likely in weapon release and placement.

With respect to the harmful impact of the politically imposed LoC constraint on the IAF's tactical flexibility, India's minister for external affairs during the Kargil War later recalled in his memoirs: "There were but two routes for the air force to operate on, and both were extremely narrow funnels. Our missions could fly in this narrow corridor either west or east or reverse." He further recalled: "The fact of the LoC not being a visibly marked line on the ground compounded difficulties."

Relatedly, because the decree prevented the IAF from operating on the Pakistani side of the LoC, the conduct of Operation Vijay remained limited to the immediate terrain from which the Indian Army sought to evict the intruders, while the most lucrative targets associated with providing logistical sustenance to the intruders enjoyed an inviolate sanctuary in Pakistani-occupied Kashmir. In particular, the town of Skardu on the Pakistani side of the LoC was only 108 miles from Kargil and had all the needed facilities for providing logistical and artillery support to the Pakistani intruders. Had the IAF been permitted to cross the LoC, it could have spared the Indian Army the need for its costly frontal assault against the Pakistanis by leveraging its asymmetric advantage to attack their source of resupply in Pakistani-occupied Kashmir, in effect imposing an aerial blockade. That, however, would have risked escalation to a wider war, perhaps one involving the PAF, which the Vajpayee government was determined to prevent at every cost.

Moreover, the man-portable surface-to-air missiles that the intruders wielded had an effective slant range that was sufficient to require the IAF's fighter pilots to remain 6,000 to 8,000 feet above the high ridgelines at all times in order to stay safely outside their threat envelopes, which increased the aircraft's turn radius, rendering some targets unserviceable from the air because of the prohibition against any crossing of the LoC. On top of that, when bombs were dropped, their delivery accuracy was degraded at higher release altitudes. Because of the extreme elevation at which most of the fighting took place, the IAF's munitions did not perform aerodynamically to their familiar specifications for lower release altitudes.

The reduced air temperature and density above the Kargil heights altered drag indices and other performance parameters that had never before been calculated for those conditions, causing weapons not to guide as predicted and requiring adaptation of delivery techniques through real-time improvisation. More to the point, as a result of the reduced aerodynamic drag caused by the surrounding thin air at higher altitudes, unguided munitions tended to overshoot their intended aim points. Precision munitions tended to have greater trajectory inertia, which translated into an increase in the weapon's normal circular error probable.

The man-portable surface-to-air missiles that the intruders wielded had an effective slant range that was sufficient to require the IAF's fighter pilots to remain 6,000 to 8,000 feet above the high ridgelines at all times in order to stay safely outside their threat envelopes, rendering some targets unserviceable from the air.

In addition, as noted above, the thinner air required pilots to release their weapons and initiate a pullout sooner than they normally would in airspace closer to sea level, further degrading delivery accuracy.

On a number of occasions, Indian ground units were alleged by some to have aborted close air support attacks in progress at the last minute out of concern that a fratricide incident might occur as a result of the inaccuracy of the IAF's unguided bombs.

In fact, the only reason that any close air support missions in progress were aborted (all were preplanned and coordinated in advance with 15 Corps) had to do either with intervening weather at the last minute or with friendly ground units that had not yet removed themselves from dangerously close proximity to enemy forces. The IAF's appreciation of this legitimate concern over the ever-present danger of fratricide and its unerring air discipline were such that, in the words of the AOC-in-C of Western Air Command at the time, "there was no case [throughout the campaign] of a blue-on-blue kill in spite of possibly high inaccuracies in the hills."

Stark terrain folds in the Himalayas tended to obscure the enemy from aerial observation and to mask the effects of bomb detonations, rendering even near misses ineffective.

Complicating matters further, the Pakistanis' individual troop positions were small and generally well-concealed, making them often so resistant to visual acquisition and targeting that the IAF's pilots, according to one analysis of the campaign, "did not provide reliable and consistent close support" to 15 Corps's engaged units. Stark terrain folds in the Himalayas tended to obscure the enemy from aerial observation and to mask the effects of bomb detonations, rendering even near misses ineffective. They also served to canalize aerial approaches to targets, dictating aircraft ingress and egress headings and, in the process, making IAF fighters predictable and hence more susceptible to ground fire.

A SUCCESSFUL ENDGAME FOR INDIA

By the time Operation Vijay had reached full momentum in early June, the Indian Army had marshaled nearly a corps' worth of dedicated troop strength in the Kargil area, including the Third and Eighth Mountain Divisions and a substantial number of supporting artillery units. The overriding objective of those forces was to recapture the high ground from which the intruders had a direct line of sight to highway NH1A, allowing them to lay down sustained artillery fire on it and on adjacent targets. Toward that end, after more than a week of hard fighting, units of Eighth Mountain Division recaptured the strategically important Tololing ridge complex and the adjacent Point 5203 in the Batalik sector on June 13, in what one informed account later described as "probably the turning point" in India's land counteroffensive.

Four days later, on June 17, another important breakthrough in the joint campaign was achieved when a formation of 7 Squadron Mirage 2000Hs struck and destroyed the enemy's main administrative and logistics encampment at Muntho Dhalo in the Batalik sector by means of accurately placed 1,000-pound general-purpose bombs delivered in high-angle dive attacks using the aircraft's computer-assisted weapons-aiming capability. For this pivotal attack, the IAF waited until the encampment had grown to a size that rendered it strategically ripe for such targeting. The AOC-in-C of Western Air Command at the time, Air Marshal Patney, affirmed later that the essentially total destruction by the IAF of the NLI's rudimentary but absolutely life-sustaining infrastructure at Muntho Dhalo "paralysed the enemy war effort, as it was their major supply depot." In characterizing the attack as "perhaps the most spectacular of all the [campaign's air] strikes," a serving IAF air commodore reported at the end of 1999 that it resulted in as many as 300 enemy casualties within just minutes. Pre-and post-strike aerial imagery of the enemy camp at Muntho Dhalo. In the first image, a dense array of tents and structures, as well as tracks leading up the hillside from the encampment, are clearly visible. In the second, after completion of the IAF's attacks, all that remain are bomb craters and rubble.

A week later, on June 24, a two-ship element of Mirage 2000Hs, in the first-ever combat use of laser-guided bombs by the IAF, struck and destroyed the NLI's command and control bunkers on Tiger Hill, the direction center for the forward-based artillery that had been fired against the Indian Army's brigade headquarters at Dras. They used two 1,000-pound Paveway II laser-guided munitions, with other fighters striking additional targets with unguided bombs. In these attacks, the target was acquired through the Litening pod's electro-optical imaging sensor at about 12 miles out, with weapon release occurring at a slant range of about 5 miles and the aircraft then turning away while continuing to mark the target with a laser spot for the weapon to guide on.

The following day, Mirage 2000Hs and Jaguars initiated around-the-clock bombing of enemy positions throughout the Batalik and Dras subsectors. Mirage 2000Hs struck as many as 25 separate designated aim points toward the campaign's end, including at Muntho Dhalo and the equally important Point 4388 overlooking Dras.

The air support provided by the IAF almost instantly boosted the morale of India's beleaguered ground troops and facilitated an early recapture of their outposts at Muntho Dhalo and Tiger Hill.

The air support provided by the IAF almost instantly boosted the morale of India's beleaguered ground troops and facilitated an early recapture of their outposts at Muntho Dhalo and Tiger Hill. After an exhausting struggle, Tiger Hill was retaken on July 4, and by July 8, 15 Corps reported that its units had recaptured 99 percent of the Batalik-Yaldor subsector and 90 percent of the Dras area, leading Prime Minister Vajpayee to declare that "there is going to be a great victory." The next day, the IAF received this congratulatory message from the Indian Army's field headquarters:

You guys have done a wonderful job. Your Mirage boys with their precision laser-guided bombs targeted an enemy battalion headquarters in Tiger Hill with tremendous success.... The enemy is on the run. They are on the run in other sectors also. At this rate, the end of the conflict may come soon.

Other than for an inconsequential brief delay due to weather, IAF combat operations continued without interruption for seven weeks. At the height of Operation Safed Sagar, the IAF was generating more than 40 fixed-wing combat sorties a day in both direct and indirect support to 15 Corps. Western Air Command was not the sole provider of IAF assets to conduct these daily missions. Because of its depth with respect to India's western border, the service's Central Air Command headquartered at Allahabad in Uttar Pradesh has traditionally been the repository of such major IAF strategic assets as the since-retired Mach 3–capable MiG-25R high-altitude reconnaissance aircraft and the Mirage 2000Hs. It was under Central Air Command's aegis that the MiG-25R was pressed into a unique medium-altitude tactical reconnaissance role to meet the needs of Operation Safed Sagar. The Mirage 2000Hs of the IAF's 7 Squadron were also Central Air Command's assets and were seconded to the operational control of Western Air Command for their use in the Kargil fighting. There was reluctance at first to employ the Mirage 2000Hs, as some in the IAF's leadership wanted to save the fighters in case the conflict escalated. For that reason, the aircraft were never fully committed to the fight. If they had been, according to the parent command's AOC-in-C at the time, they might have yielded "even better results than those achieved in Operation Safed Sagar."

Aerial strike operations ended on July 12. In all, IAF fighters flew more than 1,700 strike, combat air patrol and escort, and reconnaissance sorties throughout the campaign's course, including around 40 at night during the final weeks of fighting.

A breakdown of the total numbers of IAF sorties flown throughout the campaign by aircraft type. Although the IAF's Mi-17 helicopters were not used in an armed role after one was lost to an enemy surface-to-air missile during the air offensive's third day, they continued to play a vital part throughout the remainder of the campaign in conducting airlift, casualty evacuation, and reconnaissance missions.

At long last, "yard by bloody yard," as a retired Indian Army general later described the effort, the Kargil ridgelines were recaptured from the intruders through a heroic Indian infantry counteroffensive facilitated from its first days onward by supporting IAF airpower. By July 26, Indian forces had reclaimed a majority of their seized outposts above Kargil and driven the enemy troops that had occupied them back to their own side of the LoC, with all remaining Pakistani forces subsequently vacating the still-occupied positions under the weight of diplomatic pressure from the United States. In the end, by its official afteraction count, the Indian Army suffered 471 troops killed in action and 1,060 soldiers wounded during the Kargil fighting.

INITIAL AIR OPERATIONS

Less than a week before the start of Operation Vijay, on May 21, the IAF had launched a Canberra PR57 from 106 Squadron to conduct a reconnaissance of the besieged area that overlooked highway NH1A and the adjacent town of Kargil. While descending to 22,000 feet just two miles from the LoC, which put the aircraft as low as 4,000 feet above the highest ridgelines, the Canberra sustained a direct hit in its right engine by what was later determined to have been a Chinese-made Anza infrared surface-to-air missile. From that moment onward, the IAF leadership knew without doubt that it was nearing the brink of a major combat involvement.

The initial attacks marked the first time that the IAF had expended ordnance in combat in Kashmir since its early-generation Vampire jet fighters destroyed Pakistani bunkers in the Kargil sector in December 1971.

Kinetic air operations began in earnest at 0630 on May 26 with six attacks in succession by two-ship elements of MiG-21, MiG-23, and MiG-27 fighters against intruder camps, material dumps, and supply routes in the general areas overlooking Dras, Kargil, and Batalik. These initial attacks marked the first time that the IAF had expended ordnance in combat in Kashmir since its early-generation Vampire jet fighters destroyed Pakistani bunkers in the Kargil sector in December 1971. The IAF fighters that were pressed into these first-day attacks conducted 57mm rocket attacks and strafing passes against enemy targets. A second wave of air attacks began that afternoon, followed by high-altitude reconnaissance overflights by Canberra PR57s and subsequent low passes by MiG-21Ms to conduct near-real-time battle damage assessment.

Nearly all of the targets selected for attack in those initial strikes were on or near jagged ridgelines at elevations ranging from 14,000 to 18,000 feet. The stark backdrop of rocks and snow made for uncommonly difficult visual target acquisition, complicated further by the small size of the enemy troop positions dispersed against a vast and undifferentiated snow background. Inspired by the unique view from the cockpit of a fighter flying high over the rugged terrain, the IAF codenamed its contribution to the campaign Operation Safed Sagar—Hindi for "white sea."

During the second day of surface attack operations, the IAF lost two fighters in close succession. The first, a MiG-27 from 9 Squadron, experienced an engine failure while coming off a target after its pilot had just conducted a successful two-pass attack with 80mm rockets and 30mm cannon fire on one of the enemy's main supply dumps. The ensuing in-flight emergency resulted in the pilot ejecting safely after several unsuccessful airstart attempts, only to be captured by the Pakistani intruders almost as soon as he hit the ground. Air Chief Marshal Tipnis later reported that the pilot had fired his rockets well outside the operating envelope stipulated for the weapon, causing the engine to flame out. The sudden loss of power in the thin Himalayan air could have resulted from rocket exhaust gas having been ingested through the engine's air inlets on either side of the aircraft. (The MiG-27 was flying at an altitude well above that at which the rockets had been cleared to be fired.)

The second fighter loss, a MiG-21 from 17 Squadron flying top cover for the strikers, sustained an infrared surface-to-air missile hit while its pilot was flying over the terrain at low level to assist in the search for the downed MiG-27 pilot. The pilot, Squadron Leader Ajay Ahuja, also succeeded in ejecting safely but was executed shortly after he was captured following his landing. His body was subsequently returned bearing fatal bullet wounds and clear signs of brutalization.

On the third day of air operations, an IAF Mi-17 helicopter was downed, again by an enemy shoulder-fired Stinger surface-to-air missile while conducting a low-level attack. The ill-fated helicopter had been the last in a four-ship flight of armed Mi-17s flying in trail formation and was the only aircraft in the flight that had not been configured with a self-protection flare dispenser to draw away any incoming heat-seeking missiles.

The stark backdrop of rocks and snow made for uncommonly difficult visual target acquisition, complicated further by the small size of the enemy troop positions dispersed against a vast and undifferentiated snow background.

The IAF's pilots quickly understood what the Israelis had learned at great cost during the Yom Kippur War of 1973, when Egyptian and Syrian surface-to-air missiles and antiaircraft artillery downed nearly a third of the Israeli Air Force's fighter inventory (102 aircraft) before the three-week war finally ended in victory for Israel. Demonstrating its adaptability, the IAF moved with dispatch to equip all of its participating fighters with flares in order to provide an active counter-measure against any enemy infrared-guided missiles. It also called a halt once and for all to any further use of slow-moving and vulnerable Mi-17 helicopters in an armed fire-support role and directed that all target attacks by IAF fighters be conducted from outside the lethal threat envelopes of enemy shoulder-fired surface-to-air missiles. In all, enemy forces fired more than 100 surface-to-air missiles at IAF aircraft throughout the conflict. After the service's first three days of combat operations, however, not a single one of its aircraft was downed or sustained battle damage.

Throughout the campaign, whenever IAF reconnaissance or ground attack operations were under way in the immediate combat zone, Western Air Command ensured that MiG-29s or other air-to-air fighters were also airborne on combat air patrol stations over the ground fighting on India's side of the LoC to provide top cover against any attempt by the Pakistan Air Force (PAF) to enter the fray in a ground attack role. PAF F-16s to the west typically maintained a safe distance of 10 to 20 miles on the Pakistani side of the LoC, although they occasionally approached as close as 8 miles away from the ongoing ground engagements. The PAF's director of operations during the Kargil War later reported that there had been isolated instances of IAF and PAF fighters locking on to each other with their onboard fire control radars, but that caution had prevailed on both sides and that "no close [air-to-air] encounters took place." IAF fighters never joined in aerial combat with the PAF F-16s due to the Vajpayee government's strict injunction that Indian forces not cross the LoC. Seven years later, however, Air Chief Marshal Tipnis recalled that he had personally authorized his escorting fighter pilots to chase any Pakistani aircraft back across the LoC in hot pursuit were those pilots to be engaged by enemy fighters in aerial combat.

In all, the IAF flew some 460 fighter sorties throughout the campaign dedicated exclusively to maintaining battlespace air defence. These medium-and high-altitude defensive combat air patrols and offensive fighter sweeps, typically entailing four-ship flights of MiG-29s, took place not only in the immediate area of ground fighting in the Kargil sector but throughout Western Air Command's area of responsibility. As Operation Vijay's air component commander later recalled, he was not just concerned about Kargil or the Kashmir region but had a potentially larger-scale war in mind: "I was working on a much bigger canvas.... I was fully conscious that as we hit and killed enemy soldiers, there was every possibility for escalation, possibly outside the immediate combat area, and it was my job to be ready with adequate remaining resources for that eventuality."

IAF strike aircraft operated primarily from three northern bases, Air Force Stations Srinagar, Avantipur, and Udhampur. The closest of those to the fighting, Srinagar, was more than 70 miles away from the war zone. Within just days after the full extent of the Pakistani incursion was confirmed and well before the formal start of Operation Safed Sagar, the MiG-21bis squadron permanently stationed at Srinagar was joined by additional MiG-21M, MiG-23BN, and MiG-27ML squadrons, while additional squadrons of MiG-21Ms and MiG-29s deployed northward to Avantipur. By the time Operation Safed Sagar had reached its full stride, the IAF had deployed some 60 of its frontline aircraft to support the war effort, making for about a quarter of Western Air Command's combined fighter inventory. As they awaited mission tasking, those squadrons committed to the campaign initiated special training aimed at better acclimating their pilots to conducting night attacks under moonlit conditions. Such combat operations by fighters over high mountainous terrain at night had never before been attempted in the IAF's history.

Because of their rudimentary bomb sights, the inaccuracy of their unguided weapons, and the ruling against crossing the Line of Control, MiG-21, MiG-23, and MiG-27 pilots typically achieved only limited effectiveness when attempting to provide close air support against enemy point targets.

Increasingly as the joint campaign unfolded, most Indian Army operations were preceded by preparatory air strikes, each of which was closely coordinated beforehand between 15 Corps planners and the AOC for Jammu and Kashmir. Because of their rudimentary bomb sights, the inaccuracy of their unguided weapons, and the ruling against crossing the LoC, MiG-21, MiG-23, and MiG-27 pilots typically achieved only limited effectiveness when attempting to provide close air support against enemy point targets.

Rapidly adapting to these constraints, on May 30, just four days after the start of Operation Safed Sagar, Air Chief Marshal Tipnis decided to take action to help correct the problem of inaccuracy. He chose to commit IAF Mirage 2000H fighters capable of delivering laser-guided bombs to ground attack operations in the Kargil sector. The fighters first had to be configured to deliver the bombs, so Air Headquarters launched an accelerated effort to do so at Air Force Station Gwalior, where the Mirage 2000Hs were principally based.

India's Aircraft System Testing Establishment (ASTE) in Bangalore was well along in a developmental program to integrate Israeli-made Litening electro-optical targeting pods onto the Mirage 2000H and Jaguar fighters. To support the accelerated effort at Gwalior, ASTE began a full-court press to prepare selected Mirage 2000Hs from 7 Squadron to be fitted with Litening pods for use over Kargil. At the same time, ASTE helped modify the Mirage 2000H's centerline weapons station to carry 1,000-pound U.S.-made Paveway II laser-guided bombs instead of the IAF's French-produced Matra precision munitions, which were prohibitively expensive. Concurrently, the IAF's elite Tactics and Air Combat Development Establishment located at Air Force Station Jamnagar took the lead in developing and validating best tactics, techniques, and procedures for delivering the Paveway II. By June 12, the upgraded Mirage 2000Hs were ready to commence precision strike operations in anger for the first time in IAF history.

In the meantime, air operations against identified intruder positions and support facilities continued in the Jubar and Mashkoh Valley sectors between May 28 and June 1. Throughout the first week of June, inclement weather hindered such operations and persisted to a point where a cloud deck below the ridgelines precluded air attacks entirely on June 10 and 11. Fortunately, 15 Corps had no urgent target servicing requirements for the IAF during those two days.

FUTURE WARS AND AIR POWER

Given the increasing vulnerabilities of modern states, whether developed or developing, to even conventional war and the limitations intrinsic to small professional high-cost forces, it is inevitable that states will seek to adopt doctrines and strategies for prevention of war rather than seek war as an instrument of politics. Deterrence, therefore, is likely to assume greater importance in the coming decades.

War in the traditional and classical sense will be less viable in the 21st century as an instrument of politics since states are increasingly vulnerable to the effects of even conventional wars. Combined with technological and cost imperatives, this is shifting the locus of armed conflict from traditional regular war to the use of military power on the pattern of modern "gunboat" coercive diplomacy. Long-range strike capabilities, reinforced as they have been by advances in sensor technologies and precision guided munitions, now make it possible to attack targets across long distances which earlier would have required close combat. The era of wars of occupation has long passed into history. Even traditional territorial wars are already a phenomenon of the past, except possibly armed clashes where energy resource base still makes control of territory important. This does not necessarily mean that regular wars have become obsolete. What it implies is that highly professionalised high-cost militaries, serious difficulties of re-supply and replenishment, deepening vulnerabilities of modern states and society (to even conventional war), and the fear of losing parts or the whole of precious military capability combine to reduce the probability of conventional war. But if and when it does take place, war will be sharp and swift, and rely much more on superior technology, while the impact of its outcome will be far more crucial than what is generally believed.

In essence, countries will increasingly seek to avoid war as we have seen it; and rely even more than before on deterrence. The most significant characteristic of the changing nature of war is the growing accuracy of weapon systems and the ability to strike at long range with great precision almost independent of weather. Increase in accuracy and range has historically increased the risk of pre-emption. Surprise may appear an even more attractive option because of the smaller size of military forces. Land forces have inherent friction in war that operates limits on their flexibility especially to surprise attacks. Air power, on the other hand, possesses intrinsic attributes to respond rapidly across a vast range of contingencies spanning large distances. The quantum of firepower per unit of air power assets has been increasing. Air power is also at its best in achieving effective results when faced with mobile forces—a scenario almost inevitable in a hostile surprise attack seeking a breakthrough.

Warfare since World War II has been increasingly shifting towards greater mobility and firepower. Air power, by its nature, is more effective in a manoeuvre warfare situation rather than in situations of static warfare. This is largely due to its ability to disrupt and destabilise the momentum of manoeuvre besides its ability to impose kinetic shock. Mechanised warfare creates the conditions for air power to maximise its effect, and mechanised warfare is also the form of fighting most vulnerable to air power. Reduction in the size of military forces will tend to shift force structures more toward mechanisation in the coming decades. Mechanised warfare is also heavily dependent on mobile and large logistic assets without which mobility is deeply affected, nullifying the very utility of mechanisation. This opens up additional areas of opportunities for air power to influence the course of warfare on the ground.

The time-space dimension of warfare has been undergoing some marked shifts during the 20th century. Earlier, wars were compressed in space and spread out in time. Technology has been reversing this equation. Increasingly, future wars are likely to be expanded in space and compressed in time. This fundamental change in the time-space paradigm of warfare places a heavy premium on the information-action cycle. Increasing pace of warfare in the years ahead implies a greater rate of change in the military situation (in air and sea warfare), and, consequently, greater challenges arising therefrom, thus, demanding an accelerating speed in response. It has been argued that the real revolution in military affairs now taking place is not so much a revolution in information warfare as conventional wisdom would have us believe, but that in the control and management of time. Air power is the only component of military force that is capable of meeting the challenge of accelerating speed of response needed if destructive power has to be applied effectively on the inside of the enemy's information-decision-action cycle.

The future of deterrence and successful warfighting rests heavily on accurate long-range strike capabilities, whether conventional and/or nuclear armed. At the same time, the preferred method of employing military power for political purposes will centre on the use of force that does not lead to continued armed conflict. This, coincidentally, requires similar capabilities: high-technology long-range, "surgical" accurate strikes, which are best undertaken by (and in many cases, only by) air power. The very nature of these capabilities is such that defence against them will need to rely on similar capabilities for deterrence in future. Strategically, air power will assume increasing importance in the coming years. During the Cold War, air power was the primary vehicle for strategic nuclear deterrence to avert war. In the years ahead, air (and missile) power will be the central tool for conventional deterrence, as well as controlled punitive strikes for coercive diplomacy. Naval power in this regard, would come a close second.

It is, therefore, not surprising that Asian countries from Israel to Japan are already placing greater emphasis on stronger air forces (including missile capabilities) and naval forces. China's military modernisation and arms acquisition programme relies heavily on upgrading its air and naval capabilities, besides long-range nuclear delivery systems. In spite of a substantive cut back in defence posture worldwide, the US decided to create a new naval fleet (whose primary role would be to apply its powerful integral combat air power) after the end of the Cold War. In the process, power projection dynamics are changing from the traditional means and goals related to territorial wars to functional power projection with capabilities that can strike accurately at long distances, even if staying power remains limited. Sensor technologies provide an important additional dimension in enhancing reconnaissance surveillance, and target acquisition capabilities while precision guidance of striking power adds greater accuracy and lethality at long ranges.

3

Modernising the Indian Air Force

The induction of the first fourth-generation aircraft, the Su-30 MKI began in 1997 and the IAF is expected to build-up to full strength of 230 by 2014. It is understood that another 42 have been ordered taking the total fleet strength to 272 aircraft. There is a proposal from Russia to eventually upgrade the IAF Su-30 MKI fleet to fifth generation standards.

In the meantime, the MiG-23 fleet has already been phased out and the MiG-21 fleet with its different variants would be extinct in another five to seven years at best. The fleet of Jaguars, MiG-27, MiG-29 and even the Mirage-2000 all with upgrades, would last for another 10 to 15 years; but being of third generation vintage, would not really be able to project frontline capability. The strength of the combat fleet currently is reported to be down to 34 squadrons as against the authorised 39.5 and by 2015, is expected to reduce further to possibly well under 30 seriously eroding combat capability of the IAF. This situation will be incongruous for an emerging regional power and catastrophic in two-front war scenario.

The emerging geopolitical and security scenario requires our nation to possess comprehensive military capability, characterised by flexibility and speed of response, the mobility and transportability of all forms of national power, long-reach, precision targeting, minimum collateral damage and reduced visibility. Aerospace power fits the bill perfectly. The 21st century belongs to aerospace power and given the Indian situation, concerns and aspirations, the need for a strong and comprehensive aerospace capability is inescapable

There is therefore an imperative need for total revamp of the fleet with fourth and fifth generation aircraft beginning not later than 2015 and to build-up to the sanctioned level of 42 squadrons by 2022. Backed by a resurgent economy, two decades into the post-cold war era, India is beginning to emerge as a regional power and given competent political and bureaucratic management, has the attributes to rise to the status of a super power. The growing status of the nation is accompanied by enhanced responsibilities wherein India may be called upon to intervene decisively in the region militarily to safeguard national interests that transcend our geographical boundaries and extend from the Persian Gulf to the Strait of Malacca. As a regional power, the nation may be called upon to respond to calamities, man-made or natural, to humanitarian crisis, to restore order or to ensure peace and stability.

While economic strength is the main pillar of national power, the military capability of a nation must be enhanced in tandem to secure its economic status and provide the environment for further growth. This philosophy was echoed by Air Chief Marshal F H Major, the then Chief of Air Staff, Indian Air Force (IAF) on the occasion of its platinum jubilee celebrations in October 2007 when he said "The emerging geopolitical and security scenario requires our nation to possess comprehensive military capability, characterised by flexibility and speed of response, the mobility and transportability of all forms of national power,

long reach, precision targeting, minimum collateral damage and reduced visibility. Aerospace power fits the bill perfectly. The 21st century belongs to aerospace power and given the Indian situation, concerns and aspirations, the need for a strong and comprehensive aerospace capability is inescapable".

Stated in simple terms, the nation's aerospace power must possess the capability to project power effectively in the region for which it must have combat aircraft with adequate reach, lethal firepower through modern stand-off / precision guided munitions and stealth characteristics. It must have strategic airlift aircraft with the capability to move large forces by air over long distances, tactical transport aircraft to operate over shorter distances and a fleet of helicopters to provide mobility and firepower in the tactical battle area. Two things follow from this, one being that the nation must possess multi-layered air defence system to protect its offensive operations capability and secondly that development of aerospace power must not only cater to perceived threats but more importantly, must be capability-based to respond to a wide variety of threats, existing or unforeseen.

IAF MODERNISATION: AN OVERVIEW

In the words of the Air Chief Marshal Norman Browne, Chief of the Air Staff (CAS) of the IAF, the "IAF is witnessing an unprecedented phase of modernisation and capability enhancement [which can be] witnessed across the capability spectrum ..." The most vital capability enhancement is perhaps the IAF's modernisation of its fighter fleet, which has caused some concern in recent years due to the shrinking number of combat squadrons. According to the Parliamentary Standing Committee on Defence (15th Lok Sabha), the present number of combat squadron has dwindled to 34 against the sanction strength of 42. Moreover, the number is likely to reduce further to 31 during the 12th Plan (2012-2017). To arrest the declining trend, the IAF has made a two-prong approach: upgrading existing fighters (MiG-29, Jaguar and Mirage 2000) while inducting new ones. The aim of the IAF is to increase its combat squadron strength to 40-42 by the end of 14th Plan (2022-27) and eventually to 45 squadrons by the 15th Plan (2027-2032).

Upgrades

The contract for upgrading MiG-29s was signed in 2008 with RAC MIG of Russia at a cost of US $964 million. This program is to be completed by 2014. The first three upgraded MiG-29s (known as MiG-29UPG) were handed over to India by the Russian company in December 2012. Three more fighters are to be upgraded in Russia and the remaining 63-odd planes are to be upgraded in India with support from the Russian partner. The service life of the upgraded aircraft has been extended to 40 years. Among other features the upgraded MiG include Phazatron Zhuk-M radar, beyond-visual-range combat ability and the mid-air refuelling.

The contract for modernising Jaguars to DARIN-III Standard was signed with India's state-owned Hindustan Aeronautics Ltd (HAL) in 2009 at the cost of Rs 31.1 billion. The work is scheduled for completion by 2017. The first upgraded Jaguar was successfully flight tested by the HAL on November 28, 2012. Among other features the upgraded aircraft incorporates new state-of-the-art avionics architecture including Mission Computer (MC), Engine and Flight Instrument System (EFIS), and autopilot. The retrofitted Jaguar will "result in a major operational improvement with regard to all weather air to ground, air to sea and air to air capabilities through incorporation of multi mode radar", says R. K. Tyagi, Chairman, HAL.

In July 2011, the MoD signed a $2.4 billion contract with French companies Thales, and Dassault Aviation and HAL for upgrades to the IAF's Mirage-2000 fleet procured in eighties. As per the contract, out of 50-odd fighters, two will be upgraded in France, two at HAL with French support, and the rest by the HAL. The entire process is expected to be completed by 2021. The improvements include new avionics, radars, mission computers, glass cockpits, helmet-mounted displays, electronic warfare suites, weapon delivery and precision-targeting systems, which will bring the fleet to Mirage 2000-5 standards and extend the service life by 20 years. A separate contract valued €959 million has also been signed with MBDA to provide 450 MICA missiles to arm the upgraded fighters.

Fighter

The IAF is all set to induct in its fleet over 400 new fighters that include three new types of combat planes - Light Combat

Aircraft (LCA), French Rafale and Fifth Generation Fighter Aircraft (FGFA) – and an additional 42 SU-30MKIs. The additional SU-30 MKI is part of the $4.5 billion defence deal signed between India and Russia during President Putin's December 2012 visit to New Delhi. The newly contracted SU-30 MKI will be license produced by the HAL, taking Indian aerospace company's total order of the fighter to 222, and the total cost of procurement of 272 Su-30MKIs to $12 billion.

Beginning with inductions of new type of fighters, the IAF has already placed orders for 40 LCAs (20 each in Initial Operational Clearance (IOC) and Final Operational (FOC) standards) of MK-I version with GE404 engine. These planes are planned for induction in the 12th Plan (2012-2017). There is also a further plan to induct more LCAs of MK-II version with superior GE F414 engines, 99 units of which have been contracted for $800 million. All together, as many as six LCA squadrons (108 fighters) are to be inducted by the end of the 13th Plan (2017-2022).

The much touted approximately $20 billion medium multi role combat aircraft (MMRCA) deal, in which French Rafale emerged as the winner, looks set for contract finalisation in early part of the next financial year (2013-14). As per the plan, the first Rafale squadron comprising of 18 aircrafts will be inducted in 3-4 years after contract signing. The rest 108 aircraft, which will be manufactured by the HAL under the transfer of technology agreement with France, are to be inducted in the following seven years.

The induction of LCA and MMRCA is soon going to be over-shadowed by what is poised as India's biggest ever defence programme to acquire 200-250 Fifth Generation Fighter Aircrafts (FGFA) – though in a recent interview the Air Chief has however indicated a lower figure of 144 fighters. Consequent to 2007 inter-governmental agreement between India and Russia for joint development of FGFA, both the sides signed a Preliminary Design contract in 2010 at the cost of $295 million to be shared equally. Drawning upon the basic structural and systems design of the Russian PAF-FA, the FGFA for the IAF is now visualised as a single seat fighter with advanced features such as stealth, super-cruise, and ultra-manoeuvrability. HAL, the Indian joint partner in the developmental efforts of the FGFA, has committed $6 billion dollars for the initial developmental efforts. Total programme cost on the Indian side including for the induction is estimated to be $30 billion. The IAF is hopeful of inducting the aircraft from 2020 onwards.

COMBAT FLEET OF THE IAF

The IAF went through a partial upgrade of its combat fleet between the period 1979 to 1989 when its fleet of *Gnats, Hunters* and *Maruts*were approaching the end of their Total Technical Life and were due to be phased out leaving only the *MiG-21* as the mainstay. In this period, the combat capability of the IAF was upgraded through the induction of the British *Jaguar*, Russian *MiG-23, MiG-27, MiG-29* and the French *Mirage-2000.*

The *C-130J* has the capability to undertake deployment of Special Forces in all-weather conditions by day or night even in complete darkness. It is capable of receiving fuel in flight at low level and apart from special operations, can be employed for airborne assault, air transported operations

The induction of the first fourth-generation aircraft, the *Su-30 MKI* began in 1997 and the IAF is expected to build-up to full strength of 230 by 2014. It is understood that another 42 have been ordered taking the total fleet strength to 272 aircraft. It is also understood that there is a proposal from Russia to eventually upgrade the IAF *Su-30 MKI* fleet to fifth generation standards. In the meantime, the *MiG-23* fleet has already been phased out and the *MiG-21* fleet with its different variants would be extinct in another five to seven years at best. The fleet of*Jaguars, MiG-27, MiG-29* and even the *Mirage-2000* all with upgrades, would last for another 10 to 15 years; but being of third generation vintage, would not really be able to project frontline capability. The strength of the combat fleet currently is reported to be down to 34 squadrons as against the authorised 39.5 and by 2015, is expected to reduce further to possibly well under 30 seriously eroding combat capability of the IAF. This situation will be incongruous for an emerging regional power and catastrophic in two-front war scenario. There is therefore an imperative need for total revamp of the fleet with fourth and fifth generation aircraft beginning not later than 2015 and to build-up to the sanctioned level of 42 squadrons by 2022.

As there was considerable uncertainty at the turn of the century with regard to the operationalisation of the indigenous Light Combat Aircraft, *Tejas*, over a decade ago, the IAF had projected a requirement of six squadrons of fighter aircraft to replace part of the *MiG-21*fleet being phased out. It has been five years since the tender was issued by the Ministry of Defence and nine months since selection of the French *Rafale* was made public, contract with Dassault is yet to be signed. If all goes well, the contract may be concluded sometime in 2013 at the earliest and delivery will commence four years later. Thereafter it may take a decade for the *Rafale* fleet to reach full strength and operational status. All this presuming that there are no fresh impediments.

In the meantime, Hindustan Aeronautics Limited (HAL) has entered into a contract with Russian companies Rosoboron export and Sukhoi to develop the Fifth Generation Fighter Aircraft (FGFA), a stealth fighter in the class of the American *F-22 Raptor*. A derivative of the Russian *PAK FA* whose single-seat prototype *T-50* is already undergoing flight tests, the FGFA will be a twin-seat version customised to conform to the new doctrine of the IAF. To be produced in India by HAL, the initial order by the IAF will be for 214 aircraft (roughly ten squadrons) at a cost of US$ 100 million per aircraft and the total outlay of US$ 25 billion apart from development cost. Series production of the FGFA is scheduled to commence in 2019. The IAF can hope to have the complete initial order delivered and squadrons fully operational by 2029 at the earliest.

ARMY'S CAPABILITY ACCRETION

The challenges that the army is expected to face in the next decade are not likely to be any less formidable. An appraisal of the emerging threats in fact indicates an increasing complexity of the missions that the army may be expected to execute. The basic character of the Army's responsibilities is unlikely to witness significant changes. Till the boundary disputes with China and Pakistan remain unresolved, Army's most important role of ensuring the nation's territorial integrity will retain primacy.

Concurrently, as in the past, the Army will continue to remain embroiled in combating militancy, insurgency and terrorism. With the prevailing instability in the immediate and near neighbourhood, and the growing regional and global role of our country, the Army must also be prepared to undertake missions beyond our borders. It may be added that however much the Army may want to resist, it will continue to be drawn to tackle internal law and order situations and national manmade or natural calamities.

How has the Army fared in the last two decades in the discharge of its responsibilities? At considerable cost to itself it has barely managed to keep the lid on. Given the serious shortage of junior officers, and the indifferent and insufficient weaponry at its disposal, the Army it can be contended, has done exceedingly well. Regrettably the problems of the Army, and the stresses it is subjected to, are understood only by those who are in it. The MOD and the political leadership, or for that matter also the strategic community have a vague awareness, nowhere close to the ground realities. This explains the decades of inertia.

Exploiting the progressive decline of our conventional military capability all through the decade of the eighties, Pakistan launched a well orchestrated offensive through irregulars in Kashmir from about the beginning of 1990. When the momentum of this offensive seemed to be petering out Pakistan did not hesitate to gamble for higher stakes by resorting to Kargil. The Kargil fiasco and the growing domestic instability, however, did not dampen Pakistan's appetite for fomenting trouble for us. The terror attack on our Parliament in 2001 and 26 Nov. 2008-Mumbai is still fresh in our memory.

Over the last few years China too has begun to demonstrate bellicosity, tinged with arrogance, against us. Border intrusions with the purpose of intimidation coupled with force accretions in Tibet and along the LAC, portend problems for us. Its aggressive posturing on other fronts compounds the basket of our concerns. Viewed from the national security perspective it emerges that our concept of military deterrence has failed or is failing. Clearly then, the Army's conventional war fighting capabilities must be brought to levels that promise if not absolute, sufficient deterrence.

So how do we go about building a credible dissuasive conventional military deterrence? For the past two to three decades the three services have been unsuccessfully trying to drive the process. It would be mindless to persist with the same approach. The responsibility must shift to the PM and his Cabinet Committee on Security. This is not going to happen without some precipitate action. How this is to be brought about is a matter that the services must address?

The Army could do with a totally fresh appraisal to cover its overall strength, its structure and equipment profile, the quality of its man power, its leadership and its training. Such a review could perhaps be relevant and necessary for the Navy and the Air Force as well. Technological advancements are taking place rapidly. Correspondingly the rate of obsolescence is also increasing. It is therefore imperative that we manage change with much greater sophistication so as to ensure available funds are utilized optimally. It follows that individuals charged with formulating qualitative requirements, induction plans and evaluation of systems must be competent and have the requisite grooming and experience. Even though this issue has been debated before no concrete remedial steps have yet been taken.

INFANTRY

The Infantry is the largest arm of our Army and the only arm which has perhaps never had a respite from combat from the time the Naga insurgency began in the fifties. Matters worsened when we sent the expeditionary force to Sri Lanka for Operation Pawan. Ever since, the Infantry has continued, without break, to climb the stress ladder.

Considering the Infantry's constant engagement, aware that all Army Chiefs from the early nineties have sought to give the Infantry the highest priority in terms of equipping and modernizing it. But if we were to carry out a critical appraisal of the Infantry in 2010 the report card of twenty years effort would be quite dismal. How ironical, especially when costs are lower and the systems involved are relatively not so complex? The story is eloquent testimony to the manner in which the country's higher defence management works. Almost everything that a soldier needs, from the clothes and boots to the weapon he carries, is at present well below par.

Consider the 5.56 family of weapons that the Army is currently equipped. The Army was virtually bulldozed into accepting these weapons. It was told that indigenous R&D must be encouraged. Promises were made that in the production models the user will get a much improved and more reliable version and that a superior Mark 2 will follow. The DRDO also hinted that high volume orders from many foreign customers would be placed soon after the Indian Army accepted the induction and placed orders for delivery. The Army had no choice but to accept though none of the commitments materialized. It has lived with these weapons for more than a decade and paid an incalculable price. A good and reliable personal weapon we know does wonders to a soldier's confidence and morale. But we have failed in giving him such a weapon. Shouldn't there be review and people held accountable?

Conceptually the start point of capability-building and modernization has to be the individual soldier. So we must begin by giving him the best we can. Essentially what the soldier needs is a good and reliable personal weapon, comfortable clothing with stealth and concealment features designed to ergonomically accommodate everything he has to carry, the best protection (body armour) that portable weight permits, stabilized helmet mounted computer screens, sensors and night vision devices for observation and using his weapons, effective communications and position locating/ situational awareness systems. In addition he requires a host of sundry items like eye protection goggles, contemporary light bag pack equipment etc. The approach should be to look at the tactical vest and the helmet (protective gear) as a platform on which the future soldier systems are embedded so that weight reduction and mobility improvements issues are optimally addressed.

The resolve to modernize the infantry soldier has been there for long, but the process has been painfully slow. Ways have to be found to accelerate the process and do it comprehensively. We must therefore begin as of yesterday.

When considering assault rifles we have quite a few options available; each having its unique features. Let us briefly look at the 21st century trends in assault rifles. Essentially they are refinements to the systems developed in the previous decades. Some exciting options that could be considered are:-

- *Heckler & Koch HK 416 firing the 5.56x 45 or the HK 417 firing the 7.62×51 NATO rounds.* Both these weapons have updated features with Picatinny rails, a drop free magazine release, and some other smart features.
- *Israel's IMI Tavor TAR-21.* It has a compact bull pup design and uses the NATO 5.56x 45 cartridges. It can easily be set up for right or left handed shooters and has several modular variants that come with a standard reflex sight.
- *XM 8 from the US.* This has quite a few modular variants with inbuilt electronics such as a laser sight, round counter and integral infra red and visible sights.
- *South Korea's XK11.* This is an interesting new rifle that has a ballistic computer, a laser range finder and a digital scope that provides the soldier with combat data and enables night firing through thermal imaging sights. The product is still at a prototype stage but has considerable promise.
- *The AK Series.* The Kalashnikovs family of assault rifles is much too well known.

An important trend in small arms in the 21st century is that sophisticated electronics is now being built into the design of these weapons. There could be some justification for the approach we have now adopted. A few years ago we had considered integration of night sights in our tender for assault rifles. At that time there weren't many who were offering such embedded systems. To my mind the idea was right though the timing was wrong. But now, with most weapon manufacturers developing weapons with built in electronics.

Given the current employment of the Army and looking at the two vital needs of the infantry soldier i.e. his personal weapon and his body armour, it is difficult to decide which merits greater priority. What is but evident that on both counts the establishment has been found wanting.

Today we have all of the Rashtriya Rifles and a significant proportion of the Army deployed in combating militancy, terrorism and insurgencies. Of these how many of their personnel, are equipped with suitable body armour? And what are the constraints to procuring body armour? On both counts we will get answers that are far from convincing, particularly when today we have a host of companies in India manufacturing body armour and combat helmets. With a dynamic and inclusive approach we can harness the capabilities of these companies to give us quality protection suits and helmets at competitive prices. As a matter of fact with some support in terms of investment in R&D and inducements of assured orders, our companies can well become global leaders in protective solutions.

Assessments suggest that in the development of 'small arms protective inserts' (SAPI), technology today is at only the 40 percent level. Both in the case of X SAPI-silicon carbide and ceramic and E SAPI, and high molecular weight polyethylene (HMW-PE) and aramid fibers, there are possibilities that by improving the quality of resins and making the weave more unidirectional, weight to protection ratios can be substantially improved.

The infantry also needs to acquire better surveillance and target acquisition capabilities as well as more potent fire power at the section level and above. A mission, terrain and adversary based analysis may suggest the induction of special weapons and surveillance systems on a regional basis. It can be assumed that such an exercise would have been undertaken.

MODERNISATION OF IAF

With all this in mind the Indian Air Force also has a major transformation plan in place. This is three-pronged. The first is to preserve and maintain what they have. This is achieved with a well-conceived product and maintenance support plan.

Secondly, they plan to selectively upgrade and improve the lethality of their assets that have adequate residual life left. Some of the fleets and assets that are being upgraded are:

a. Upgrade of the MiG-29 series by 2014. Upgraded aircraft will be available by 2017.
b. Technical upgrades of Mi-17 upgrade.
c. In fact, upgrades of Su-30 are already in the pipeline and in various phases.
d. In parallel, MAFI (Modernisation of Air Fields Infrastructure) programme for upgradation of airfield and maintenance infrastructure is also being progressed.

The third prong of the transformation is to progress the acquisitions and replacements where no residual life is left:

a. The final round of the procurement of 126 Medium Multi-Role Combat aircraft is on with Rafale.
b. Procurement of additional Su-30 is under progress. Our total numbers are going to be in excess of 270 Su-30s.
c. The LCA (Light Combat Aircraft) IOC certification was done in Jan 2011. There are delays. Induction is expected in this year, by which time all teething issues should hopefully be sorted out.
d. RFP for six additional Flight Refuelling aircraft was re-issued in Sep 10. FETs (Field Evaluation Trials) have been completed.
e. 10 C-17 Globemaster III Heavy Lift Aircraft.

f. Induction of new Medium Lift Helicopters (Mi-17 V5) has already commenced.
g. Induction of Combat helicopters and Heavy Lift Helicopters is being progressed.
h. Contract for Spyder LLQRMs has been signed and the first squadron is expected soon.
i. All the three AWACS aircraft have been delivered. Contract for Medium Power Radars, Low Level Transportable Radars and Low Level Light Weight Radars has been signed and delivery has commenced.
j. MTA (Multirole Transport Aircraft) and FGFA (Fifth Generation Fighter Aircraft) programmes are being progressed with Russia. FGFAs will be available around or just after 2017. The requirement is for about 200 to 250 aircraft.

MODERNIZING ARTILLERY : RETROSPECT AND PROSPECT

The images of field guns firing in Kargil in 1999 with a devastating effect at the target end are still afresh in the mind of the Indian public. That was also the time when India was recovering from the economic crisis of the early 1990s when the foreign exchange reserves had dwindled to dangerous lows to even think of acquiring defence equipment through imports. The Kargil crisis compelled the politico-military establishment to reassess the country's defence and security policies, not just to replace the Soviet vintage equipment with the Armed Forces but in terms of their modernization. In the subsequent years as part of its overall modernization effort, a Field Artillery Rationalisation Plan was introduced; the same also formed basis for the Artillery modernization plans.

Consequent to the experience in Operation Parakaram, the Indian army revised its doctrine in 2004 to respond to the realities of a tough neighbourhood. As a result, a Cold Start doctrine was articulated which had several premises. Evidently, a doctrine draws from experiences of previous wars and can be aspirational as it defines the objectives that should be chosen for the future and the operational concepts to be followed to attain goals. In this mode, a doctrine drives the nature of organization, force structure and training.

The Cold Start doctrine enunciated by the Indian Army rests on rapid mobilization, concentration and launch of operations in a seamless continuum. The other planks of the doctrine are:

- Multiple thrusts with divisional sized integrated battle groups.
- Broad front, shallow depth, limited objectives.
- Pivot corps offensives supplemented with available Integrated Battle Groups from Strike Corps resources.
- Strike reserve largely uncommitted.
- Aims at attrition and capture of territory.
- Cognizant of possible nuclear thresholds.
- All weather, day night operations; air drops and heliborne operations; IW and EW; massed firepower ('100 guns' concept); operational fires.

Massing of accurate and heavy volume of firepower, coordinated with combined arms operations including the air support would be a necessary condition for achieving the objectives of a Cold Start doctrine in real-time. The Artillery doctrine no doubt will flow out of the conceptual and doctrinal issues for combined arms operations emanating from the Cold Start precepts.

Lack of adequate artillery firepower would definitely restrict the freedom and movement of own forces whereas enhanced enemy artillery fire power will also add to difficulties of own forces' manoeuvre. The Cold Start doctrine requires a massive artillery support ab initio to neutralise the enemy defences in the shortest possible time without giving him much reaction time.

Further, the India Army Chief has recently talked about the changing geo-political and strategic environment and the need to be prepared for a range of security threats and challenges including the possibilities of a need to deal with two fronts. He also reflected upon the Out of Area Contingencies which may necessitate employment of forces. Therefore the gaping voids in our field artillery need to be filled up in a hurry to meet the likely threats to the defence of the realm. The artillery rationalization plan's key objective was to standardize the equipment profile from a multitude of calibre of guns to a single calibre. There are advantages to be gained in terms of streamlined logistics, easy maintenance and repairs including standardization of ammunition.

While, this plan was outlined at the turn of the century with ambitious goal of implementing it in three to four plan periods of Five Year Defence Plans, no progress could be made due to several contextual factors. The major factor being the ghost of Bofors (payoff allegations in their mid-1980s deal) exacerbated further by allegations of corruption in some of the subsequent potential artillery acquisition deals.

However, as a first step towards modernization of field artillery almost over a decade after enunciation of FARP, there is silver lining on the cloud. Finally, the government has decided to buy 145 M777 ultralight howitzers from the US-based entity of the BAE Systems through the government-to-government Foreign Military Sales (FMS) route. The FMS route avoids all the ills and impediments associated with India's Defence Procurement Procedure which has been continually revised but has not delivered especially on the artillery procurement. A Fast Track Procedure is also part of the DPP but that has also not helped meet India's burgeoning defence acquisition needs.

An indication that the above deal of 145 light Howitzers may be clinched was a notification by the Pentagon to the US Congress in the second half of January 2010 of a possible sale of 145 state-of-the-art lightweight towed Howitzers to India.

The Defence Security Cooperation Agency rationalized to the Congress, "India intends to use the howitzers to modernise its armed forces and enhance its ability to operate in hazardous conditions. The howitzers will assist the Indian Army to develop and enhance standardisation and to improve interoperability with US Soldiers and Marines who use the M777 as their primary means of indirect fire. India will have no difficulty in absorbing these weapons into its armed forces." That it also makes a good commercial sense and an important breakthrough in the Indian defence bazaar can not be mentioned in the solemn note to the Congress.

There are reports however, on another level, that the deal may not come through as a result of the recent strategic side-lining of India in the London Conference on the Afghanistan imbroglio. There are unconfirmed reports that the Indian policy establishment is considering as to what strategic leverages India has to ensure its meaningful role in unfolding scenarios in Afghanistan where the dominant discourse is being dictated by the US, notably the Pentagon. Some years back, before the Indo-US defence Framework Agreement was signed in 2005 and the Ministry of Defence had drawn out ambitious defence acquisition plans, a retiring Defence Secretary had remarked that defence purchases from abroad should be used a strategic leverages in consonance with our policy objectives. If such recourse is adopted it would further delay the process of procurement.

But then this is not the end of the massive requirements of Indian field artillery for either ultra light howitzers or for that matter other type of guns. There are four other types of 155 mm guns which are to be acquired as part of the long-term artillery modernization plans.

While the acquisition of 145 Howitzers would be sufficient only to equip seven artillery regiments after catering for General staff reserves and would fill existing voids or provide replacements for mountain artillery units to be converted to 155 mm calibre as part of FARP, additional requirements have also arisen because of the governments decision to raise two mountain divisions and a fourth artillery division to support operations in the mountainous areas. This would translate into a requirement of ultra light howitzers for four mountain artillery brigades which would mean acquisition of additional 290 pieces that would have to be spread over 12th, 13th and 14th Five Year Defence Plans.

As part of the first phase of FARP, besides the 145 pieces, a requirement of 158 Towed and wheeled guns, 100 tracked guns to support the mechanized formations and 180 wheeled guns with armour protection has been spelt out. Hopefully, these guns would be acquired in the current 11th Five Year Plan (2007-2012). Last year, the Defence Acquisition Council had included a fifth category classified as Mounted Gun Systems. These howitzers, mounted on wheeled chassis, would have a shoot and scoot capability with the crew remaining mounted on the vehicle.

Looking at the overall requirements the estimates of the number of guns to be inducted to complete the rationalization plan range from 2700 to 3600 guns in the long term perspective of 15 to 20 years costing between Rs 22,000 crores to Rs 30,000 crores. These demands are based on the total number of artillery regiments which are 200 or so, and the additional artillery units planned to be raised. Such mammoth requirements also predicate that India has to indigenize the production of 155 mm guns as it can remain an importer if it has any pretensions of becoming a major power.

Defence Minister A K Antony though has already stated that the policy now was to acquire every important system with Transfer of Technology (ToT). Indian artillery immediately needs 400 towed 155 mm guns as no such guns have been acquired since the Bofors were inducted in 1987. Induction of these guns would be followed by indigenous production of 1580 guns of this type.

The acquisition process was suspended after dealings with Singapore's ST Kinetics (and six other companies) were put on hold due to allegations of corruption involving Ordnance Factories Board (OFB)'s top executive. That in fact led to a single vendor situation, and that is best avoided, according to the procurement manual. The results of the investigations (by India's Central Bureau of Investigation, or CBI) are not known but till the companies involved are not cleared of the allegations or suspicions, no contracts would be signed by them. However, pending the completion of the process, the procedural system has okayed that the trials of equipment offered by these companies could go on so as not to cause further delay. A deal could and would be signed only after these companies are cleared of any charges of wrong-doing.

Accordingly, the government has approved the trials of the Towed guns from SK Kinetics and BAE Systems with the caveat that trials are subject to clearance of allegations of corruption (in the case of SK Kinetics). Indian Army Chief Gen Deepak Kapoor (a gunner himself) had admitted the development to be of a particular concern as the Army has not been able to purchase a single gun in the last 23 years. Earlier Denel of South Africa was blacklisted on similar charges which led to the current re-tendering process. The second category is of Tracked guns mounted on tank chassis for supporting the mechanized formations for five artillery regiments to be acquired to the extent of 100 155mm/52 calibre guns to replace the existing 130mm Catapult and 105 mm Abbot Guns.

There is the third category of wheeled 155 mm guns mounted on a six-wheeled vehicle with armour protection to the extent of 180 (as mentioned earlier). The fourth category of ultralight howitzers. And the last and the fifth category is the mounted gun system, The artillery modernization includes off-the-shelf purchase of 200 155mm/52-calibre mounted gun systems to be followed by indigenous manufacture of another 614 such howitzers under transfer of technology. The 17-tonne motorized howitzers will arm 40 regiments. A rough glance would suggest that the overall requirement would easily surpass a figure of 3000 guns.

Concerned about fast depleting stocks including war wastage reserves of field artillery, the Army Headquarters has mooted a proposal for the induction of 80-100 pieces of 130 mm medium guns from old stocks lying with former Soviet Republics, as a desperate last resort, to have something at least ASAP. Though of World War II vintage, the 130 mm gun was imported and inducted into the Indian artillery in the 19060s. It is a rugged and a reliable gun which has seen action in all the terrains as obtaining in India including the Sia Chen Glacier base, high altitude areas and deserts. However, it lacks the sophistication and mobility of the modern artillery guns, and has a limited range of the types of ammunitions it can fire.

The Army headquarters is being forced to adopt such a measure for earliest making up of critical deficiencies and building already depleted war wastage stocks. It needs to be underscored that except for upgradation of a limited number of 130 mm guns to 155mm by Soltam of Israel, a project that received mixed reviews, the Indian army has not inducted or upgraded an artillery gun for nearly three decades. In fact, OFB tried to sell the upgunned 130mm to the Gulf countries, but there was no interest in an old system here.

With indigenous production at standstill, in the Artillery faces a real precarious situation and hence this desperate and some say counterproductive measure. It is learned that the issue was discussed in recent Defence Acquisition Council meeting with final decision still pending.

Enunciation of the Cold Start doctrine could not have served its purpose of strategic communication to our potential adversaries unless the voids in fire power are made up in double quick time. The acquisition decisions on procurement of 155 mm 52 calibre towed howitzers, SP tracked and wheeled guns, and mounted gun systems as also ultralight howitzers must be taken on priority for the Artillery to play its role in a future war imposed on India.

MODERNISING THE INDIAN INFANTRY

Why has it taken the Army so long to conceive an upgrade package for the oldest, most potent and intensely employed fighting arm, the Infantry, even after the so-called revolution in military affairs? The foot soldier, the original and most versatile weapon system that is always taken for granted, has emerged from the dubious shock and awe strategy of recent campaigns as its ultimate arbiter. India has paid dearly for the neglect of its infantry in terms of cost, casualties and over-stretch of battle. But the Infantry has never let us down. Kargil was its finest hour. Gen VP Malik, the Army Chief of the time, wryly noted: "We will fight with what we have."

So when for the first time an international conference of Army and defence industry was launched last week to put the forgotten soldier centre-stage, some misgivings were natural. While Army Chief Gen JJ Singh outlined his vision for the soldier system of the future, the conspicuous and total absence of Government - MoD - robbed the conference of any sanctity. In sharp contrast, for a MoD-sponsored defence finance seminar earlier in the month, Government officials and ministers were stepping over each other at Vigyan Bhavan.

Free India's Army came into being in 1947 and within weeks, the Infantry soldiers landed in Srinagar to save J&K from being gobbled up by Pakistani tribal raiders. Since then, the Infantry has not ceased fighting proxy wars there and later, elsewhere too. A former Army Chief, Gen SR Choudhury, who was not from the Infantry, described the Infantry as the Army and vice versa. Field Marshal Montgomery said: An army is considered only as good as its Infantry. The experience of four wars, several border skirmishes, two out-of-area missions, the ceaseless campaign to counter cross-border terrorism in Kashmir, numerous other insurgencies in the North-East, internal stability operations elsewhere in the country and UN peace keeping operations make the Indian Infantry the most battle-hardened and combat rich force in the world. The simple and uncomplaining infantryman has given so much to so many for so little. The modernisation of the infantry was first attempted - halfheartedly - in the mid-1980s by the Perspective Planning branch of the Army Headquarters. The bias for mechanised warfare, zealously pursued by Gen Sundarji, was so pronounced that the Infantry modernisation plan was skipped altogether. Guns, tanks, APCs were the weapons in demand. The Infantry was ignored. Had a modest upgrade package been undertaken at that time, infantry would have been more combat contemporary and effective.

Instead, till recently, some soldiers were still using World War II equipment and clothing. Shameful as it was, soldiers had to buy rucksacks and other accoutrements from the market. DRDO is still to come out with a light bulletproof vest. The Army failed to accurately visualize the nature of combat it would fight in the future. Pakistan-sponsored insurgency in Punjab did not alert the nation and the Army to the proxy war brewing in J&K. We defaulted on both counts - anticipating low intensity conflict and cross border terrorism and preparing the Infantry for it.

Despite the sustained counter-insurgency and counter-terrorism campaign in J&K and the North-East since the 1990s, the Army was sluggish in investing in the infantry. The first Gulf War reintroduced the fiction that wars could be won from the air. The air campaigns in Bosnia and Kosovo temporarily turned fiction into reality. But 9/11 broke the myth of supremacy of air power. Operation Enduring Freedom in Afghanistan lasted 76 days; 65 of these were air operations.

The 11-day land offensive secured a temporary and incomplete victory against the Taliban. Operation Iraqi Freedom on the other hand, fought for 20 days was bereft of any preparatory air campaign though a secret air war preceded it. Unhappily for the US/NATO-led coalition forces, despite their pyrrhic military victories, low intensity wars in Afghanistan and Iraq are continuing in full blaze.

The recent 34-day war in Lebanon and the ongoing campaign in Gaza demonstrate the limits of Israel's military power. Used to decisive victories in less than 10 days, Israeli Defence Forces (IDF) were badgered by Hassan Nasrallah's jihadi militia. Reliance on air power, tanks and guns in Lebanon as substitute for ground troops - infantry - was motivated by casualty aversion. We too have to be sensitive to casualties.

The wars in Lebanon, Iraq and Afghanistan spurred by the growing cult of Osama bin Laden and Hassan Nasrallah require a redefinition of the concept of power and military success. Success would necessarily be an inclusive military victory encompassing post-conflict stability and reconstruction. For this we need Infantry.

The Indian Army should not get overly seduced by high-sounding warfare like 'netcentric' that the West is being diverted into. This is not to suggest we ignore the strides in high-tech warfare. But as a former US NATO Commander noted recently: "This netcentric stuff is great but our men in Baghdad are being blown up with their Humvees by IEDs." He suggested that we address the battle we are fighting before switching to the one we will fight in the future. India's supreme operational challenge is and will be the maintenance of internal security. Just last month, Prime Minister Manmohan Singh stated this ground reality. The Infantry is at the heart of counterinsurgency and counter-terrorism operations and may well get sucked into anti-Naxal operations as well. Keeping the Army operationally ready for both conventional and unconventional missions is imperative but the emphasis has to be on the business of the day: CI and CT.

The Indian Infantry is belatedly embarking on a modernisation programme to enhance its combat skills through increased lethality, communications, surveillance, mobility and suvivability. These force multipliers will enable the soldier to fight all-weather, 24x7 and on any terrain in the right battle-configuration albeit with the accent on LIC.

The GSQR for the Future-Infantry-Soldier-As a System (F-INSAS) must empower not encumber the soldier. DRDO must compete with domestic and international industry. DRDO has one more chance to make amends for its omissions and commissions. F-INSAS must strike the right balance between the surge of technology and sensibility of the soldier keeping the battle of the future in mind. Defence Minister AK Antony should accord F-INSAS the highest strategic priority.

ARMY AVIATION CORPS (INDIA)

The Army Aviation Corps is a component of the Indian Army, formed on 1 November 1986. The aviation arm is headed by a Director General of the rank of Lt General at the Army HQ, New Delhi.

History

In 1984, the Indian Army's Northern Command inducted the HAL Cheetah into the Siachen Glacier. The pilots were put to the ultimate test professionally and also in terms of human endurance. In 1986, the "Air Observation Post" units were transferred from the Indian Air Force to the Indian Army to form the Army Aviation branch.

Using nine helicopter squadrons, Army Aviation has supported ground units by carrying men and material in the highest battlefield on earth, culminating in the conquest of the entire 72 km of the Siachen Glacier. Innumerable skirmishes and confrontations are taking place in the ongoing operations in the Siachen Glacier and the Army Aviation Corps is providing the required support for sustenance of our troops.

The Sri Lankan operations saw full-fledged jungle warfare application of the army's aviation resources in extremely hostile conditions. The Corps won laurels for its daring performance in the face of all odds. The Corps has also been operating in the jungle, mountain and riverine terrains of India since long.

A unit of the Army Aviation Corps had the unique distinction of operating in Somalia, as part of UNOSOM-II (United Nations Operation in Somalia-II), from October 1993 to November 1994. During these operations, the flight flew over 2000 hours without any accident and maintained 100% serviceability in an environment akin to desert terrain. Army aviators have also been operating in the desert areas since long. In fact, some of the Army's biggest battles and peacetime exercises have been carried out in the deserts and areas contiguous to the plains of Punjab. The Corps has an exposure of participating in a war-like scenario in Operation Vijay - 1999 (Kargil Conflict).

Today

Role

The army aviation pilots are drawn from other combat arms, including artillery officers, to form a composite third dimensional force for an integrated battle. IAF operates & flies attack

Helicopters like the Mil Mi-25/Mi-35 which are owned and administered by the Indian Air Force, but under the operational control of the Army & play a major role to support the armoured columns and infantry. Apart from the attack role, helicopters like the HAL Chetak (Aérospatiale SA 316 Alouette III), HAL Cheetah (Aérospatiale SA 315 Lama) and HAL Dhruv provide logistical support for the Indian Army in remote and inaccessible areas, especially the Siachen Glacier.

Army Aviation Corps(AAC) also perform tasks like CSAR, artillery lift, Combat transportation, logistics relief, military prisoner transportation and Medical evacuation(MEDEVAC) during war and in the case of natural calamities.

Training

Training is imparted to all candidates at the Combat Army Aviation Training School (CATS) at Nashik. The Army Aviation training was previously conducted in School of Artillery, Deolali. But now it is carried out in an independent Combat Air Training School also at Deolali.

The Cheetah helicopter simulator has been set up at Combat Army Aviation Training School (CATS). It is expected to reduce substantial cost in training and also to reduce pilot risk during training.

The simulator is designed to expose the trainee to different weather conditions like snow, rain, storm and different terrains in addition to night flying training in handling emergencies, tactical handling of the flying machine, its different maneuvers and more. The project to install a simulator was proposed in December 2000 and approved in April 2002, with CATS Nashik chosen as the centre for installation. Macmet Technologies Ltd, which won the bid over Hindustan Aeronautics Limited (HAL), completed the project by 2005 at a cost of Rs 16.26 crore. After stringent checks, the facility was accepted by the army in December 2005.

Aircraft

The Indian Army operates around 136 helicopters.

COMBAT AIRCRAFT

The IAF is preparing to expand its area of operations and power-projection capability well beyond its immediate neighbourhood by 2022. From a sanctioned strength of 39 fighter squadrons, the IAF is down to around 32 following decades of neglect. But it hopes to augment its strategic makeover by increasing this to 42 squadrons of 700-800 frontline combat aircraft over the next decade through an ambitious $50 billion procurement drive.

Besides 272 imported and licence-built Sukhoi Su-30MKI MRCAs that will form the backbone of the fighter fleet, this expansion includes the acquisition of 126 Dassault Rafale-B/C/M (the exact variant to be acquired by India has yet to be announced) fighters and around 214 Fifth-Generation Fighter Aircraft (FGFA) which could increase to around 250 or even 300 platforms.

Both latter projects, however, are delayed. The IAFs Medium Multi Role Combat Aircraft requirement-likely to rise to around 205 Rafales is postponed due to complex negotiations over the technology transfer to Hindustan Aeronautics Limited (HAL) in Bangalore which will build 118 Rafales (the rest will be built in France) and the sudden death in October 2013 of the official negotiating the tender.

Furthermore, the $35 billion FGFA programme is deferred because of complications in finalising its $11 billion Research and Development contract that is to be equally shared between India and Russia. This, in turn, would postpone the arrival in India of three FGFA prototypes based on the Sukhoi T-50 PAK-FA MRCA for flight testing by the IAF between 2014 and 2019 to determine its final configuration before manufacturing begins. As part of its moderinsation, the IAF is upgrading its 51 Mirage 2000H MRCA to Mirage 2000-5 status in a $3 billion deal being performed by Dassault and Thales and 67 MiG29B/S MRCAs including eight MiG-29U/B trainers for $964 million in a 2009 contract agreed with manufacturers, Russian Aircraft Corporation.

The Mirage-2000Hs are to be fitted with advanced avionics, mission computers and a pulse Doppler radar capable of identifying objects at a range of 70 nautical miles (130 kilometres), all of which would provide IAF commanders the flexibility to commit fewer aircraft on combat missions for higher success rates. The retrofit would also keep the Mirage-2000Hs operationally relevant for another two decades. The upgrade includes a $48.3 million outlay to augment HAL's capabilities to retrofit 47 Mirage-2000Hs in Bangalore in as many months after four were readied in France within 40 months of the deal being inked. The MiG-29s, including eight MiG-29U/B trainers, will be equipped with new Klimov RD-33 Series-3 turbofan with digital fuel injection, the Phazotron Zhuk-ME phased array radar and the Vympel R-77 Beyond Visual Range (BVR) air-to-air missile.

The IAFs 125-strong SEPECAT Jaguar IS/IB/IM fleet is being retrofitted with HAL's Display Attack Ranging Inertial Navigation III (DARIN-III) system whilst manufacture of the locally designed 'Tejas' Light Combat Aircraft (LCA), also built by HAL, will begin in early 2014, shortly after it secured its long- postponed initial operational clearance in December 2013. The LCAs Final Operational Clearance (FOC) will only obtained in late 2014 after it has successfully integrated its weapons suite, radars and sensors to enable it to fire rockets, laser-guided bombs, BVR missiles and perform aerial refuelling.

The IAF will initially induct 40 LCAs powered by General Electric F404-GE-IN20 turbofans with a limited 80-85 kilonewton (KN) thrust that restricts its weapons load and angle of attack in accordance with the IAFs qualitative requirements. The follow-on circa 100 LCAs will be fitted with the General Electric F414-GE turbofan with a 90-100 Kilonewton (KN) thrust that will significantly overcome these two limitations. By 2022 the IAF plans to induct seven LCA squadrons to replace its MiG-21 ground attack jets whose operational life has been extended well beyond their retirement date until 2022-24 in order to maintain numerical platform superiority over Pakistan.

Special Missions

In August 2012 India's Defence Research and Development Organisation's (DRDO) Centre for Airborne Systems in Bangalore took delivery of the first of three Brazilian Embraer 145 AEW aircraft to integrate all mission systems including the DRDO's indigenously-developed active antenna array radar pending its eventual introduction into the IAF. Once completed the EMB-145 AEW aircraft will offer endurances in excess of five hours and provide 240 degree surveillance at distances between 135-202nm (250-374km) officials said.

The three EMB 145 platforms were acquired for $210 million in 2008 and will eventually supplement a similar number of Israel Aircraft Industries (IAI) Elta Systems-built Phalcon radars mounted on Ilyushin Il-76 turbofan freighter; the ensemble being known as the A-50EI. The IAF is to acquire two similar follow-on AEW systems for an estimated $800 million by 2020-22 to further augment its surveillance and power projection capabilities.

Freighters

Nevertheless, the IAFs strategic lift capability, currently dominated by Soviet-era platforms, has received the biggest boost with the induction of two types of US military freighter at Hindon Air Base on Delhi's outskirts. These included six Lockheed Martin C-130J-30 Hercules turboprops acquired at a cost of $1.2 billion and specially configured for use by India's Special Forces, and three of an eventual ten Boeing C-17 Globemaster III turbofan freighters acquired in 2011 for $4.1 billion.

The IAF created history in August 2013 by landing a C-130J-30 at the Daulat Beg Oldie advanced landing ground, the world's highest airstrip in the northern Himalayan Ladakh region, adjoining China's unsettled frontier, displaying the IAFs growing strategic reach which can now support army formations deployed in this inhospitable, largely snow-bound terrain all year round. Meanwhile, in December 2013 the IAF signed a $1 billion contract for six additional C-130J-30s via the FMS programme. To be delivered within three years the supplementary transports will be based at Panagarh in eastern India, the headquarters of the Indian Army's new Mountain Strike Corps for employment against China. Delivery of the remaining seven C-17s will be completed by the end 2014 after which the IAF plans to order six more to replace the circa twelve IL-76s which entered IAF service in 1985. The arrival of the six add-on C-17s will make the IAF their largest operator after the US Air Force.

Furthermore, in May 2013 the Ministry of Defence dispatched a tender to eight overseas vendors to supply the IAF with 56 medium transport aircraft with a 6,000-8,000 kilogram (13,200-17,600lb) payload and a cruise speed of 432 knots (800 kilometres-per-hour) and through a Joint Venture (JV) with an indigenous private sector manufacturer.

The tender has been dispatched to Alenia Aeromacchi (Italy), Antonov (Ukraine), Boeing (USA), Airbus Military (Europe) and Illyushin (Russia). Under the terms of the tender, these overseas vendors will tie-up with private Indian companies to form the JV, designated the Indian Production Agency (IPA).

Sixteen of the selected platforms will be acquired off-the-shelf and the remaining 40 will be built locally under the JV but the programme is facing powerful resistance from HAL which was deliberately omitted from the project because of its poor serviceability, soaring costs and deadline overruns. This was the first instance of the IAF looking exclusively to India's private sector to build the cargo aircraft instead of HAL, which for decades, has monopolised the licenced production of all Indian military aircraft.

But backed by the federal Industries Ministry HALs involvement in the programme is under active consideration. Eventually, these 56 platforms will supplement the long-delayed Multi-role Transport Aircraft (MTA) under joint development by India and Russia. Sustaining the transport and fighter fleets will be six Airbus Military A330 Multi-Role Tanker Transport (MRTT) jets which the IAF selected in late 2012.

Trainers

Additionally, the IAF is in the process of inducting 75 Swiss-designed Pilatus PC-7s basic turboprop trainers, 20 more BAE Systems Hawk Mk132 jet trainers for its Surya Kiran Aerobatics Team (SKAT) taking the total to 123 Hawks. The IAF is also taking delivery of 80 Russian Mi-17V5 medium-lift armed helicopters with a 19,685ft (6000m) operational ceiling acquired in December 2008 for $1.34 billion. The deal for another 71 Mi-17V5 platforms for $1.53 billion, which would include 59 for the IAF, was agreed during President Vladimir Putin's visit to Delhi in December 2012.

IAF officers said the Mi-17V5 fleet will be deployed on special airborne operations; for the transportation of troops and materiel; search and rescue missions; casualty evacuation and possibly even anti-insurgent operations. Air Chief Marshal Norman Browne, Chief of Staff of the Indian Air Force, said in October 2013 that price negotiations for 22 Boeing AH-64E Apache attack helicopters and 15 Boeing CH-47 Chinook heavy-lift helicopters were concluded and their procurement had been forwarded to the Federal Finance Ministry for approval.

Away from airframes, replacing obsolete air defence capability and high altitude radar, upgrading 30 airfields and resurrecting long-disused advanced landing grounds near the precipitous Chinese frontier to support air operations are also IAF priorities. The IAFs long-delayed modernisation drive is aimed at bolstering its depleting combat squadrons, augmenting its strategic transcontinental reach to manage out-of-area contingencies and to extend its power-projection capability well beyond its immediate neighbourhood. By the end of India's 13th Five-Year Finance Plan in 2022, the IAF envisages a combat strength of around 40 frontline, multi-role combat aircraft squadrons. This will comprise 700-800 aircraft with BVR capabilities acquired via imports, joint ventures with overseas manufacturers and technology transfers, and moderately through indigenously developed platforms with high foreign content.

FUTURE OF THE ARMY AVIATION CORPS

The army is currently evaluating helicopters from Kamov, Eurocopter and AgustaWestland for the 197 light helicopter contract for lifting supplies for the troops stationed at high altitudes. The $750 million deal for the 197 helicopters for the defence forces aims to replace the aging 1970s-vintage Chetak and Cheetah helicopters and will be for high altitude, surveillance and logistics.

The successful bidder will provide 60 helicopters in a flyaway condition, while the remaining 137 aircraft will be licence-produced by Hindustan Aeronautics Limited (HAL). Under the offsets clause, the winning bidder must also invest at least 30% of the contracted cost in India.

In December 2014, Kamov Ka-226T was selected for the role of Light Utility Helicopter and as an initial replacement for Obsolete Chetak and Cheetah, while the LUH is under development. Kamov would set up a production plant in India and around 197 would be procured under the "Make in India" program.

The army is also planning to acquire HAL Light Combat Helicopter, which is under development by the Hindustan Aeronautics Limited to meet its requirements for an attack helicopter which can operate at high altitude (16,300 feet) to fit into an anti-armour and anti-infantry role. The army is also planning to acquire a 3-tonne single-engine HAL Light Utility Helicopter which is also under development for recce and observation role. As of 2007 the Army Aviation Corps modernisation plans were:

Other future acquisition plans are:

- Reconnaissance and surveillance helicopters – HAL Dhruv will replace the existing fleet of Cheetah and Chetak helicopters. While some helicopters will be procured as 'Buy' category, others will be 'Designed and Developed' by HAL as 'Make' category. RFP for the former has been issued and the procurement was likely to commence soon.

- Tactical Battle Support Helicopter - This is being developed as a tri-services project by HAL. The helicopter will be called Indian Multi Role Helicopter. By 2007 the procurement process had already been "set into motion" for battle support helicopters. These machines should be capable of carrying 10–12 men into the battlefield.
- Special operations squadron - A special operations squadron is being raised to provide dedicated integral aviation support to the Para Commandos (India).
- Heli-borne early-warning – Raising of a heli-borne early warning flight has been planned for employing electronic warfare.
- The government of India, on 2 July 2014, approved purchase of 39 Apache helicopters.
- Light fixed-wing aircraft – The army is also planning to induct light fixed-wing aircraft in future for surveillance and communication tasks.
- DRDO Imperial Eagle

4

Structure of the Indian Air Force

RECRUITMENT AND TRAINING

Recruitment is through three military related academies. These include the National Defence Academy, Indian Military Academy and Officers Training Academy.

For entrance, one must display that they are both physically and mentally fit to be in the military by sitting examinations and undergoing medical checkups. The complete list of institutions training Indian army were listed in Military academies in India section.

Indian Army

Strength: During a conflict, the air-arm of the Indian army plays a crucial role in providing essential supplies and air cover to the ground forces. Shown here is the Indian Army's HAL Dhruv.

Indian Army Statistics

Active Troops	1,325,000 (2nd)
Artillery	7100
Battle Tanks	5010
Aircraft	52 squadrons of helicopters
Surface-to-air missiles	90,000+

The Indian Army is the world's second largest army in terms of military personnel (after China). It is a completely voluntary service, the military draft having never been imposed in India. The army has rich combat experience in diverse terrains, due to India's diverse geography, and also has a distinguished history of serving in United Nations peacekeeping operations.

The force is headed by the Chief of Army Staff, currently General Deepak Kapoor. The highest rank in the Indian Army is Field Marshal, but it is a largely ceremonial rank and appointments are made by the President of India, on the advice of the Union Cabinet of Ministers, only in exceptional circumstances. (See Field Marshal (India)). General S.H.F.J. Manekshaw and the late General K.M. Cariappa are the only two officers who have attained this rank.

The Indian Army has seen military action in the Indo-Pakistani War of 1947, the Indo-Pakistani War of 1965,the Indo-Pakistani War of 1971, and others such as Operation Polo in 1948, the Sino-Indian War in 1962 over the McMahon Line, and the Kargil War against Kashmiri insurgents and the Pakistan military personnel

Currently, the Indian army has dedicated one brigade of troops to the UN's standby arrangements. Through its large, sustained troop commitments India has come in for much praise for taking part in difficult operations for prolonged periods.

The Indian Army has participated in several UN peace-keeping operations, including the ones in Cyprus, Lebanon, Congo, Angola, Cambodia, Vietnam, Namibia, El Salvador, Liberia, Mozambique and Somalia. The army also provided a paramedical unit to facilitate the withdrawal of the sick and wounded in Korea.

INDIAN AIR FORCE: IS IT AN EXPEDITIONARY FORCE?

Doctrinal Background

Whilst it is true that the IAF now has the assets to function effectively in 'Out of Area Operations' (such as Aerial Refuellers, strategic airlifters like the C17s, the AWACS, Special Forces aircraft like the C130 Js and long-range fighters such as the Sukhoi 30s), India's polity does not expect the IAF to function in an expeditionary role.

This is reinforced in the Union War Book and the RM's Op Directive emanating there from. An Air Expeditionary Force (AEF)-the USAF recently and the Allied Air Forces during WWII would fall under this definition-is one that, in today's' context, is capable of deploying a package of 'shooter' air power, including air-to-air, precision air-to-ground and defence suppression aircraft into a theatre to begin delivering combat air power within a short period-48 hours or so.

For the USAF, an expeditionary element has been a long felt need, mainly on account of their shrinking overseas basing infrastructure. Thus they look to expeditionary elements to give them a 'plug-and-play' 911 policing capability in a theatre in keeping with their strategy of global engagement'.

This, in effect, gives them the option, in a contingency, of not having to rely on direct overseas deployment of air power from mainland US. Hence the evolution of their expeditionary air elements to seek to provide rapid, responsive air power tailored to the obtaining geopolitical situation-read 'adventurism by a rogue nation' in US parlance-often to give them a 'filler' capability to overcome naval air power gaps such as absence of an aircraft carrier in the vicinity.

The genesis of the USAF Expeditionary Air Force can be traced to Gulf War II around Oct 1994 when Saddam's forces were threatening to invade Kuwait for a second time a la Gulf War I in 1990, and the USAF had to re-position itself in the region at short call. Later, USAF's AEF II deployed to Jordan for several months in 1996.

These deployments indeed demonstrated the real 'speed' characteristic of air power. Now, the IAF is firstly not geared for a theatre type of military scenario, not still having a CDS nor Theatre Commanders yet. Nor does our country officially advocate functioning like a regional policeman, regardless of what we may have done over the Maldives during Op Cactus Lily or Sri Lanka during Op Pawan, enforcing the writ of the Indian State over a 'rogue' neighbouring State.

Out of Area Ops vs. Expedition

So what is the real difference between having Out of Area air capability and being an expeditionary air force? Clearly, it is the prevailing political stance that governs IAF's operational employment. Like we do not subscribe to employing air power against our own citizens, our country surely would not like to be seen as a regional hegemon that enforces its political will through use of offensive air power, as the US is wont to do globally, especially post 9/11. Also, the USAF sees the AEF as a via media for coalition-building and regional cooperation. The IAF may have carried out a Maldives, a Goa or a Sri Lanka, but an expeditionary military is not in our national psyche. That is not to say that a repeat air action as was done in the cases mentioned is not foreseeable or doable. However, should the Indian government decide in the future to task the IAF with an expeditionary role, the IAF will not only have to buttress its Out Of Area capabilities in terms of further increased inventory in key assets, but more importantly perhaps, exercise the same periodically, to be effective when called upon to do so. There are several aspects to an expeditionary role than just deploying Out of Area. There are airfield management, academic and doctrinal training, flight safety and ground safety, joint exercises etc. to be considered. Incidentally, the USAF expeditionary elements do not believe in having 'full spectrum' capability, so as not to lose out on staying 'lean and mean'. This again is an area that would demand rigorous planning and training, were the IAF to assume on an expeditionary avatar.

Other Challenges for an AEF

Another factor in an Air Expeditionary Force deployment is pre-positioning. Whereas the US could facilitate pre-positioning in concerned sectors thanks to their military and foreign policies such as the Status of Forces Agreement (SOFA), what can India do in our vicinity? Would any country in the zone from the Persian Gulf to the Malacca Straits be willing to extend such a facility to us? Prepositioning becomes critical especially for stores such as armament and servicing equipment. An option is to coax friendly neighbours to oblige with similar equipment in their inventory or civil infrastructure/lab facilities, but this would only be wishful thinking in our operational scenario.

One gets the uneasy feeling that, possibly with the recent induction of American-origin assets such as the C-130J and the C-17, we have willy-nilly started toying with ideas such as 'expeditionary' roles. We have to make a clear distinction and find a balance between our in-country security requirements, from counter-insurgency to anti-terror/anti-hijack operations, wherein our long range assets come into play, and the urge to opt for diplomatic 'Gun Boat' options. An expeditionary air force also calls for extensive reorganisation down the command chain, such as setting up Expeditionary Wings and theatre commands. Besides, a high degree of coordination and symbiosis between existing Air Commands and any proposed expeditionary elements would be called for. Another factor that needs consideration in this context is the additional costs involved in such Out of Area Operations. Air lift costs themselves would be considerable for a country like India with its constraints in defence budgeting.

The Roles and Missions Debate

After its experience with four recent Expeditionary Air Missions, considerable debate exists in US military circles on the viability of an expeditionary force in today's context. Some of their C-in-C s still feel that the capability could be sustained in theatre rather than in mainland US. It would be a folly, therefore, for the IAF not to think through roles such as 'Expeditionary Air Elements'. We fortunately have a clear definition of our roles and missions (amply articulated to the government through the IAF Doctrine IAP 2000). The IAF does not need to confuse itself with roles which are firstly highly unlikely in our environment and secondly against our national ethos. Similar capabilities could be achieved and maintained without projecting ourselves as an Expeditionary Air Force. It is highly undesirable for any fighting service to be confused about its roles and missions, as military history over the years bears out. It is to be hoped that the reportage mentioned at the beginning of this piece is only an ill-informed aberration and not anything constituting a 'company policy' for the IAF.

TRAINER FLEET OF IAF

IAF's fleet of HPT-32 trainer aircraft has been grounded since August, 2009 after a crash of an aircraft on 28th July, 2009 due to engine failure. In order to improve the reliability of the engine, Hindustan Aeronautics Limited (HAL) is implementing certain modifications on the engine and air frame including integrating a system called Aircraft Parachute Recovery System.

The Request for Proposal (RFP) for procurement of Basic Trainer Aircraft (BTA) for the Indian Air Force was issued on 16th December 2009. In response techno-commercial proposals were received from Korean Aircraft Industries, South Korea; GROB Aircraft, Germany; EADS PZL, Poland; Hawker Beechcraft, United States of America; Alenia Aerammachi, Italy; Aerostar of Romania; and Pilatus, Switzerland. The proposal for procurement of the trainer aircraft is being progressed in accordance with the Defence Procurement Procedure-2008.

No issues which are considered critical to flight safety had emerged during the technical evaluation of the aircraft.

The estimated cost of the procurement is Rs2900 crore. The proposal is expected to be finalized during the current financial year.

Purchase of 10 C-17 Globemaster III Aircraft

The government has accorded approval to buy ten C-17 Globemaster-III aircraft for the Indian Air Force. The Letter of Offer and Acceptance (LOA) for procurement of these aircraft along with associated equipment was signed on 14th June 2011.

The cost of the procurement is US$4.116 billon. The delivery of these aircraft will commence from June, 2013 and is expected to be completed by June, 2015.

Purchase of AJTs

In March 2004, government had signed a contract with BAE Systems and Rolls Royce Turbomeca UK for procurement of 24 Hawk Advanced Jet Trainers (AJT) and with Hindustan Aeronautics Limited (HAL), Bengaluru for the licence manufacture of another 42 AJTs under Transfer of Technology from BAE Systems for the Indian Air Force (IAF). All the 24 direct supply aircraft have been delivered by BAE systems while 28 out of 42 aircraft contracted with HAL had been delivered till July, 2011.

In July 2010, government signed another contract with HAL for procurement of additional 57 Hawk AJTs from HAL. Of these, 40 are for the IAF and 17 are for the Indian Navy. The delivery of these aircraft will commence from 2013 and is expected to be completed by 2016.

Summery

A major responsibility of the IAF in the future would be in the area of strategic airlift. Internal security compulsions will place growing demand for the movement of quick reaction as also regular security forces within the country on short notice.

Given its emerging regional power status and the newly forged strategic partnership with the US if not abrogated by the incoming administration, India may be called upon to project power in the region which may involve airlift of large military forces to areas of interest of either of the partners in the region outside our borders and to provide sustained logistic support. Strategic airlift capability of the IAF would therefore need to be built up practically from scratch as the existing fleet is fast approaching the end of its total technical life.

At the tactical level, the IAF should be equipped with a fleet of medium tactical transport aircraft and helicopters capable of speedy response with special forces over shorter ranges.

The IAF has taken some baby steps towards acquiring the capability of projecting combat power in the region. At this point in time, the capability is limited to a token force and cannot be described as significant. However, while steps are in hand to augment the existing fleet of long range combat aircraft as also to acquire a new fleet, the capability of power projection would in the ultimate analysis be limited by the size of the fleet of in-flight refuelling aircraft. This fleet would have to be suitably enlarged for any meaningful power projection that is capable of making an impact.

The IAF needs to enhance some of the force multipliers already on the inventory as also to develop a range of new capabilities both in the strategic and tactical regimes. At the strategic level, the IAF must be able to provide the nation with credible nuclear deterrence against Pakistan and China. Also, it should be capable of power projection in its perceived area of national security interests and those of our ally in the region beyond the national borders with combat aircraft, in-flight refuelling and strategic airlift capability. These forces should be geared to provide swift response to a crisis situation and be able to provide logistic support to sustain forces for significant length of time. For strategic strike deep into enemy territory, the IAF needs to have a combination of missile based and airborne platforms, the latter with powerful electronic warfare equipment to suppress and defeat enemy air defence systems. Tactical roles may be transferred to UCAVs and helicopters.

To provide effective air defence of the homeland, the IAF needs to acquire a fleet of AWACS and AEW aircraft over and above the few already on order to enhance surveillance capability at low level. New generation area and point defence missile systems need to be inducted to replace the ageing and obsolete systems currently deployed. For strategic and tactical intelligence, the IAF must have its own satellite systems and a fleet of UAVs with a range of advanced sensors to provide all weather day and night capability. The fleet of UAVs should be adequately supported by appropriate ground infrastructure for automated and speedy processing of intelligence information, and fleet of tactical transport aircraft and helicopters for quick response with special forces.

PRACTICAL CONSIDERATIONS UNDERPINNING THE FORCE STRUCTURE

It has been emphasised by the Indian government that India's nuclear weapons are not country specific. However, a military force structure can only be configured to neutralise specific current threats and must be made flexible enough to be adaptable to meet emerging challenges. Without going into specific details of the nuclear threats faced by India, an aspect that requires a separate analysis, it could be stated that the nuclear weapons possessed by both China and Pakistan, when placed in the context of their unresolved territorial and boundary disputes with India, are definitely a threat in being while those possessed by the other NWS that are distant from India are far less hazardous. Hence, a realistic force structuring option would be to base India's deterrent on the nuclear weapons stockpile of China as a planning parameter.

How Many Cities should be Targeted?

The key decision to be made in working out a nuclear force structure for India is regarding the number of nuclear warheads necessary for a retaliatory strike with a counter value strategy that emphasises attacks on large cities and industrial centres. At the heart of the planning process is the question: how many such targets must Indian nuclear forces plan to destroy in order to ensure that deterrence works? Would it be adequate to target one large, metropolitan-cum-industrial centre with thermonuclear weapons, or would it be necessary to plan to destroy ten, twenty or more such complexes? Is the level of deterrence proportionately dependent on the number of targets in the adversary country that one's nuclear force is capable of destroying or, does the law of diminishing returns apply after the capability to destroy a certain number of targets has been acquired? These are complex challenges to resolve and several reputed nuclear strategists have attempted to find the answers through intuitive as well as mathematical solutions based on econometric models and the "innovative use of statistics". There is, perhaps, something to be said for the theory of diminishing returns. Quoting Bernard Brodie, Bharat Karnad has written:

> Brodie, in one of his most memorable series of insights, noted that in the nuclear age, "the potential deterrence value of an admittedly inferior force may be sharply greater than it has ever been before," in the event, that "a menaced small nation could threaten (a big one) with only a single thermonuclear bomb" directed at its premier city, which he contended "would be a retaliatory capability sufficient to give the (aggressor) government pause." Further, that ten thermonuclear tipped ("city busting") missiles aimed at the same number of the enemy's cities "would no doubt work still greater deterrent effect." But, increase in the deterrent effect, he surmised, would be "less than proportional to the increase in magnitude of potential destruction" in part because the deter-er would run out of high-value enemy metropolitan centres to hit. It amounted to saying that too large a nuclear arsenal would only fetch diminished deterrence.

However, Herman Kahn, another prima donna of nuclear theology, disputed Brodie's logic. He explained that, as the efficiency of a ballistic missile is the square of its accuracy as represented by its CEP, ten ballistic missiles aimed at ten cities would not deter an adversary who could be reasonably sure that given a CEP of one to two km, a large number of them are bound to fall substantially away from the city centre and may be only partially effective or completely ineffective. Hence, for credible deterrence to be achieved, the adversary must be certain that India would be in a position to ensure that three to four nuclear warheads can be delivered with the required accuracy on every selected target. The comparatively greater density of population per square kilometre in Asian cities is another factor that must be taken into account while deciding the number of cities that must be targeted for effective deterrence.

Despite Mao's assertion that "300 million Chinese would survive" nuclear war, it could be argued that the fear of losing some of its modern showpieces on the eastern coast, combined with the certainty of horrendous civilian casualties due to extremely high population densities, would be adequate to deter China from being the first to begin nuclear exchanges that are bound to escalate to city-busting strikes. The China scholars at IDSA hold sharply divergent views on the number of Chinese cities that need to be targeted to ensure deterrence. Sujit Dutta is of the opinion that China would be deterred if its leadership were convinced that its adversary could destroy even three major cities. M.V. Rappai concurs with this view and argues that the Chinese are taking their economic development very seriously and would not do anything to jeopardise the future of their thriving population and industrial centres. Swaran Singh advocates the targeting of five cities for effective deterrence but feels that rather than the ability to target a number of cities, India's overall nuclear capability should be built up for effective deterrence. However, Srikanth Kondapalli holds the view that perhaps even the credible targeting of 15 to 20 Chinese cities may not be adequate for deterrence as the Chinese would not hesitate to take whatever military action they might consider necessary if, in their view, their national security interests were to be seriously threatened.

In the context of China, India's major nuclear adversary, the targeting of only three to five cities may be inadequate as totalitarian regimes are known to have high tolerance levels. In the absence of hard intelligence about what would deter the Chinese, it would be appropriate for a nuclear planner to err on the side of caution and plan on overkill to ensure that deterrence does not fail. Hence, it could be argued that India should plan on the assured destruction of about 10 to 12 major population and industrial centres (including two to three high priority military or counter force targets such as SSBN bases and nuclear command and control centres) in a retaliatory strike. This should definitely be adequate for the purposes of credible deterrence in the 2000-2010 timeframe. As China develops further into a major industrialised nation, the possible destruction of even three to five major population-cum-industrial centres would be adequate for deterrence. In the case of Pakistan, the destruction of an even lesser number of carefully selected targets would mean that Pakistan would ultimately cease to exist as a nation. An assured destruction capability in respect of eight to ten major value targets would be recognised in advance by India's adversaries as a catastrophic disaster of unmanageable proportions. Such a capability would constitute adequate deterrent threat to qualify the likely damage as unacceptable.

Are Megaton Monsters Necessary?

The next major issue that needs to be resolved is whether the Indian deterrent should be built with 'megaton monsters' or be limited to boosted fission kiloton weapons with yields ranging from 20 to 30 Kt with current technology. It can hardly be disputed that the deterrence value of thermonuclear weapons is much greater than that of fission weapons due to their far greater destruction potential. However, the key question is whether such destructive potential is militarily necessary. Solly Zuckerman has stated that "There is built into nuclear weapons greater destructive power than is necessary for military purposes and their secondary, non-military effects overshadow those which relate specifically to their military use." nation with a limited availability of fissile material, that has opted to suffer what may be a disarming first strike and must, for that reason, stockpile at least twice the number of warheads than what it may actually need for deterrence, has no choice but to opt for thermonuclear weapons in the megaton class. Another compelling reason for thermonuclear weapons in the megaton range is that their larger lethal radius can achieve the desired results with lesser numbers even when the accuracy of delivery is low, that is, the CEP is one to two km. A megaton warhead-tipped ballistic missile would cause horrendous damage even if it detonated well off a city centre and would, therefore, contribute far more to deterrence than fission or even boosted fission bombs. Dr. G. Balachandran argues succinctly for India to base its deterrence on high-yield thermonuclear weapons.

"... India cannot rely on a nuclear deterrent based on weapons of the types tested, that is, fission weapons in the range of 20 Kt. Even with accurate long-range missiles, with a CEP of the order of 200 metres, the (fissile) material requirements are far in excess of the current inventory... It should be understood that increasing the yields of pure fission type of weapons would not solve the problem. On the contrary, the use of fission devices of higher yield will require larger stockpile of W-Pu (weapons-grade plutonium). For instance, for a soft point target at large distances, with a CEP of 1,000 metres, one would require either 10 weapons with a yield of 20 Kt (each) or one with a yield of one megaton. 10 x 20 Kt weapons would require 30 kg of W-Pu... one pure fission weapon with a yield of one megaton would require 150 kg of W-Pu. A thermonuclear weapon, of course, requires far less fissile material for high yields with resultant reduction in the weight of the weapon. Therefore:

- The first requirement for an effective and credible nuclear deterrent is the need for the Indian nuclear arsenal to be based on high yield thermonuclear weapons.
- The second requirement... is to accelerate the missile development programme, especially the development of ICBMs... India cannot be said to have a truly effective nuclear delivery system against China. Its delivery systems are not yet adequately developed.

Citing a Harvard Nuclear Study Group report on the politics of nuclear weapons, Bharat Karnad writes about a 'nuclear paradox': "Nuclear weapons can prevent aggression only if there is a possibility that they will be used, but they should not be made so usable that anyone is tempted to use them... The decision to launch city-busting hydrogen bombs and thermonuclear warheaded ICBMs in a direct attack on the enemy homeland would, on the face of it, be more onerous and far-reaching and, hence, will be more difficult to make than, say, a decision to loose off a theatre nuclear weapon or a tactical nuclear salvo on a peripheral target. And for this reason, thermonuclear weapons, theoretically speaking, would be under tighter command and control and would more easily help stabilise the security situation vis a vis a bigger nuclear power." Also, as thermonuclear weapons do not cost substantially more than fission weapons, it would make sense to optimise India's meager fissile material stockpile by producing sufficient thermonuclear weapons in the megaton class to equip at least all ballistic missiles with them. However, though the requirement is apparently justified, since the demonstrated thermonuclear capability is limited to only 200 Kt warheads, India will have to make do with 200 Kt weapons till (and if) further testing enables the development of megaton class warheads. On the other hand, if in future it is possible to improve the accuracy of India's IRBMs to a CEP of less than 0.01 percent (50 metres at 5,000 km; the Minuteman-III ICBM of the US is reported to have a CEP of 120 metres at a range of 13,000 km), though they would still not be ideal, 200 Kt thermonuclear warheads would be adequate to meet the requirements of deterrence.

The Need for a Triad

Many analysts, particularly those in the West, have interpreted the National Security Advisory Board's reliance on a triad in the draft Nuclear Doctrine as one of the main areas of concern for a likely arms race in Southern Asia. Criticism has centred around the view that a doctrine of 'minimum deterrence' does not need a triad of delivery systems. Their main bone of contention is that SSBNs with SLBMs are not essential for India's nuclear force. All such criticism is obviously ill informed and without objective analytical basis. It would be unrealistic to base India's retaliatory strike force mainly on bomber/fighter-bomber aircraft and land-based ballistic missiles. While all possible targets inside Pakistan can be fully covered by the deep penetration aircraft in service with the Indian Air Force (IAF), they lack the range necessary to hit high-value targets deep inside 'Han' China, including Beijing, and the rapidly modernising cities on the east coast. Air-to-air re-fuelling capability is also not available.

It is often said that a SU-30 on a one way mission to Beijing can reach its target and that there would be no dearth of pilots in the IAF to volunteer for such a suicide mission. While that may be true, it would be foolhardy to base deterrence calculations on such a course of action. Though the SU-30 is a multi-role aircraft, due to the paucity of numbers presently available and those on order, a SU-30 deep strike mission would require a large number of specialised air defence and electronic warfare-capable aircraft as escorts to negotiate vast stretches of the increasingly well defended Chinese air space.

The escort aircraft with the IAF are mostly capable of only tactical ranges and during the final and the most crucial portion of the flight, the SU-30s would have to fly very much on their own. If the Su-30s were launched un-escorted, their chances of survival would be rather slim during war and their contribution to furthering the cause of deterrence would remain completely doubtful during peace. In view of the fact that an Indian strike would be a retaliatory one, the risk of SU-30 airbases in eastern India being rendered unusable due to the preceding nuclear as well as conventional strikes, would also have to be vectored into the planning parameters.

A substantial proportion of the land-based ballistic missile force is also likely to be destroyed in a disarming first strike or even a conventional strike during war before the nuclear threshold is crossed. Missiles of the Agni-I class can be made road-and rail-mobile and can be moved around over large areas in a random, un-predictable manner without a discernible pattern, though they would be vulnerable to attacks by terrorists and insurgent groups. They can also be housed in hardened, over-ground shelters and moved frequently from one shelter to the other or emplaced in fixed silos designed to withstand the overpressures likely to be generated by nuclear explosions of 20 to 30 Kt. Hardened shelters can be easily spotted by modern satellites and can all be destroyed in a disarming first strike. To ensure that not all the missiles are so destroyed, such shelters will need to be constructed at the scale of at least two to three per missile, including some realistic dummy shelters that may not be hardened but must be equipped with dummy missiles mounted on actual tractor erector launchers (TELs) being moved into and out of them so as to enhance their credibility as real missile shelters. Though mobile missiles are harder to locate and track and are less vulnerable at present, surveillance and target acquisition technologies are improving rapidly and adversaries planning first strike strategies may be expected to make the required investments in them.

Fixed silos capable of withstanding a nuclear attack are extremely costly to construct and maintain. So far it has not been possible even for advanced Western countries to construct shelters capable of withstanding the blast of thermonuclear weapons in the megaton range, because such silos are a technological challenge and are prohibitively costly.

Should India's adversaries choose to employ such weapons in future, fixed silos would be virtually useless. Hardened shelters for mobile missiles and fixed silos for the Agni-II and larger class of missile will have to be constructed over huge areas with wide gaps between them to ensure that an attack on one shelter or silo does not destroy more than one missile.

They also have to be secured against stand off and commando type ground attacks by terrorists and insurgent groups. Despite all these measures, it would be fair to assume that up to 40 to 50 percent of the strategic missile force would still be destroyed in a disarming first strike as, despite the US failure to destroy Iraqi Scud launchers during the 1991 Gulf War, modern surveillance capabilities are continuously improving and new military satellites will enable the constant tracking of an adversary's missile force.

There is apparently a need to hedge against the destruction of land-based ballistic missiles by distributing them between static silos, hardened shelters and rail-and road-mobile storage. At the same time, there is a need to build into the force structure sufficient reserves to cater for pre-launch losses. Nuclear deterrence does not come cheap.

Since air bases are susceptible to destruction in a disarming first strike and India's strategic aircraft themselves have limited range and are vulnerable to in-flight interception by the enemy's air defences, and a large proportion of the land-based ballistic missiles may be destroyed before they can be launched, there is no option for India but to go in for submarine launched ballistic missiles (SLBMs) on nuclear-powered submarines (SSBNs) as soon as both SSBNs and SLBMs can be developed.

As is well known, SSBNs are fairly safe from detection even with state-of-the-art reconnaissance, surveillance and target acquisition (RSTA) means, not vulnerable to a 'zero warning' surprise attack, and are not affected by increases in the adversaries' missile accuracy except those that may be anchored in a submarine base at the time of attack. They also have their limitations, not the least of which include the technological complexity of achieving the desired missile launch accuracy from a mobile platform that can never be as sure of its location (and depth) as a fixed silo and the difficulty of communicating targeting information and executive orders to them once they are submerged.

Also, in the Indian context, SLBMs would provide value for money only if they could be developed to reach ranges in excess of 5,000 km so that they can reach all likely targets from their patrolling bases well away from the shores. The SSBNs should be capable of operating from patrolling bases in the Indian as well as the Pacific Oceans and should be equipped for spending at least 30 to 40 days continuously at sea.

As stated earlier, Brigadier Vijay Nair is of the view that India needs four SSBNs, each with 16 SLBMs; Bharat Karnad wants five SSBNs in India's nuclear force, each with 12 SLBMs and Rear Admiral Raja Menon has recommended a force of six SSBNs (with two 'on station' at all times), each equipped with 12 SLBMs.

Six SSBNs would obviously be preferable to four or five as they would provide greater redundancy and flexibility. However, the difference in capital costs would be considerable and four SSBNs (with a minimum of at least one on patrol at all times) should meet India's requirements of deterrence well into the first few decades of the 21st century.

FORCE STRUCTURE PROPOSALS OF INDIAN ANALYSTS

Throughout the 1980s and the 1990s (up to mid-1998), the Indian nuclear debate concentrated mainly on striving for universal nuclear disarmament, nuclear free zones, whether India should join the Non-Proliferation Treaty (NPT) and the Comprehensive Test Ban Treaty (CTBT), the advantages and disadvantages of exercising the 'nuclear option', the finer nuances of 'opaque', 'non-weaponised', 'recessed' and 'existential' deterrence, and the need to work for a global 'no first use' commitment. Very little was either discussed or published even in academic journals and by security studies think tanks on a nuclear strategy for India and a viable force structure to give effect to that strategy. The anti-nuclear lobby, the so-called 'doves', was so strong that few editors would have dared to publish an article specifying the nuts and bolts of a nuclear arsenal for India. As such, few Indian analysts have written on the subject and there is not much to go by.

K. Subrahmanyam has written that "... if a country can project an image of having around 500 nuclear warheads, which India can build in twelve to fifteen years time if it were to set out on the programme and disperse them on its vast area, the country will have a credible deterrent." Even after the Pokhran-II tests, while explaining that minimum deterrence is not a numbers game, he wrote: "Whether it is 150, 250 or 300, the Indian deterrent will still be a minimum one compared to others except Pakistan." However, he is known to believe that "... a force of around 60 deliverable warheads could meet adequately India's need for a minimum deterrent." For delivering these 60 warheads, Subrahmanyam advocates the development of 20 Prithvi missiles and 20 Agni missiles; the remaining 20 warheads are to be delivered by air force bomber/fighter-bomber aircraft. Subrahmanyam argues that "If India were to develop a modest force of 20 Agni missiles, the India-China ratio in deterrence capability will still be higher than the present China-US ratio." He does not visualise the need for SSBNs armed with SLBMs. He does not make a major distinction between low-yield fission weapons and those in the thermonuclear class, but instead emphasises the criticality of solid-fuel missiles: "Whether the warheads are of 15 kilotons-fission or 120-150 kilotons (thermonuclear warheads), both are bound to have a deterrent effect... What is absolutely crucial for credible deterrence is the solid-fuelled missile of appropriate ranges. That is what India needs to concentrate on."

Jasjit Singh also advocates a minimalist approach and a time period of 15 to 20 years for the Indian arsenal to stabilise. He writes. "The exact size of the arsenal needed at the end-point will need to be worked out by defence planners based on a series of factors. But at this point it is difficult to visualise an arsenal with anything more than a double-digit quantum of warheads. It may be prudent to even plan on the basis of a lower end figure of say 2-3 dozen (survivable) nuclear warheads by the end of 10-15 years. It is necessary to keep in mind the fact that with the passage of time, deterrence decay factors will lead to the requirement of a smaller arsenal rather than a larger one." Though he bases his force structure on a triad for delivery, he feels that "It would indeed be infructuous to pursue the development or possession of an intercontinental capability to do so," and that intermediate range ballistic missiles (IRBMs – with a range between 500 and 5,000 km) would be adequate for India's requirements. Maharajkrishna Rasgotra is of the view that "Some 30 bombs of Hiroshima strength committed against five major targets in Pakistan, 60 deployed against eight to ten targets in China, and another 30 held in reserve for contingencies and deployment at sea, should adequately meet the needs of minimum deterrence. This number (120 warheads in all) allows for possible losses in an enemy first strike and leaves enough for a devastating counterattack."

General K. Sundarji, a former Indian Chief of the Army Staff and a perceptive military thinker, was perhaps the first analyst in India to write about the military aspects of India's nuclear deterrence. He advocated a nuclear force structure of approximately 150 warheads mounted almost entirely on a Prithvi-Agni missile force. Brigadier Vijay K. Nair has suggested a force level of 132 nuclear warheads of different types, including weapons in the megaton range. For delivery, besides bomber/ fighter-bomber aircraft, he recommends five SSBNs (each with 16 SLBMs) and 48 ballistic missiles (12 SRBMs and 36 MRBMs). He writes: "India must ensure adequate reserves to provide fail safe assurance of her strategy and yet maintain an adequate force structure after hostilities cease. An additional reserve of two weapon systems is required for each planed autonomous strike and a minimum of 20 percent of the entire force structure should be available for post-strike security imperatives." Out of a total requirement of 111 nuclear warheads for retaliatory strikes against Pakistan (17 targets) and China (eight targets), he feels that 37 warheads are required for strikes and an additional 74 as "65 percent reserve for reliability". He adds another 22 as a "post-war reserve", taking the total to 132 warheads.

Rear Admiral Raja Menon (Retd.) recommends that India's nuclear arsenal should be based primarily on SSBNs from about 2020 onwards. Till then, he feels that India's nuclear deterrent should be based only on ballistic missiles. He excludes bombers/fighter-bombers from the deterrence calculus because of the destabilising impact of the short flying time (20 minutes) between Pakistan and India's forward airfields and the inducement for the early use of nuclear weapons even in a conventional conflict. He supports the elimination of air delivered nuclear weapons from the arsenals of both India and Pakistan under mutually agreed nuclear risk reduction measures (NRRMs). He writes: "If both India and Pakistan can resist the temptation to field some kind of nuclear weapons urgently and postpone their arsenals to a less vulnerable set of missiles, the total number of nuclear weapons would be reduced; and, the inducement to a first strike would also vanish." While the logic may be impeccable, practical realities preclude the adoption of such an option. Till the Agni-I and Agni-II IRBMs become fully operational and the Indian Navy begins to acquire SSBNs, India has no option but to base its deterrence against China solely on air delivered nuclear warheads. Indian bombers/ fighter-bombers such as SU-30s, Jaguars and Mirages can effectively reach value targets in the Chinese hinterland. However, it would be wishful thinking to assume that Pakistan would accept that India might retain nuclear-capable/nuclear-armed aircraft in the eastern theatre while removing them from its western borders under mutually agreed NRRMs.

Admiral Menon has estimated that the modernised Chinese arsenal would comprise 596 warheads after 2010. Up to 2030, he suggests that an all-missile, land-based force should comprise five regiments of 12 missiles each (with survivability being ensured by concealment and rail-garrison mobility) and fifty percent of them should have up to four independently targetable warheads each. He feels that these would suffice to withstand a first strike by China with the maximum number of warheads that China may decide to launch and yet have enough missiles remaining to inflict unacceptable damage. He feels that some hardened silos may need to be provided "if the rate of degradation of the rail garrison missile force is judged to be too rapid." Against Pakistan, he proposes a force of 200 cruise missiles, 36 of them nuclear tipped, as cruise missiles are the least provocative. He visualises the "handing over of Indian deterrence from the land-based force to the sea-based force... over a ten year period... (to be) completed by 2030" and suggests a nuclear force of six SSBNs, each armed with 12 SLBMs. Each SSBN will carry at least 12 missiles and, in his view, as India has MIRV (multiple, independently targetable re-entry vehicles) ambitions, each missile could carry up to ten 250 to 400 Kt nuclear warheads. "Such a force would give India a warhead strength of 216 (6 x MIRV) in a pre-launch scenario and probably 380 warheads in a scenario with adequate strategic warning and with five boats deployed. This could be the entire Indian deterrence till the middle of the 21st century."

It is indeed intriguing that Admiral Menon does not visualise a need for air-delivered nuclear warheads for the Indian deterrent. He writes: "With opposing airfields separated by barely 20 minutes flying time, it would be a case of use-them-or-lose-them for Pakistan, a fear reinforced by the threat of capture by armoured forces, in a country handicapped by lack of strategic depth. An airdropped bomb is perhaps the farthest from a second strike weapon on the Subcontinent. It contributes nothing to deterrence stability and, if at all the weapon is discussed in a worsening crisis, it can only be in reference to a first strike." Besides their dual-use capability and the "sunk costs" already incurred in the acquisition of nuclear capable bombers/fighter-bombers, it must be remembered that unlike ballistic missiles, aircraft are recallable even after they have taken off with nuclear weapons on board.

They present a cost-effective solution to India's immediate deterrence requirements till the Agni-I and Agni-II series of ballistic missiles can be made fully operational. As for the proclivity to use-them-or-lose-them, the analogy is suggestive of flippant nuclear decision-making. There is no reason to believe that the Pakistani leadership, military or civilian, will act irrationally and set off nuclear exchanges merely because they would be worried about their forward airfields being put temporarily out of commission by the Indian Air Force. India will need air-delivered nuclear warheads in its arsenal not only against Pakistan, but also against China for a long time to come as they offer a here-and-now solution and are akin to a bird in hand.

To base the entire Indian nuclear force only on SSBNs would not be appropriate for the following reasons:

- Flexibility of targeting options for targeting individual targets with a variety of weapons platforms to achieve better strike assurance would not be available.
- The problems of communicating with submerged submarines are well known.
- It is becoming increasingly easier to locate and track submarines and by 2020-30 advanced navies such as the US Navy may be able to map and track the position of every submarine in any of the oceans.
- The Indian hinterland provides adequate depth and area to disperse widely India's ballistic missiles and the rail and road networks provide ample opportunity to keep moving the missiles at random, though with

attendant problems of command and control and missile launch inaccuracies.

- The force structure would lack inter-Services balance, which in itself is not desirable.

Bharat Karnad follows what has been dubbed a 'maximalist' approach to nuclear deterrence and strongly advocates the need for megaton-class thermonuclear weapons in the Indian arsenal. He assumes that the primary and secondary target lists could contain about 60 locations that need to be hit. In order to ensure that each of these targets can be destroyed with an acceptable assurance level so that deterrence is credible, he recommends the targeting of each with four nuclear weapons, each of which has a two mile (approximately three km) CEP (circular error probable—a measure of the accuracy of delivery; it denotes the distance from the point of impact to the centre of the target as the radius of the circle within which, on average, 50 percent of the missiles aimed at the target will fall). Bharat Karnad suggests that India's nuclear arsenal be gradually built up over a period of three decades to a total of 328 nuclear warheads.

Leaving out the 50 reserve warheads, Bharat Karnad has suggested that, out of the remaining 278 warheads, 253 should be thermonuclear. Hence, in his view, all the warheads in the Indian arsenal, with the exception of 25 ADMs, should be thermonuclear. He writes: "If a counter-cities or counter-value nuclear bombardment strategy is the only one that makes sense, then thermonuclear bombs, with megaton yields, are the most convincing instruments of this strategy." It is difficult to dispute the logic of this statement. However, India's 45 Kt, two-stage thermonuclear explosion during the tests of May 1998 has the potential to be upgraded to a practical capability of about 200 Kt only. For weapons in the megaton class to be developed, further refinement of the design and additional physical testing would be necessary. As India has unilaterally renounced further nuclear tests, it is doubtful if such a capability can be created. Also, as missile accuracies continue to improve and CEPs drop to hundreds of metres and lesser, the trend among the P-5 is to limit warhead yields to between 200 to 300 Kt. Yields in this range should be adequate for India's purposes also for a counter-value strategy provided India can develop ballistic missiles with a CEP of less than 500 metres. As for ADMs, their use in Tibet, as suggested by Bharat Karnad to stop a major Chinese offensive, would prove to be counter-productive as the waters of almost all the rivers in Tibet flow into India and it would hardly be prudent to pollute those waters with long-lasting nuclear radiation by creating landslides on the snow covered mountainsides and endanger life in the northeastern states. Besides, it would be a major environmental disaster. R.R. Subramanian, a senior analyst at the Institute for Defence Studies and Analyses (IDSA), New Delhi, and a physicist by training, is of the opinion that India needs at least 425 warheads if the combined efficiency (accuracy, reliability, in-flight interception) of the delivery systems is taken to be 0.3. He feels that with an efficiency of 0.3, approximately 125 to 130 warheads could be counted upon to destroy their intended targets. Of these, he is of the view that 25 to 30 are needed to target Pakistan and about 100 are required against China. To assume that India's nuclear force would deliver an overall efficiency of only 0.3 would appear to be overly pessimistic. However, in the absence of accurate factual information about individual components of the nuclear force, primarily the targeting and delivery systems, it is possible to neither prove nor disprove this contention.

Lieutenant General Pran Pahwa (Retd.) recommends that India's deterrence be based on 182 warheads. He bases his calculations on the assumption that China is likely to employ two warheads each to destroy every Indian warhead and that 20 percent Indian warheads would survive a Chinese first strike which would be essentially a counter force one. He feels that if India had 182 warheads, China would need to fire 364 warheads and, given a Chinese arsenal of 400 warheads, it would be left with 36 to India's surviving 36 warheads. Since the numbers remaining would be matched, China would be deterred from launching a first strike. This argument gives the

Chinese an excessive 80 percent success rate and does not take into account the possibility that a Chinese first strike is likely to combine counter value with counter force targets.

It emerges that Indian analysts have widely varying views on the number of nuclear warheads that India needs for its minimum deterrent. The figures vary from the low double digits ("two to three dozen") at the lower end to just over 400 at the upper end. Suggestions for weapons yield range from 15 to 20 Kt fission weapons to thermonuclear weapons in the megaton range. The recommended delivery vehicles embrace the entire range of the triad including ICBMs and cruise missiles. The sole purpose of India's nuclear weapons is to deter the use and the threat of use of nuclear weapons. Minimum deterrence is not a numbers game. Its ends are served if the adversary is deterred from crossing the nuclear threshold and from threatening to do so. As Kenneth Waltz famously said, "More is not better if less is enough." What matters is to find a rational way to determine how much is enough.

STRUCTURE OF THE IAF

The President of India is the Supreme Commander of all Indian armed forces and by virtue of that fact is the notional Commander of the Air force. India's Ministry of Defence under the Defence Minister oversees the Air Force, by way of direct civilian leadership. The Prime Minister and the National Security Council provide indirect leadership by shaping government security policy. A Chief of the Air Staff in the rank of Air Chief Marshal commands Air Head Quarters and provides military leadership. He is assisted by six officers: a Vice Chief of the Air Staff, a Deputy Chief of the Air Staff, the Air Officer in Charge of Administration, the Air Officer in Charge of Personnel, the Air Officer in Charge of Maintenance, and the Inspector General of Flight Safety. In January 2002, the government conferred the rank of Marshal of the Air Force on Arjan Singh making him the first and only *Five Star* rank officer with the Indian Air Force and ceremonial chief of the air force.

Bases

The IAF operates over 60 air bases, with more being built or planned. They are grouped under one of the five Regional Air Commands. Western Air Command is the largest Air Command. It operates 16 Air bases from Punjab to Uttar Pradesh. Eastern Air Command operates 15 Air bases in Eastern and North-eastern India. Central Air Command operates 7 Air Bases in Madhya Pradesh and surrounding states of central India. Southern Air Command, a strategically important Air command, in line with India's latest doctrine of protecting the vital shipping routes. It operates 9 Air bases in Southern India and 2 in the Andaman and Nicobar Islands. South Western Air Command is the front line of defence against Pakistan, this important Command operates 12 air bases in Gujarat, Maharashtra and Rajasthan.

Commands and Structure

The Indian Air Force is divided into five operational and two functional commands.

Operational Commands	Functional Commands
• Central Air Command (CAC), headquartered at Allahabad, Uttar Pradesh • Eastern Air Command (EAC), headquartered at Shillong, Meghalaya • Southern Air Command (SAC), headquartered at Thiruvananthapuram, Kerala • South Western Air Command (SWAC), headquartered at Gandhinagar, Gujarat • Western Air Command (WAC), headquartered at Subroto Park, New Delhi	• Training Command (TC), headquartered at Bangalore, Karnataka • Maintenance Command (MC), headquartered at Nagpur, Maharashtra

Each Command is headed by an Air Officer Commanding-in-Chief in the rank of Air Marshal. The purpose of an operational command is to conduct military operations using aircraft within its area of responsibility whereas the responsibility of functional commands is to maintain combat readiness.

Aside from the Training Command at Bangalore, the center for primary flight training is located at the Air Force Academy in Hyderabad, Andhra Pradesh, followed by operational training at various other schools. Advanced officer training for command positions is also conducted at the Defence Services Staff College; specialized advanced flight training schools are located at Bidar, Karnataka, and Hakimpet, Andhra Pradesh (also the location for helicopter training). Technical schools are found at a number of other locations.

Wings

Wing is a formation intermediate between Command and Squadron. A Wing generally consists of two or three IAF Squadrons and Helicopter Units and along with the Forward Base Support Units (FBSU). FBSUs do not have or host any Squadrons or Helicopter units but act as transit airbases for routine operations. In times of war, they can become full fledged air bases playing host to various Squadrons. In all, about 47 Wings and 19 FBSUs make up the IAF.

Squadrons

Squadrons are the field units and formations attached to static locations.

In other words, a Flying Squadron is a sub-unit of an air force station which carries out the primary task of the IAF. All fighter squadrons are headed by the Commanding Officer with the rank of Wing Commander. Some Transport squadrons and Helicopter Units are headed by the Commanding Officer with the rank of Group Captain.

Within this formation structure, IAF has several service branches for day to day operations. They are:

Flying Branch	Technical Branch	Ground Branch
• Flying	• Engineering • Logistics	• Administration • Accounts • Education • Medical & Dental • Meteorological

The rank structure of IAF is based on the rank structure of the Royal Air Force.

The Air Force has a strength of 170,000 personnel. The highest rank attainable in the IAF is Marshal of the Indian Air Force conferred by the President of India after exceptional service during wartime. MIAF Arjan Singh is the only officer to have achieved this rank. The head of the Indian Air Force is the Chief of the Air Staff. The Air Chief Marshal is Fali Homi Major. The members of the IAF are commissioned or enlisted in one of the service branches.

Officer

Anyone holding the citizenship of India can apply to be a an officer in the Air Force as long as they satisfy the eligibility eligibility criteria. There are four entry points to become an officer. Male applicants, who are between the ages of 16½ and 19 and have passed high school graduation, can apply at the *Intermediate* level. Men and women applicants, who have graduated from college (3 year course) and are between the ages of 18 and 28 years, can apply at the *Graduate* level. Graduates of engineering colleges can apply at the *Engineer* level if they are between the ages of 18 and 28 years. The age limit for the flying and ground duty branch is 23 years of age and for technical branch is 28 years of age.

After completing master's degree, men and women between the ages of 18 and 28 years can apply at the *Post Graduate* level. Post graduate applicants do not qualify for the flying branch. For technical branch the age limit is 28 years and for the ground duty branch is 25. At the time of application all applicant must be single. From the applicants the IAF selects candidates for officer training. After complition of training, the applicant becomes an officer.

Airmen

The duty of an airman in the Indian Air Force is to make sure that all the air and ground operations run smoothly. From operating Air Defence systems to fitting missiles, they are involved in all activities of an air base and give support to various technical and non technical jobs.

The recruitment of personnel below officer rank as an Airman in the IAF is conducted through All India Selection Tests and Recruitment Rallies. All India Selection Tests are conducted at the Airmen Selection Centres (ASCs) located all over India. There are 14 Airmen Selection Centres, spread all over India. These centres are under the direct functional control of Central Airmen Selection Board (CASB) with administrative control and support by respective commands. The role of CASB is to carry out selection and enrolment of airmen from the Airmen Selection Centres for their respective commands.

Candidates initially take a written test at the time of application. Candidates passing the written test undergo physical fitness test, an interview, conducted in English, and medical examination.

Candidates for training are selected from individuals passing the battery of tests based on their performance. Upon completion of training, an induvidual becomes an Airman.

Some MWOs and WOs are granted honorary commission in the last year of their service as an honorary Flying Officer or Flight Lieutenant before retiring from the service.

NON COMBATANTS ENROLLED AND CIVILIANS

Non Combatants Enrolled (NCs(E)) were established in British India as personal assistants to the officer class, and are equivalent to the *orderly* or *sahayak* of the Indian Army.

Almost all the commands have some percentage of civilian strength which are Central Govt. Employees. These are regular ranks which are prevalent in ministries. They are usually not posted outside their stations and are helpful in administration and usual office and technical work. More than 250 different designations exists.

IAF Aircraft

The Indian Air Force has a strength of over 1,500 aircraft. Most of the IAF's aircraft are of Soviet/Russian origin. The Air Force also operates some aircraft from Britain and France. Hindustan Aeronautics Limited under licence produce some of the Russian and British aircraft in India. The exact number of aircraft in service with the Indian Air Force cannot be determined with precision from open sources. Apparently reliable sources provide notably divergent estimates for a variety of high-visibility aircraft.

Air superiority and multi-role combat aircraft:

- IAF Su-30 MKI
- IAF Jaguar
- Il-78 landing at Lajes, Portugal

These aircraft are primarily for air defence and superiority purposes. However, most of them have significant strike, offensive support capabilities. The IAF possesses several multi-role fighter jets that perform these functions.

The Sukhoi Su-30MKI is the IAF's prime air superiority fighter. The Su-30K variant was first acquired in 1996. In 1996, the IAF signed a US$1.6 billion contract with Russia for the supply of 50 Su-30MKIs and the technology transfer and license to manufacture 140 Su-30MKIs by Hindustan Aeronautics Limited.

The twin seater, multi-role fighter has a maximum speed of 2500 km/h (Mach 2.35) and has a service ceiling of 20,000 meters. The aircraft, with one mid-air refuelling, can travel as far as 8000 km, making it an effective platform to deliver strategic weapons. In 2007, US$700 million were spent to upgrade IAF's remaining 10 Su-30Ks & 8 SU -30MKs to MKI Std variant and signed a contract for the supply of 40 additional

MKIs with Russia. MiG-29s are dedicated air superiority fighters of the IAF. The MiG-29 (NATO: *Fulcrum*) has a top speed of 2,445 km/h (Mach 2.3) and is armed with a 30 mm cannon along with R-60 & R-27 R missiles. The IAF was began deploying MiG-29 in 1984 and was the second air force to do so. Since their induction, the IAF's MiG-29s have undergone a series of upgrades including more efficient and powerful radar (Zhuk-ME), weapons system and upgraded engine.

Mirage 2000s, capable of flying at 2,500 km/h (Mach 2.35), are the IAF's premier multirole fighter jet. These aircraft can carry a wide range of weaponry including two 30 mm integral cannons, two *Matra Super 530D* medium-range missiles, two *R550 Magic* close combat missiles and various ground attack munitions.

Since 1963, over 450 MiG-21 combat aircraft have been serving the IAF.

Most of these MiGs have been upgraded since induction. In 1996, India signed a US$300 million deal with Russia to upgrade 125 MiG-21 *Bis* and a multi-million dollar deal was awarded to Israel's Elta for upgrading the avionics of the MiGs. Due to their frequent crashes, the MiG-21s have been dubbed *flying coffins* by the media. As of 2007, about 250 MiG-21s remain in service with the Indian Air Force and are planned to be replaced by the indigenously-built HAL Tejas starting 2010.

ORGANISATIONAL AND STRUCTURAL CHANGES

The IAF is likely to resolve its current manning issues through the induction of women in all branches and jobs, while at the same time evolving a gender neutral short-service cadre that is assisted to find employment in other sections of the economy post tenure. This would form a ready reserve force for recall during periods of hostility with a permanent commission cadre at its core. There is also likely to be greater emphasis on multi-skilling of personnel from the initial training period itself in order to improve upon productivity and efficiency of

IAF manpower. The IAF should also be in the process of completing a re-organisation of its organisational structure and cadre to promote flexibility and efficiency while minimising costs.

The transformation of the IAF will, however, be dependent upon and be influenced by a few major factors:

- The growth of the Indian economy: only robust growth of the economy can ensure adequate funding for the various projects already sanctioned or awaiting final clearance.
- Fructification of a few long period indigenous technology development initiatives, especially in sensors and their integration.
- The geo-political scenario: an increased perceived threat of military confrontation with India's neighbours would spur on the programmes discussed above, while a benign security situation would lead to less urgency to build up capabilities rapidly. The latter situation may further result in other military or non-military programmes taking higher priority for allotment of resources, possibly leading to inadequate allotment of funds and consequent slippages in schedules for IAF's modernisation.
- Any serious natural disaster could potentially disrupt the transformation process both directly (through the impact of such a disaster on the laboratories, etc., involved in the work) and indirectly (through the need to re-prioritise the entire national effort and resources towards disaster alleviation efforts).
- A major unforeseen technology breakthrough in India or abroad that could make the entire transformation effort redundant.

The IAF's transformation process is likely to progress in the manner indicated above. It is important to note that true technology co-operation with foreign vendors who have access to advanced technology is likely to be the greatest challenge and opportunity for foreign as well as Indian companies operating in the aerospace field.

INDIAN AIR FORCE WILL BE SPENDING US$70 BILLION ON PROCUREMENT AND UPGRADES IN THE NEXT DECADE

THE threat scenario is periodically reviewed by the Indian Air Force and steps taken to meet any eventuality. This includes induction of new aircraft and air defence assets as well as upgrade of the operational capability of existing assets.

The IAF has prepared a comprehensive Long Term Perspective Pan (LTPP) till the year 2027 for modernization of its fleet to meet the security challenges. The IAF is in the process of inducting various types of fighter aircraft like Medium, Multi Role Combat Aircraft (MMRCA), Light Combat Aircraft (LCA), SU-30 MK1 and Fifth Generation Fighter Aircraft (FGFA). The Government has allocated adequate funds for the purpose.

The Indian Air Force (IAF) has ambitious plans to transform itself into one of the most modern air forces in the world by acquiring capabilities across the entire spectrum of war fighting over the next decade. Indian Air force will be spending US$70 billion on procurement and upgrades in the next decade.

The IAF envisages transforming itself into a potent and networked aerospace power through three aspects.

For decades the IAF had largely been tethered to one non-western source. Much of the inventory acquired through this route has now been overtaken by obsolescence. As a result, in recent years, there has been an alarming erosion in combat power and other capabilities. Even after prolonged and reportedly vigorous effort, the indigenous Research & Development Organisations and the Aerospace Industry have not been able to provide a respectable degree of self reliance to the IAF. The near total dependence on foreign sources for cutting edge technology and frontline equipment is potentially perhaps the most debilitating factor that often threatens to seriously undermine the capability of the IAF.

First and foremost priority for IAF has been to induct and integrate new technology weapon platforms and upgrade the existing inventory. IAF has a long list of acquisitions which includes 126 MMRCA; 214 fifth generation fighter aircraft which will be coming around 2017; additional 42 SU30's for which IAF has already issued RFP to HAL; 75 trainers for which process is well on its way; two more AWACS of IL-76 base; ten C-17s; 80 + 59 medium-lift helicopters; 22 attack helicopters; 12 VVIP helicopters.

There are upgrades also going on for weapon systems: 63 MiG-29's, that upgrade is well on its way in Russia. Mirage 2000 upgrade has gone to the CCS and Jaguar re-engineering, that is another major project for which a new RFP has been issued already.

In the Missiles segment, IAF has 18 firing units of MRSAM (Medium Range Surface to Air Missiles), four Spyders, 49 SR-SAM that is short range, 8 Aakash missiles. There are different stages of missiles coming — a multi-layered defence which is what is desirable in air defence. Plus it has the AWACS and from the AWACS to the IACCS.

In radars, IAF has got Rohinis, aerostats, medium-power radars, low-level tactical radars, low-level light weight radars, AFNET which is already active, besides the MAFI (Modernisation of Airport Infrastructure) which is going on. The first airfield to convert on to MAFI would be Bhatinda. IAF has the IACCS which is active, so all-round development of the Indian Air Force is in the offing.

IAF radars have complete coverage at medium and high levels. It has some gap at the low levels because the capability of ground base radars is limited because of the earth's curvature. To fill these gaps, IAF has many other schemes in place. Firstly low-level radars, the medium-power radars, the LLTRS, the LLWRs, they fill in the low-level gap. It has got the AWACS and the aerostats which actually raises the platform of the radar so it increases the range of the radar. Most of them are on track and 2012 onward, they will start ramping up. The first medium-powered radar at Naliya - was inaugurated earlier this year.

The second important aspect is the induction and training of manpower to handle the new inventory. Though the manpower intake has improved a little bit, but it is still not up to the desired standards. IAF is taking various measures such as inducting candidates before their 12th standard and degree and giving them a degree in the Air Force. IAF is approaching various regions to find new talent. Also, the emphasis is been made to retain them. It is improving the training patterns.

Not surprisingly, in the last three financial years the IAF has been allocated more money for capital acquisition than the other two services and is likely to get more funds than the Army and the Navy in the next few years.

Despite the limitations, the IAF has managed to attain and project an image of a potent force capable to preserving the sovereignty of the Indian skies and in more recent times, to project power albeit limited in quantum and reach. And even in the future there appears to be no option but to procure advanced technology and hardware from abroad. There is however an attempt to indigenize products through co-development, co-production and the difficult, but innovative, concept of "Offsets". This route is the most expedient under the circumstances to accord military hardware a semblance of Indian character.

Life of a modern weapon system is in the region of thirty years which is normally extendable by another 10 to 15 years after a mid-life upgrade. New equipment procured for the IAF over the next decade will remain operational up to 2050 at the very least, possibly up to 2060. As the nature of warfare itself is undergoing transformation, it is necessary to make a comprehensive reassessment of the contours of the operational scenario that the IAF will have to contend with and reconfigure its inventory accordingly. To do this at this point in time, the IAF needs to take note of India's regional power status in the emerging world order and assess its possible role and responsibility in the new geopolitical and geostrategic environment.

Tejas—India's Big Defence Leap

The Indian Defence industry has posted a significant milestone on January 10, when the Indian Air Force formally granted initial operational clearance to the country's first indigenously manufactured light combat aircraft, marking the culmination of nearly two decades of work by Indian defence scientists and technicians. Named the Tejas, the aircraft will initially form one squadron (20 aircraft) in the IAF.

The Tejas was designed by the Aeronautical Development Agency (ADA) under the Defence Ministry-controlled Defence Research and Development Organisation. The project was conceived and launched in 1983, with an expected budget of Rs560 crore (about $5.6 billion), but test flights weren't launched until 2001.

The project, which has its fair share of critics in India—and even within the Indian Air Force—has seen numerous ups and downs during the course of its long journey to service. But 10 years after the initial test flights, the fourth-generation plus aircraft has finally arrived. Admittedly, there are still some doubts over the fact that the LCA's engine, radar, some navigation technologies and some of its displays are imported. But officials at the ADA asserted ahead of the launch that the design, development, testing, certification and mastery of the system engineering are completely Indian.

There are just six to eight countries in the world that can design, develop, test and certify a fighter aircraft—India is now one among them. ADA already has a road map in place for future development of the Tejas. Over the next five years, the Tejas will be completely indigenous and the higher variant will be ready by 2014. Even without any further refinement, the current batch of Tejas aircraft is comparable with Sweden's Gripen, the Chinese-Pakistan J-17 Thunder and the South Korean T-50 jets. If all goes well, over the next decade, both the manufacturers and the Indian Air Force are planning to increase that number to 200 aircraft, if not more. But even without these kinds of numbers, India's Defence Ministry will be celebrating the induction of the LCA Tejas as a major turning point in its effort to indigenise the country's defence production sector.

Procurement of Combat Aircraft

Su-30 MKI aircraft and Tejas Light Combat Aircraft are the major modern combat aircraft that have been contracted for induction into the Indian Air Force (IAF). The total cost of procurement of the Su-30 MKI is over Rs55,717 crore while the cost of procurement of the Teja Light Combat Aircraft is about Rs8691 crore.

Capacity for design and manufacture of modern combat aircraft involves development of very high and sophisticated technology skills which is a gradual process.

Technology denial regimes have thwarted this effort in the past. The Defence Procurement Procedure provides for procurement of aircraft and their subsequent manufacture in India. Hence, major aircraft procurement programme entail a mix of outright purchase from abroad and subsequent manufacture in India with increasing levels of indigenization. Hindustan Aeronautics Limited (HAL) is already manufacturing the Su-30 MKI aircraft as well as the Tejas Light Combat Aircraft for the IAF. Further, HAL would also eventually be manufacturing the Medium Multi-Role Combat Aircraft (MMRCA) and Fifth Generation Fighter Aircraft (FGFA) planned for induction into the IAF.

Trainer Fleet of IAF

IAF's fleet of HPT-32 trainer aircraft has been grounded since August, 2009 after a crash of an aircraft on 28th July, 2009 due to engine failure. In order to improve the reliability of the engine, Hindustan Aeronautics Limited (HAL) is implementing certain modifications on the engine and air frame including integrating a system called Aircraft Parachute Recovery System.

The Request for Proposal (RFP) for procurement of Basic Trainer Aircraft (BTA) for the Indian Air Force was issued on

16th December 2009. In response techno-commercial proposals were received from Korean Aircraft Industries, South Korea; GROB Aircraft, Germany; EADS PZL, Poland; Hawker Beechcraft, United States of America; Alenia Aerammachi, Italy; Aerostar of Romania; and Pilatus, Switzerland. The proposal for procurement of the trainer aircraft is being progressed in accordance with the Defence Procurement Procedure-2008.

No issues which are considered critical to flight safety had emerged during the technical evaluation of the aircraft.

The estimated cost of the procurement is Rs2900 crore. The proposal is expected to be finalized during the current financial year.

Purchase of 10 C-17 Globemaster III Aircraft

The government has accorded approval to buy ten C-17 Globemaster-III aircraft for the Indian Air Force. The Letter of Offer and Acceptance (LOA) for procurement of these aircraft along with associated equipment was signed on 14th June 2011.

The cost of the procurement is US$4.116 billon. The delivery of these aircraft will commence from June, 2013 and is expected to be completed by June, 2015.

Purchase of AJTs

In March 2004, government had signed a contract with BAE Systems and Rolls Royce Turbomeca UK for procurement of 24 Hawk Advanced Jet Trainers (AJT) and with Hindustan Aeronautics Limited (HAL), Bengaluru for the licence manufacture of another 42 AJTs under Transfer of Technology from BAE Systems for the Indian Air Force (IAF). All the 24 direct supply aircraft have been delivered by BAE systems while 28 out of 42 aircraft contracted with HAL had been delivered till July, 2011.

In July 2010, government signed another contract with HAL for procurement of additional 57 Hawk AJTs from HAL. Of these, 40 are for the IAF and 17 are for the Indian Navy.

The delivery of these aircraft will commence from 2013 and is expected to be completed by 2016.

Summery

A major responsibility of the IAF in the future would be in the area of strategic airlift. Internal security compulsions will place growing demand for the movement of quick reaction as also regular security forces within the country on short notice.

Given its emerging regional power status and the newly forged strategic partnership with the US if not abrogated by the incoming administration, India may be called upon to project power in the region which may involve airlift of large military forces to areas of interest of either of the partners in the region outside our borders and to provide sustained logistic support. Strategic airlift capability of the IAF would therefore need to be built up practically from scratch as the existing fleet is fast approaching the end of its total technical life.

At the tactical level, the IAF should be equipped with a fleet of medium tactical transport aircraft and helicopters capable of speedy response with special forces over shorter ranges.

The IAF has taken some baby steps towards acquiring the capability of projecting combat power in the region. At this point in time, the capability is limited to a token force and cannot be described as significant. However, while steps are in hand to augment the existing fleet of long range combat aircraft as also to acquire a new fleet, the capability of power projection would in the ultimate analysis be limited by the size of the fleet of in-flight refuelling aircraft. This fleet would have to be suitably enlarged for any meaningful power projection that is capable of making an impact.

The IAF needs to enhance some of the force multipliers already on the inventory as also to develop a range of new capabilities both in the strategic and tactical regimes. At the strategic level, the IAF must be able to provide the nation with credible nuclear deterrence against Pakistan and China. Also, it should be capable of power projection in its perceived area of national security interests and those of our ally in the region beyond the national borders with combat aircraft, in-flight refuelling and strategic airlift capability. These forces should be geared to provide swift response to a crisis situation and be able to provide logistic support to sustain forces for significant length of time. For strategic strike deep into enemy territory, the IAF needs to have a combination of missile based and airborne platforms, the latter with powerful electronic warfare equipment to suppress and defeat enemy air defence systems. Tactical roles may be transferred to UCAVs and helicopters.

To provide effective air defence of the homeland, the IAF needs to acquire a fleet of AWACS and AEW aircraft over and above the few already on order to enhance surveillance capability at low level. New generation area and point defence missile systems need to be inducted to replace the ageing and obsolete systems currently deployed. For strategic and tactical intelligence, the IAF must have its own satellite systems and a fleet of UAVs with a range of advanced sensors to provide all weather day and night capability. The fleet of UAVs should be adequately supported by appropriate ground infrastructure for automated and speedy processing of intelligence information, and fleet of tactical transport aircraft and helicopters for quick response with special forces.

5

National Security and Indian Air Force Evolution

NATIONAL SECURITY LESSONS

The Kargil War of 1999 was a rich teaching experience for India in the national security arena in many respects. For one thing, it represented the country's first exposure to the "CNN factor," in that televised images of the fighting showcased in Indian living rooms each evening helped the government and armed forces to mobilize domestic support for Operation Vijay while, at the same time, demoralizing the literate Pakistani rank and file. Making the most of that tool, the Vajpayee government interacted skilfully with the nation's media in building domestic and international appreciation of the fact that India had been attacked without provocation by Pakistan and accordingly was in the right in its chosen response.

The Vajpayee government interacted skilfully with the nation's media in building domestic and international appreciation of the fact that India had been attacked without provocation by Pakistan and accordingly was in the right in its chosen response.

As the counteroffensive unfolded, Indian media coverage of combat events was detailed and extensive, with numerous television channels showing a constant flow of scenes from the war zone in a manner reminiscent of CNN's coverage of the

1991 Persian Gulf War. Some analysts in New Delhi suggested afterward that this media coverage helped to serve as a force multiplier for Indian combat operations, since it was more credible by far than Pakistan's version of ongoing events. It definitely served as a morale booster for the Indian populace. Shortly after the campaign ended, the Indian government convened a Kargil Review Committee, chaired by the eminent international security scholar and strategist K. Subrahmanyam, which was charged with determining how Pakistan's forces had succeeded in crossing into Indian-controlled territory and establishing a foothold there without having been detected in due time by military intelligence. It concluded on the important media-coverage count that the showdown against the Pakistani intruders was "India's first television war" and, as such, was an experience that "knit the country together as never before."

A major shortcoming highlighted by the war experience was a significant deficiency with respect to the provision of timely indications and warning of impending crises.

As for the country's vigilance over its perennially volatile border with Pakistan, a major shortcoming highlighted by the war experience was a significant deficiency with respect to the provision of timely indications and warning of impending crises. Although the Indian Army had a brigade of troops fielded in the Kargil sector to monitor activities there and the IAF possessed Canberras, Jaguars, and MiG-25Rs capable of overseeing the area by means of medium-and high-altitude aerial photography, local civilians noticed the intruders before the Indian Air Force did. In an early comment on the air contribution to the campaign, a serving IAF air commodore frankly admitted that Pakistan's intrusion into the high reaches of the Kargil sector made for "a surprise bordering on shock." A clear lesson emanating from this experience, he noted, was the "urgent requirement to improve our surveillance and reconnaissance capability. We cannot afford to be surprised again." Similarly, the Indian Army chief at the time, General Malik, later recalled that India's surprise at the incursion "reflected a major deficiency in [the country's] system of collecting, reporting, and assessing intelligence." Clearly, the IAF needed a better nationwide, real-time intelligence, surveillance, and reconnaissance capability.

As for the good-news part of the story, this intelligence, surveillance, and reconnaissance deficiency has since been substantially improved upon by India's placement of indigenous reconnaissance satellites on orbit. In October 2001, the Indian government launched its first Technology Experiment Satellite, which substantially improved the quality of its overhead intelligence product as a result of the satellite's one-meter resolution. India's spaceborne synthetic aperture radar capability provides all-weather, around-the-clock coverage, and the Indian Army also now maintains a constant vigil in the area with its inventory of Israeli-made Searcher and Heron unmanned aerial vehicles. In addition, today there are five times the number of troops permanently garrisoned in the Kargil sector than at the time of the Pakistani incursion in 1999, consisting of four brigades totaling nearly 20,000 troops.

Today there are five times the number of troops permanently garrisoned in the Kargil sector than at the time of the Pakistani incursion in 1999.

A major interservice shortcoming highlighted by the first two weeks that followed the initial detection of the incursion was the near-total lack of transparency and open communication between the Indian Army and the IAF with respect to the gathering crisis. Without question, the onset of the Kargil confrontation revealed a lack of effective air-ground integration in India's joint arena at the most senior leadership level. On this point, one IAF airman later lamented the "complete loss of synergy between air and land forces" at the start of the operation that had been occasioned by "the late induction into the fray of airpower and, hence, the denial of the optimum employment of its attributes of offensive action," notwithstanding the fact that "we were fighting a clearly defined enemy within our own territory." Another IAF airman, noting how the army at the outset had "looked to fight a classical high-altitude battle on its own," asked rhetorically whether it was, at least during the campaign's first two weeks, a case of "my war, can you help" rather than "our war, let's do it together."

This inclination at the outset to go it alone, it might be noted, was not just an idiosyncratic Indian Army trait. The since-retired director of operations of the PAF during the Kargil crisis, Air Commodore Kaiser Tufail, similarly noted the PAF leadership's "surprise" at having been told of what the Pakistan Army leaders had authorized, adding that "we all were ... piqued at being left out of the army's planning [and] were given to believe that this was a 'limited tactical action' in which the PAF would not be required." Tufail also noted that from the very start of the Kargil confrontation, the PAF "was trapped by a circumstantial absurdity—it was faced with the ludicrous predicament of having to provide air support to infiltrators already disowned by the Pakistani Army leadership." He further suggested that in the end, the PAF's "restraint in warding off a major conflagration" was "its paramount contribution to the Kargil conflict."

In their clear inclination at first to go it alone in countering Pakistan's incursion into Indian-controlled Kashmir, the Indian Army's leaders failed to honour the reasonable proposition advanced four years earlier in the IAF's first published air doctrine that "wars are rarely won ... by a single component of military force." The IAF's doctrine manual issued in 1995 had noted "the immense advantages air forces can provide *before* a surface battle begins and the major contribution air forces can make in exploiting opportunities as a result of surface action." As for the opportunity costs incurred by the Indian Army as a result of that initial failure, one was an unfortunate persistence of misunderstandings regarding the IAF's capabilities and limitations that could easily have been cleared up in ample time beforehand by more open and timely cross-service communication.

For example, of the army's insistence at the outset that the IAF employ solely attack helicopters in the close air support role, an IAF airman later wrote that *a sounder understanding of airpower capabilities [on the army leadership's part] would have dictated that the most vulnerable platforms be inducted last. Had the Indian Army taken the IAF into confidence from Day One and developed a joint plan to evict the intruders instead of trying to use it as an afterthought, armed helicopters could have joined the fight after sufficient degradation had been inflicted by fixed-wing aircraft and artillery.*

As for the complaints heard later from some army commentators that the IAF's pilots would not descend to lower altitudes from which their free-fall munitions could be delivered with greater accuracy, another IAF airman observed that "one of the valuable lessons that emerged from the Kargil operations was the need for closer joint army–air force planning and consultations from the very beginning," whereby the targeting advice of Indian airmen "could, at the very outset, be incorporated into the army's plan for ground operations."

This airman also explained why scarce air assets should not be "frittered away on insignificant targets like machine-gun posts and trenches, but [rather should be used] on large targets of consequence," such as the enemy supply camp at Muntho Dhalo and the enemy battalion headquarters atop Tiger Hill, against which it could be more effective in meeting the army's support needs at the operational and strategic levels.

After the Kargil Review Committee's report was released, the Indian Army censured the responsible division commander and relieved the brigade commander—the latter of whom since won a lawsuit in which he successfully argued that his dismissal had been without valid cause. No effort was undertaken beyond that, however, to allocate responsibility for the breakdown in jointness at the service leadership level and for the army's slowness to enlist the IAF's full involvement once an imminent clash was at hand.

A decade later, the former AOC for Jammu and Kashmir who had overseen IAF operations at the tactical level during the campaign wrote that one of the most important lessons spotlighted by the experience was the crucial need for "integration of higher military management and mission-based capability creation.

That has not yet happened." He added that the IAF and Indian Army today are definitely creating communication networks with cross-service interfaces to plug into one another's network but noted further that "whether these will work in a network-centric environment remains unknown." He also observed that the Kargil Review Committee's recommendations had still not yet been fully implemented "due to [persistent] differences between the army, navy and air force and the unwillingness of the political class to enact the binding legislation."

On the plus side, once the army got past its initial disagreements with the IAF over precisely what kind of air support it needed and just how that support might best be provided, an atmosphere of harmony largely prevailed between the two services when it came time to move ahead with the implementation of Operation Vijay.

In this respect, General Malik later recalled that once the scale and potential consequences of the intrusion had become fully understood and assimilated by the service chiefs, he went out of his way to persuade the Cabinet Committee on Security that India's substantial air and naval supremacy should be brought to bear not only in the immediate Kargil sector but also along India's entire western border.

He further recalled: "The Indian Air Force responded very quickly after the CCS approved the employment of airpower on India's side of the LoC.... After May 23, there were no professional differences whatsoever that could affect our teamwork or planning."

SECURITY ENVIRONMENT IN THE TWENTIES

To summarise, in the geopolitical, geostrategic and security environment that is likely to prevail in the 2020s, the dictates of national security would place the following demands on armed forces of the nation:-

- To be prepared for a prolonged and widespread multi front border war with China with only a remote possibility of employment of nuclear weapons.

- To be prepared for a short and intense conflict with Pakistan with the real possibility of the first use of nuclear weapons by the adversary.
- To be prepared for simultaneous conflict with both the potential adversaries acting in collusion.
- To sustain the capability to fight a prolonged low intensity conflict in Kashmir and other sensitive regions of the country in the pursuit of internal security.
- To develop and maintain the capability for rapid strategic intervention and power projection in the region extending from the Straits of Malacca to Central Asia and the Gulf to safeguard and promote national interests.
- To play a dominant role in the management of disasters and natural calamity in the region of interest.

While considerable progress has been made on the political, economic and diplomatic fronts, the overall security situation continues to remain fraught with uncertainties. India's growing political and economic stature in the world and commitments of national interests necessitates a move away from the traditional defensive mindset. India must acquire the capability for power projection in the area of interest which will require a qualitative change in the operational philosophy of the armed forces especially of the IAF. Within the broad structural framework that has evolved over the last five decades, there is a need to modify the composition and character of the various constituents of the IAF to provide extended reach and staying power. The focus must shift from the 'Tactical' to the 'Strategic' as also on 'Force Multipliers'. The IAF must also develop interoperability with other friendly powers in the region and the world for furtherance of mutual interests.

The armed forces of India have matured through the five conflicts with our neighbours in the last five decades. The IAF in particular has benefited from the lessons learnt in these conflicts and has been quick to absorb the technological advances witnessed elsewhere in the world. Undoubtedly, in the military dimension of national security, the IAF would be called upon to shoulder enhanced levels of responsibility and would have a critical role to play both during peace and war especially in situations demanding swift response. Traditionally considered outside the zone of responsibility, the IAF will be drawn increasingly in to specialised roles related to internal security. The IAF therefore needs to draw up plans to acquire the wherewithal to meet with the challenges of the 2020s. As the pace of change is slow, radical change in the broad structure is neither desirable nor possible in the timeframe under consideration. However, there is imperative need to introduce qualitative change in the capabilities of the IAF driven by the technological revolution in Air Power.

ASSESSING THE IAF'S PERFORMANCE

Both the Indian Army and the IAF were essential players in a genuinely joint counteroffensive. It would be hard to deem either as having been the more pivotal contributor toward determining the ultimate victory for India's forces.

To be sure, from a simple weight-of-effort perspective, 15 Corps artillery was the main source of direct fire support throughout the fighting, and massive barrages of it provided sustained suppressive cover under which Indian infantry teams eventually moved up the daunting terrain to recapture their former posts.

In all, 15 Corps committed 15 artillery regiments and more than 300 artillery pieces to what one account called "one of the most bitterly fought mountain battles of all times." Throughout the campaign, they expended more than 250,000 rounds of ammunition in a sustained laydown of fire on a scale not seen anywhere in the world since World War II.

But to say that the IAF turned in a "poor showing" during the Kargil War, as one otherwise insightful campaign assessment observed two years after the conflict ended, overstates the cumulative impact of the IAF's operational shortcomings by a considerable margin.9393 On the contrary, as a better-informed review of Operation Vijay concluded some time thereafter, the IAF's entry into action on May 26 and its gradual improvement in performance over time in fact "represented a paradigm shift in the nature and prognosis of the conflict."

Granted, it was only natural that India's leading airmen would lend their voices to such a self-congratulatory conclusion. For example, a decade after the war ended, the chief of the Air Staff at the time, Air Chief Marshal Fali Homi Major, suggested that the IAF's entry into the Kargil equation had "immediately altered the nature of the conflict." By the same token, during his tenure as the AOC-in-C of Western Air Command, Air Marshal Pranab Barbora volunteered at roughly the same time that "the conflict in Kargil would have gone on and on if airpower ... had not come into play." In strong supporting testimony to these observations, the Indian government's formal afteraction assessment of the campaign released on December 15, 1999, found the intervention of the IAF to have been both "unnerving" to the enemy and

> *a significant development with far-reaching consequences.... Not only did this decision send a signal to Pakistan that India would use all available means to evict the intruders, it also had a strong impact on the course of the tactical battle in terms of the interdiction of Pakistani supply lines within Indian territory ... and the lowering of the morale of the intruders.*

It was not, however, just Indian Air Force leaders who rendered such laudatory judgments regarding their service's performance. Senior Indian Army officers were likewise generous in voicing their appreciation of the IAF's combat contributions. For example, retired Major General G. D. Bakshi characterized the IAF's innovative use of airpower as "one of the excellent features of the Kargil operations," adding that "the complete domination of the sky by the IAF over the area of intrusion ... served to demoralize the [NLI] troopers" and, "in combination with artillery, served to mass effects and generate an element of shock and awe."

If the IAF was unable to provide consistently effective oncall close air support for all the prevailing multitude of extenuating factors, it certainly was effective in other air applications no less pertinent to the ongoing fighting. The IAF performed more than adequately in servicing enemy headquarters complexes, supply dumps, and other assets that were more readily accessible to aerial attack from standoff ranges. As a U.S. Army officer rightly observed in this regard, the IAF's contribution to the joint fight "grew as the campaign wore on," and fighter aircraft armed with laser-guided bombs and well-placed unguided munitions "eventually destroyed virtually all of the Pakistani supply lines and played a major role in the battle for Tiger Hill."

Furthermore, in marked contrast to what the air component commander during the Kargil fighting later characterized as 15 Corps's "profligacy in the use of artillery in a carpet-bombing mode," the IAF dropped only around 500 general-purpose bombs in all during the seventy-four-day campaign, none of which were released indiscriminately and the majority of which were deemed to have been effective against their assigned targets. As Air Marshal Patney recalled in this regard, "after every mission, the army would give us the results of the attack. In about 70 percent of the missions, we were told 'bombs on target.'"

The IAF also rapidly adapted to the campaign's unique operational challenges. The PAF's director of operations during the war was one of many who acknowledged afterward how the IAF "immediately went into a reappraisal mode [after its initial combat losses] and came out with GPS [Global Positioning System]-assisted high-altitude bombing by the MiG-21, MiG-23BN, and MiG-27 as a makeshift solution." He further acknowledged the rapid reconfiguration of the Mirage 2000H with Litening pods to allow the option of day and night laser-guided bomb delivery. Once accurate target attacks by Mirage 2000Hs and Jaguars showed their ability to achieve significant combat effects, he added, around-the-clock operations by the IAF "had made retention of posts untenable by the Pakistani infiltrators." In all, he concluded, although the Indian high command was completely surprised by the Kargil intrusion at the outset, "the IAF mobilized and reacted rapidly as the Indian Army took time to position itself."

Much of the IAF's improved combat effectiveness during the campaign over time was a direct result of Western Air Command's eventual replacement of classic manual dive bombing by MiG-23s and MiG-27s with the more accurate method of GPS-aided level bombing from safer altitudes above the effective reach of the enemy's man-portable infrared surface-to-air missiles.

As the command's AOC-in-C at the time later recalled, "when the conflict started, there was only one squadron fitted with GPS. We [accordingly] acquired hand-held GPS instruments from the market and fitted them in the aircraft," which allowed for "a somewhat ad hoc system.... With the target coordinates available, on approach to the target, pilots dropped their bombs at the determined distance from the target. We knew that if the coordinates were accurate, the results would be reasonable." Air Marshal Patney added: "We also knew that the accuracy would be much better at lower heights. That is why we resorted to night operations in those forbidding hills and at low levels of around 500 feet, something never done before anywhere in the world and that also with aircraft that had no modern aids and in an area where no radars could operate." Air Chief Marshal Tipnis later applauded this novel initiative as the air war's "biggest contribution to ingeniousness."

By the same token, once the Mirage 2000H was introduced into the daily flow of operations, the accuracy of IAF weapons deliveries against point targets increased substantially even with the use of unguided low-drag bombs, thanks to the aircraft's much-improved onboard avionics suite that features a continuously computed release point (CCRP) system which compensates for target area wind and enables near-precise weapon placement. The pilot simply designates his intended aim point through his cockpit head-up display (HUD) and then depresses a consent button on the aircraft's control stick. The computer releases the bomb automatically at just the right moment once all required delivery accuracy parameters are achieved. With the aid of this proven system, the pilot knows with high confidence that his bomb will land on the point designated by the cursor on his HUD once the weapon departs its pylon.

Further innovative real-time adaptation by the IAF occurred when MiG-21 pilots lacking sophisticated onboard navigation suites resorted to the use of stopwatches and GPS receivers in their cockpits for conducting night interdiction bombing. Yet another novel technique developed by the IAF for use in the campaign entailed selecting weapon impact points so as to create landslides and avalanches that covered intruder supply lines. Finally, to note just one of many additional examples that could be cited, the IAF pioneered during its Kargil campaign what has since come to be called nontraditional intelligence, surveillance, and reconnaissance through its use of electro-optical and infrared imaging targeting pods for conducting high-resolution aerial re-connaissance of the battlespace.

It was yet another exaggeration for two commentators, in assessing the campaign, to suggest that the IAF's leaders were "shocked" at their two aircraft losses to surface-to-air missile fire and that those same leaders "panicked" as they searched for alternative tactics, techniques, and procedures for addressing the challenge the missiles presented. In fact, what those leaders actually did in the circumstances was to consider with deliberation a surface-to-air threat that they had fully anticipated in their prior contingency planning and then to address it systematically in a solutions-oriented way. As Air Chief Marshal Tipnis told Prime Minister Vajpayee and others at a Cabinet Committee on Security meeting after the two aircraft were downed, "While I was sorry to lose two fighters, I was not overly worried. The air force knew what had gone wrong and knew what was required to be done to ensure we did not repeat the mistakes."

In this connection, as the ineffectiveness of the IAF's conventional bombing persisted for four straight days on end, Tipnis visited 15 Corps headquarters in Srinagar to confer with the on-scene army commanders and to jointly work out best alternative approaches to the satisfaction of all. It was in substantial part out of that cross-service mind meld at the tactical level that Tipnis ultimately decided to employ Mirage 2000Hs that could deliver laser-guided bombs with consistent accuracy against the most vital targets.

Partly because the IAF had not amassed a sizable inventory of laser-guided bombs at the time the crisis erupted and partly because of the paucity of targets of sufficient merit to warrant the use of such costly munitions, Western Air Command, by the recollection of its commander at the time, expended only two laser-guided bombs in all throughout the Kargil fighting, both delivered against the enemy's main forward command post on Tiger Hill. Yet even this limited use against a key NLI target dramatically altered the dynamics of the campaign. After those successful laser-guided bomb attacks, subsequent targeting pod imagery observed by IAF pilots in real time showed enemy troops abandoning their positions at the very sound of approaching fighters. Diaries kept by Pakistani soldiers that were later recovered by Indian Army units amply attested to the demoralization caused by the IAF's attacks, most particularly those conducted during the campaign's final countdown once precision munitions were introduced.

The IAF pioneered during its Kargil campaign what has since come to be called nontraditional intelligence, surveillance, and reconnaissance through its use of electro-optical and infrared imaging targeting pods for conducting high-resolution aerial reconnaissance of the battlespace.

With respect to the altitude floor imposed on IAF fighter operations by Western Air Command throughout most of the campaign out of legitimate concern over the ubiquitous enemy infrared surface-to-air-missile threat, the commander of the Indian Army's Fifty-Sixth Mountain Brigade, Brigadier Amar Aul, later blamed the ineffectiveness of many IAF attempts at close air support delivery on the unwillingness of IAF pilots to "take reasonable risks" by descending into the enemy's lethal antiaircraft threat envelope. To that all-but-express intimation of IAF cowardice in the face of enemy fire, an IAF group captain responded that such unwillingness was driven by the entirely appropriate and sensible need for the IAF to respect the effectiveness of the enemy's infrared surface-to-air missiles. "A far more serious lapse," he observed, would have been "a dogged tendency to persist in sacrificing assets when, clearly, there was a need for a reassessment."

True enough, the hard deck of 6,000 to 8,000 feet above the terrain that was imposed on the IAF's pilots after the downing of two aircraft by enemy surface-to-air missiles during the campaign's second and third days "reduced their ability to deliver effective [close air support] to [ground] maneuver units." But it also eliminated their susceptibility to an all but certain high loss rate had they persisted in attempting such foolhardy operations under the circumstances. On this point, as the above-cited group captain later correctly noted, "gone are the days of fighters screaming in at deck level, acting as a piece of extended artillery. The air defence environment of today's battlefield just does not permit such employment of airpower any more, a significant fact that needs to be understood by soldier and civilian alike."

By remaining safely outside the enemy's lethal surface-to-air-missile threat envelope, the IAF's pilots during the Kargil War were doing exactly what any professional airmen the world over would have done in similar circumstances.

In this regard, it is worth noting in passing that when the legitimate demands of threat avoidance require fighter aircraft to operate so high above a battlefield that engaged ground troops cannot see or hear them, it is only natural for the latter to suspect at some level that their promised "air support" is not there. Yet by remaining safely outside the enemy's lethal surface-to-air-missile threat envelope, the IAF's pilots during the Kargil War were doing exactly what any professional airmen the world over would have done in similar circumstances. Indeed, they did what U.S. and allied pilots have done in all major instances of aerial force employment from Operation Desert Storm in 1991 onward—unless, of course, a truly dire emergency situation on the ground should require accepting higher risk.

It also is true that the IAF's suspension of any further attempts to use armed helicopters in combat and its associated imposition of an altitude floor to keep fixed-wing fighters out of the enemy's surface-to-air-missile threat envelope "removed a large component of potential Indian firepower" from the fight, but *only* from providing effective direct fire support to friendly troops in close contact with enemy forces. Those legitimate and proper operating restrictions in no way kept IAF pilots from providing indirect support and interdiction that had a steadily mounting effect in facilitating Indian ground advances against the enemy over time. As the IAF group captain later recalled in this regard, "the series of [IAF] attacks against Point 4388 in the Dras sector was an excellent example of how lethal air strikes, combined with timely reconnaissance, detected the enemy plans to shift to alternate supply routes, which were once again effectively attacked. In this, the IAF succeeded in strangling the enemy supply arteries."

One important battlefield effect achieved by the IAF's combat air patrol operations during the campaign was their prevention of Pakistani helicopters from resupplying the NLI's outposts and conducting reconnaissance and casualty evacuation missions, an accomplishment that a retired Indian Army major general portrayed as the IAF's "most significant contribution" to Operation Vijay. Another significant IAF contribution was the successful interdiction of needed resupply to the increasingly beleaguered Pakistani intruders by destroying the NLI's logistics base at Muntho Dhalo. By one informed assessment, hundreds of enemy troops were killed by IAF air action in such attacks, and Indian military intelligence intercepted numerous enemy radio transmissions during the campaign that attested to the effectiveness of those attacks. Especially during the campaign's final days, that intercepted traffic revealed severe shortages of rations, water, medical supplies, and ammunition, as well as an inability of the occupying enemy units to evacuate their wounded. Yet another telling testament to the effectiveness of the IAF's interdiction attacks came when Pakistan's Foreign Minister Sartaj Aziz, during an official visit to New Delhi on June 12 as Operation Vijay was just reaching peak intensity, implored the IAF to "stop its air strikes" as one of three specific requests that he levied on the Indian government.

The IAF's ability to adapt to an unnatural limitation imposed by top-down civilian direction and to work effectively within the Vajpayee government's ban against any crossing of the Line of Control by Indian forces may well have been the determining factor in keeping the PAF out of the fighting and hence in maintaining escalation control throughout the seventy-four-day war.

The IAF's ability to adapt to an unnatural limitation imposed by top-down civilian direction and to work effectively within the Vajpayee government's ban against any crossing of the LoC by Indian forces may well have been the determining factor in keeping the PAF out of the fighting and hence in maintaining escalation control throughout the seventy-four-day war. After the surviving intruders were driven back into Pakistani-controlled territory and the Indian Army reclaimed and secured its positions in the Kargil heights, Air Marshal Patney reflected in this regard:

It is the nature of airpower that escalation is inherent in its use, unless its use is one-sided, as happened this time.... Before May 26, when we went into action, one of our apprehensions ... was the degree of enemy resolve and to what extent we could expect such escalation.

Patney added:

We had not planned for this kind of war. We had planned that we would use airpower in this particular area, but certainly not in the way we were required to do so.... If we were to apply airpower in its classical sense, in which we had done all our training, we would have crossed the LoC well before and crossed the [international border] as well.

In the end, however, neither development ever occurred.

The asymmetrical use of India's airpower allowed the Vajpayee government to telegraph an unmistakable signal of its seriousness to key audiences both in Pakistan and worldwide. Further, as one of the best Western accounts of the Kargil fighting from an operational perspective observed, it "had the additional domestic benefit of giving the IAF a direct role in a major national crisis, not unimportant for future bureaucratic struggles."

THE BROADER STRATEGIC OUTLOOK

As for the broader implications of the Kargil benchmark for deterrence and international security, that war was the first serious border conflict of sustained duration between two nuclear-armed antagonists that ended with a clear winner and loser at the conventional level. Although it is always risky to try to generalize from a singular and, in many ways, unique case of that sort, the Kargil War nonetheless offers much food for creative thought regarding a number of generic issue areas, such as the escalation dynamics that govern a bilateral nuclear relationship of major tension. It underlines the importance of avoiding such escalation-prone thresholds as India's crossing of the LoC to carry the fighting into Pakistan, and Pakistan's engagement of IAF fighters servicing NLI targets on India's side of the LoC. And it reminds military planners of the ever-present possibility that inadvertent leadership misjudgment on either side regarding the other's limits of tolerance could lead to a breach of the nuclear taboo that neither player wants or could possibly profit from.

The Kargil War was the first serious border conflict of sustained duration between two nucleararmed antagonists that ended with a clear winner and loser at the conventional level.

The confrontation also showed India the downside strategic consequences of an avowed nuclear no-first-use policy that necessarily put the country's government in a reactive mode when it came to the prospect of inadvertent nuclear escalation. By the same token, for Pakistan's leaders, the unexpected—and unexpectedly sharp and intense—response that their provocation prompted from the Indian Army and IAF should make them think twice about the limits of their nuclear deterrent. More to the point, it should have had a tempering influence on their initial presumptions about the extent to which merely having a credible nuclear attack capability in and of itself empowered them to try conventional acts of territorial acquisition with impunity. To that extent, it should have instilled as well a healthy once-burned, twice-shy mindset among those leaders and their successors who might be tempted to undertake a reprise of that gambit some day in the future—particularly in light of the persistent regional imbalance of conventional airpower in India's pronounced favour.

For both protagonists, the war represented a real-world battle laboratory for reconfirming something the leaders of NATO and the Warsaw Pact came to learn during the height of the Cold War in Central Europe a generation before. A stable bilateral nuclear deterrence relationship at the strategic level can markedly constrain in intensity and scale, if not inhibit entirely, recurrent flash points that, in the absence of such a relationship, might have every chance of erupting into an open-ended conventional showdown for the highest stakes. But the Kargil War demonstrated that nuclear deterrence is clearly not a panacea. The possibility of future conventional wars of major consequence along India's northern borders with Pakistan and China persists, and the Indian defence establishment must plan and prepare accordingly.

EVOLVING SHAPE OF THE IAF AIRCRAFT FLEET

The aircraft fleet of the IAF is likely to undergo major changes as well. The *Su-30MKI*, numbering about 272 aircraft, would continue to form the high and heavy end of the fleet. The low end would be comprised of the *Tejas* LCA which, by then, would be in final operational clearance (FOC) configuration. *Tejas* numbers could be expected to be in the region of 350 to 450 aircraft. The current three squadrons of *MiG-29* would be well into their upgrade and would be available in upgraded form about five years hence. Likewise, the three squadrons of *Mirage-2000H* would also be available in upgraded form in a similar timeframe.

The rotary wing fleet should retain the same inventory more or less with the most significant changes being the entry of larger numbers of *Dhruv* Advanced Light Helicopters (ALH) as well as upgraded Mi-8/17/17-1V/ 17-5V. In addition, the

Light Combat Helicopter (LCH) will be inducted starting about five years hence in parallel with the *Apache Longbow-III* attack helicopters.

In the fighter category, the most significant change should be the completion of the development of the Indian Fifth Generation Fighter Aircraft (FGFA) from the *Sukhoi* T-50/ PAK FA baseline by the end of this decade and the commencement of induction of FGFAs into service starting about ten years hence against a total order of 250 or more. Older aircraft types would be retired in a phased manner so that the available numbers of aircraft to the IAF does not fall excessively until the force level required has been built up with new inductions.

This could see the *MiG-21 Bison*, *MiG-29* and *Mirage 2000* upgrades continue in service well into the 2020s, with carefully staggered retiring of these fleets commencing from 2025.

The IAF's airlift capability would also be considerable as, in the next five to ten years, all 16 C-17 aircraft and a total of nine to twelve *C-130J* would be in service and be supplemented slowly with the Indo-Russian collaboratively developed Multi-role Transport Aircraft (MTA). The*Il-76* should be commencing retirement from service about the same time.

Weapon induction should also see a change with the indigenous Astra missile becoming the standard fit Beyond Visual Range (BVR) standardised across all IAF aircraft fleets in the next ten years.

The short range close combat missile of choice is likely to be the Russian *R-73* and its newer variants. Once the *Astra* is in service, there could be indigenous development of short range close combat missiles either derived from it or developed independently. For precision attack, the *Helina* (an air launched variant of the *Nag* anti-tank missile) with an imaging infra red (IIR) seeker backed by an upgraded variant of the currently available algorithm able to discriminate targets including moving targets even in heavy clutter, should be the standard fit across all types of IAF aircraft. Indigenous Precision Guided Munitions (PGMs) with satellite navigation-laser designation/

terrain matching/optical hybrid guidance systems developed indigenously should become available in the five to ten year period given that work on such weapons is being pursued, albeit at a slow pace, because these fall under unfunded private research at a few DRDO laboratories in the absence of firm IAF orders and sanction to develop such weapons.

Network Centric Warfare Capabilities

Within five years, the IAF would have its proprietary AFNET network fully in place with enhanced encryption features implemented. The Integrated Air Command and Control System (IACCS) should also be ready with all its modules including encrypted jam resistant wireless component, thus giving the IAF full networked war fighting capabilities.

The data link system embedded in the IACCS architecture would enable high situational awareness for all war fighters and the battle commanders even at "remote from the battlefield" locations.

The IAF would, in ten years, be moving towards dynamic targeting of ordnance. It would be in the process of developing capability to data link with, say a missile in flight, to reassign its target or modify its attack profile on the fly.

The IAF would be developing Two Stage to Orbit (TSTO) craft in consultation with and through the DRDO and ISRO, to ensure assured space access when required.

Interest in micro-satellites for defence support tasks is also likely to increase in view of the fact that such small satellites can be launched by lower lift capability launchers or even from aircraft with suitably modified boosters at much shorter notice than heavy satellites. Such raid satellite launch capability is likely to be crucial for a networked organisation to operate effectively. Ten years from now this project could be expected to be at technology demonstration stage. The IAF should also at this time be commissioning dedicated research into Directed Energy Weapons (DEW) at institutes of higher learning and research centres in the country.

What Needs to be Kept in Mind?

There are a few salient features of the planned transformation of the IAF over the next five to ten years that merit attention.

- The IAF is moving towards advanced capabilities in platforms and systems.
- The focus is slowly shifting towards indigenisation, i.e., production of all major and crucial systems within the country.
- Between license production (which leads to obtaining "know how"), technology transfer, and "know why" (which leads to actual technology transfer and gains in design and development skills), the latter are being preferred. For instance, this aspect may have played a part in the choice of the PAK FA over the F-35 JSF offer from the US. The MTA, LRSAM and other projects also demonstrate a bias towards collaborative development rather than "buy and make" as seen in the MMRCA deal; this MMRCA license manufacture agreement may have been found acceptable in view of the great time pressure to induct aircraft at the earliest given the currently falling numbers of fighters due to unplanned retirement of a few squadrons from IAF service.
- Several high-end systems for the IAF have been developed totally indigenously in the public and the private sectors of the Indian Aerospace Industry. These include the secure and encrypted pan Air Force wide area network (WAN), AFNET, IACCS, and the Advanced Command Air Tasking System (ACATS), to name a few. Other noteworthy indigenous systems in or about to enter service are the *Reporter* and *Rohini* radars, Tejas LCA, Dhruv ALH, LCH and EMB-145 based AEW&C system.
- Purchases of defence and civil equipment from foreign sources are now accompanied with offset clauses varying from 30 to 50 per cent.

- There are great opportunities for foreign companies to enter into genuine collaboration with Indian players in the public and private sectors of the aerospace industry in India to design and develop new systems and platforms leading to a win-win situation for both sides, given India's proven "frugal engineering" and Information Technology (IT) skills. Just these two proven skills available in India justify the setting up of joint ventures (JVs) in the aerospace field by foreign technology giants with Indian companies, quite independent of bidding for any civil or military contract and its offset requirements.
- Foreign governments and companies will require to shed their erstwhile "sell and maybe give a license to make" policy in favour of genuine from-the-ground-up collaborative design and development. A step in this direction has been made by the Indo-Russian *Brahmos project*. More than the original *Brahmos* project, this is more applicable to the new hypersonic variant of the Brahmos missile being developed jointly. The Indo-Russian collaboration for the PAK FA fifth generation fighter aircraft (FGFA) wherein India is partly funding a substantial part of the project in exchange for design involvement and development of a variant to meet India's specific needs is another tentative step in this direction.

PEACE KEEPING, ANTI-PIRACY, AND EXPLORATION MISSIONS

United Nations Peacekeeping

India has been the largest troop contributor to UN missions since inception. So far India has taken part in 43 Peacekeeping missions with a total contribution exceeding 1,60,000 troops and a significant number of police personnel having been deployed. India has so far, provided one Military Advisor (Lt Gen R K Mehta), one Police Adviser (Ms Kiran Bedi), one Deputy Military Adviser (Lt Gen Abhijit Guha), 14 Force

Commanders and numerous Police Commissioners in various UN Missions. Indian Army has also contributed lady officers as Military Observers and Staff Officers apart from them forming part of Medical Units being deployed in UN Missions. The first all women contingent in peacekeeping mission, a Formed Police Unit from India, was deployed in 2007 to the UN Operation in Liberia(UNMIL). It also suffered 127 soldier deaths while serving on peacekeeping missions. India also provided army contingent performing a peacekeeping operation in Sri Lanka between 1987 and 1990 as Indian Peace Keeping Force and in November 1988, India also helped restore government of Maumoon Abdul Gayoom in Maldives under Operation Cactus. As of June, 2013, about 8000 Indian UN peacekeepers, both men and women, are deployed in nine missions, including Congo, South Sudan, Liberia, UNDOF, Haiti, Lebanon, Abeyi, Cyprus and Cote de Ivoire.

Anti-piracy Mission

India sought to augment its naval force in the Gulf of Aden by deploying the larger INS *Mysore* to patrol the area. Somalia also added India to its list of states, including the U.S. and France, who are permitted to enter its territorial waters, extending up to 12 nautical miles (22 km; 14 mi) from the coastline, in an effort to check piracy. An Indian naval official confirmed receipt of a letter acceding to India's prerogative to check such piracy. "We had put up a request before the Somali government to play a greater role in suppressing piracy in the Gulf of Aden in view of the United Nations resolution. The TFG government gave its nod recently." In November 2008, an Indian navy warship destroyed a suspected Somali pirate vessel after it came under attack in the Gulf of Aden. In a report on Somalia submitted to the Security Council, UN Secretary General Ban Ki-Moon said "*I welcome the decision of the governments of India and the Russian Federation to cooperate with the Transitional Federal Government of Somalia to fight piracy and armed robbery against ships.*" India also expressed consideration to deploy up to four more warships in the region. On 2010-09-06, a crack team of Indian marine commandos(MARCOS) boarded MV Jag Arnav and overpowered attacking pirates - seven heavily armed Somalians and one Yemeni national. As part of the Indian response to the piracy menace in the area, the Indian Navy has escorted over 1,200 ships so far.

Relief Operations of IAF

Indian Air Force provides regular relief operation for food and medical facility around the world by its cargo aircraft most notably Ilyushin Il-76. The most recent relief operation of the IAF was in Kyrgyzstan. During the 2010 Ladakh floods, two Ilyushin Il-76 and four Antonov-32 aircraft of the IAF carried 30 tonnes of load, which include 125 rescue and relief personnel, medicines, generators, tents, portable X-ray machines and emergency rescue kits. A MI-17 helicopter and Cheetah helicopter were pressed to increase effectiveness of the rescue operations. During 2013 Uttrakhand Floods, Indian armed forces demonstrated heroic courage in rescue operations. By 21 June 2013, the Army had deployed 10,000 soldiers and 11 helicopters, the Navy had sent 45 naval divers, and the Air force had deployed 43 aircraft including 36 helicopters. From 17 June to 30 June 2013, the IAF airlifted a total of 18,424 people - flying a total of 2,137 sorties and dropping/landing a total of 3,36,930 kg of relief material and equipment.

IAF Efforts in Eclipse Study

The Indian Air Force successfully undertook sorties to help Indian scientists study the total solar eclipse that took place on 23 July 2010. Two separate missions from Agra and Gwalior were flown along the path of the moon's shadow, a mission that was deemed hugely successful by scientists associated with the experiment.

While one AN-32 transport aircraft carrying scientific equipment, cameras and scientists that took off from Agra landed back after a three-hour flight, a Mirage-2000 trainer from Gwalior took spectacular images of the celestial spectacle from 40,000 feet. With weather being clear at such altitudes and coordinates planned by the IAF pilots, both AN-32 and Mirage-2000 pilots were able to accomplish the mission successfully.

Indian Navy Exploration

The Indian Navy regularly conducts adventure expeditions. The sailing ship and training vessel INS Tarangini began circumnavigating the world on 23 January 2003, intending to foster good relations with various other nations; she returned to India in May of the following year after visiting 36 ports in 18 nations. Lt. Cdr. M.S. Kohli led the Indian Navy's first successful expedition to Mount Everest in 1965. Another Navy team also successfully scaled Everest from the north face, the technically more challenging route. An Indian Navy team comprising 11 members successfully completed an expedition to the Arctic pole in 2006. The Indian Naval ensign first flew in Antarctica in 1981. The Indian Navy succeeded in Mission Dakshin Dhruv by traversing to the South Pole on skis in 2006. With this historic expedition, they have set the record for being the world's first military team to have successfully completed a ski traverse to the geographic south pole.

6

Indian Air Force in the 21st Century: Challenges and Opportunities

GLOBAL

One of the defining characteristics of the contemporary global geo-political environment is that a nation's power is increasingly determined by its economic might and technological prowess, rather than by its military strength. Though interdependent, the most fundamental is economic strength, without which, none of the other indices of power can be created or sustained. At the same time economic growth is not guaranteed without the protective cover of military power, in what is referred to as its 'peace dividend'.

Popular phrases that describe today's world are interdependence, global village, flat world etc. Certainly, there is heightened interaction and cross-pollination in every sphere. This interdependence leads to a 'balancing of interests'; instead of 'balance of power'; and the politics of 'confrontation' has been replaced to a large extent by the more nuanced – 'competition and cooperation'.

Asia and India

Indeed, Asia is the current power-house and every major power has presence and high stakes here. Asian countries have greater influence around the world as well and military capabilities are now substantial on the continent. The region is also witness to conflicts & instabilities, as peoples attempt to reconfigure their settings, the reverberations of which are felt around the world. It is also a region of nuclear proliferation and increasingly, the cradle and playground of terrorism.

India is situated in a turbulent part of the continent. Its size, resources, capabilities and growth also endow it with power, visibility, influence and responsibility for a greater role in regional affairs.

Threat Perceptions

So what is the impact on our security and threat perceptions? Territorial disputes still linger, our adversaries are acquiring ever greater military capabilities. Cross-border terrorism and internal security challenges persist. At the same time trade and energy security add to our considerations and are a potential source of conflict. This encourages an outward orientation, which is good.

Ideological divisions in the modern world still exist, but in other forms, such as democracies vs autocracies or fundamentalists vs the secular. These strains and tendencies exist within and outside our country too and impact our security calculus; turning into militant aspirations, that challenge national integrity. These have in the past sought to re-draw national boundaries and many still abound, even drawing covert support from outside the country. If we were to include the proliferation of weapons of mass destruction then we collectively face a very serious threat indeed. Meeting these challenges requires understanding, as well as careful handling. Invariably, in these situations, one finds the lines between policing and military operations blurred.

Yet another area of concern for us, is ethnic Indian population, residing in other parts of the world, which at times may need protection and support. There have been instances of this in the past. On the flip-side, migrant populations have changed the demographic character of our border states and impacted their polity, with attendant security connotations. We are all aware that non-traditional threats create crisis situations that in the end require the military's organisational capabilities and technical support. Keeping the peace is yet another important international commitment for Indian Armed Forces. There is no longer the comfortable immunity from problems in some distant part of the globe. This entwining of interests and effects can work both ways and nations that anticipate and act have the advantage. It is not easy for a single nation to ensure peace and stability for itself, on its own.

This encourages, indeed demands international cooperation. This realisation or compulsion is very visible the world over. India's international cooperation too has considerably increased, translating into increased engagement in all spheres, including military exchanges and interactions. The role of military diplomacy has also been enhanced. The significance of collective security and cooperative organisations has increased over time. India too seeks increased and active part in cooperative mechanisms, though joining collective security organisations is not our policy. An associated challenge sometimes is to prevent from being subsumed by a more prolific and larger friend and retain independence.

On the whole, India is faced with the full 'spectrum of threats' from nuclear confrontation, through conventional war; to conflicts limited in area, scope or objectives; to the lower end friction, such as insurgencies, terrorism etc. Moreover, India needs to be prepared for the escalation of conflict from limited upto nuclear. The spectrum has also acquired a complexity and technological sophistication, making it prudent and necessary to move away from a 'threat-based preparation', to a more accommodative and flexible – 'capability-based approach'. This would help lessen the uncertainty and unpredictability, because capabilities could then be readily tailored to suit the challenge at hand.

Nature of Conflict

While, the probabilities of total wars and extensive

mobilisations may have reduced, India still must be prepared for a full-fledged and conventional conflict. Nuclear power-play has increased in the region and impacts postures and strategies. In a more integrated and interdependent world, the spillover of conflict in the neighbourhood and its negative global consequences makes it everybody's concern. While there would be supporters for either party, the sum of international pressure would be to end conflict. Moreover, the battle spaces are now transparent to the public, and legalities cannot be ignored. Therefore, limited, but high-tech wars of high intensity are more likely. Aerospace power has a distinct advantage in such a scenario. Determining the objectives and the end-state in a limited war is critical, but poses dilemmas. Perceptions matter too. The Indian politico-military leadership must continually work for clarity in military objectives and desired end-states.

While the future is uncertain, wars will be multi-dimensional, requiring an inter-disciplinary approach and the marshalling of all organs of national power. Military power is a critical component of national power, without which, as history bears out, progress is possible only up to the point where it clashes with the interests of another stronger nation. Often, assumptions of conflicts and military capabilities are based on the classical war scenario. However, the IAF recognises that complex military challenges require different force constructs, for different situations, ranging from highly mobile and effective conventional forces, to 'rapid - reaction joint special-forces'. It is here that Air Power could provide the crucial edge. Clearly, future conflicts are likely to be short and sharp; more challenging & unpredictable, requiring a capability for assured, clean, swift, calibrated, varied and flexible responses and a transportability of national power in all forms.

THE HARDWARE–TECHNOLOGICAL CHALLENGES

We now turn to the challenges facing the IAF. I am aware that in the challenges lie seeds of opportunity and thus how we address them will qualify our future. Technology is at the core of an air force – acquiring and assimilating it is our primary challenge. The lack of it curtails national options, impacting postures and doctrines. Denial and selective availability of technology are all enmeshed in international relations. As long as operationally feasible, the IAF supports the national quest for indigenisation. We recommend acquisition of core-technologies and core-competencies and developing emerging technologies. We also recommend a collaborative and participative approach – of partnerships between users, DRDO, the Industry, the Government and foreign vendors. In these multiple partnerships, we believe that the user must be the captain. We strongly support the Government's endeavour to transform our current 'buyer-seller' relationships to joint-ventures, co-development and co-production.

Maintenance Challenges

While our response to technological challenges will determine the 'shape' of things to come, maintenance challenges determine how long they last and their cost-effectiveness. 'Maintainability', which includes logistical issues, is therefore, crucial. IAF is proactive on this and has energised interaction with vendors and entered into 'long-term spares and repair contracts'. We have also put our materials management and equipment accounting on-line.

The People and Organisation

While hardware is important, it is converted into capabilities by people. Aerospace power requires highly-skilled and impeccably trained personnel. Also, in aviation, optimum performance usually lies close to safety margins, which brings in the concern of costs – both in human and material terms. Attracting quality youth, training and retaining them is another of IAF's challenges. Inculcating qualities of leadership and innovativeness and ushering in meritocracy and productivity are important on our agenda. However, the expanding civil aviation sector exerts a huge 'pull' on this resource and we are doing our best to blend personal aspirations with organisational compulsions. We need Government support to make this happen. Updating of skills is an associated challenge, for which international exposure has been very useful. But in the long run we might need an Air University. Again, if our manning is adequate, we would be able to send our people on sabbaticals of higher learning.

As the hardware changes, new capacities and capabilities are generated that sometimes radically alter the way we do business. And it is hard to do things differently with the old processes, interfaces and organisational structures. Keeping pace and adapting to the changes, as an organisation, is another challenge.

AEROSPACE POWER

Of all forms of military power, it is aerospace power that intrinsically possesses the characteristics that enable such responses. I am by no means lessening the import of other forms of military power, yet modern aerospace capabilities have as much, or prhaps greater impact than what maritime power did for colonising nations in the past.

Unlike the latter, whose applicability is determined by a country's geographic location; and the land forces, whose shape and size are determined by relations with neighbours, size of the country and internal security compulsions; aerospace power has a more universal applicability. That is why even armies and navies strive to assimilate organic aerospace capabilities.

Recent technological developments, including the synergy of air & space, have enhanced aerospace force unprecedently, making it astonishingly reliable, effective, clean and responsive and the 'preferred instrument', in most situations of peace or war. It has enabled effects-based operations, made simpler parallel operations and creates strategic effects with a small footprint. Aerospace power is empowering and futuristic and easily lends its strengths and capabilities to other disciplines. In the Indian context, all forms of military power are necessary and important, however, strategic aerospace power offers newer options, both for our northern concerns, as well as for our outward orientations.

I wish to highlight that aerospace power is inherently flexible and its application is not constrained by geographical areas. It can easily be assigned to any task on priority to attain the objectives – current or overall. IAF's doctrines and plans are founded accordingly. I mention this as some believe that air power doctrines are rigid and unaccommodative. Debates have taken place on 'Counter Air Operations' (the so-called air war) vs 'Counter Surface Force Operations'. It has been said that the IAF attributes less importance to the latter. But contrary to perception in some quarters, a large part of IAF's effort in past conflicts has been in support of the surface battle. Our current plans too, allocate a sizeable portion of air effort towards CSFO.

THE IAF

Evolution and Status

Lets take a brief look at the IAF, its Evolution & Status, Role and Goals. From Counter-Insurgency in its early years, to Army cooperation in WW-II, the IAF was a tactical force. Today, it is a strategic force – powerful, professional and proven. Though the transition to strategic capability has been slow in coming, the process must be sustained, if we are to effectively influence events within India's strategic boundaries.

In its 76th year, the IAF with its fine combination of Air Warriors, machines and ethos has proved itself time and again. Status of the Force and strength of the economy have boosted our International Defence Cooperation, including assistance to friendly air forces. Trans-continental reach has enabled exercises with friendly Air Forces on all Continents, which is an excellent way to train, assimilate best practices and strengthen bonds of friendship.

The IAF is also a sought-after contributor to UNPKO. Currently, we have four highly acclaimed missions in the Congo & Sudan. The IAF also remains at the forefront of the Nation's HA/DR missions. IAF's uniqueness lies in its rich all-terrain experience and its diverse inventory. Its capability and reach have enhanced significantly in the last decade.

Roles

Given our situation, concerns and aspirations, a strong and comprehensive aerospace capability is inescapable. The IAF's roles can be described as Deterrence, Punishment, Protection, Projection and Peace-time roles. It will be readily apparent, that India needs its air force to execute all of these. The IAF must be a strong 'deterrent', in a tough neighbourhood. Implicit in the deterrence is the ability for swift, calibrated, but effective 'punishment'. Our deterrence currently includes the nuclear dimension. The IAF's primary and traditional role is 'protection' or Air Defence, the scope of which will expand as do our interests and reach.

A benign presence, or assistance to friendly nations in distress, is a 'projection' of interests that IAF would be expected to execute. This requires long-range presence, persistence, 'forward-basing arrangements' etc. Perhaps the most visible demonstration and utility are 'Peace-time' applications – both internal and external. They range from airlift and surveillance, to possible offensive action. Military diplomacy is yet another aspect that has increased in recent years yielding handsome friendship dividends. Indeed, IAF today is adequately suited and structured to execute these roles, should the need arise.

Goal

If we look at the way the IAF must evolve and compare it to any other evolving air force; and the path charted by the advanced air forces – there are essential similarities. In fact, but for minor variations, we are on a globally recognised growth path. So, depending upon the circumstances, threat perceptions and resources, it is the scope and pace of growth of the Air Force that essentially remain to be managed.

Clearly, the IAF must be equipped for long-reach, persistence, all-weather, precision, air dominance, networked and space-enabled force, capabilities. I am aware that not many air forces have such capabilities, but the IAF, among the leading air forces of the world, can, with the right infusion of technology and training, attain such status. IAF is sensitive to the many competing demands on the nation and doesn't seek the 'best and now', but requisite capability, in time to keep ahead of our adversaries. 'Requisite Capability, Well in Time; Right People, Well Organised; Assured Performance' is a phrase that sums up our goal and our emphasis.

Modernisation of the IAF

Though we are a fairly balanced force – we also have shortages, reducing force-levels and gaps in our inventory, which are being addressed with all urgency and governmental support. IAF's modernisation plan, aims to sustain and enhance its operational potential and consolidate the specified force levels through judicious and cost-effective replacements and upgradation of existing resources. It is a gradual, but transformational modernisation.

The approach is three-pronged – preserve upgrade and acquire. All fleets, including transport and helicopters, with residual life, are being upgraded to contemporary standards; so also is operational and maintenance infrastructure and logistic tools. The planned acquisitions are across-the-board and include platforms, weapons, sensors and equipment; spread over the next 10-15 years.

To run through some of our programmes, the MiG-27 and Jaguar upgrades are almost done; the MiG 29, Mirage 2000 are being negotiated and the IL-76, AN-32 and the helicopter fleets will follow. Capabilities of UAVs will also be enhanced. Airfield and maintenance infrastructure are also being enhanced in a phased manner.

The response to RFP for the MMRCA is expected soon. The Hawk AJTs have been inducted. The first AWACS will be with us this year end. Additional Dorniers, Boeings and upgraded Cheetah will soon join the fleet. The contract for C-130Js has already been signed and contracts will soon be signed for Mi-17 1Vs, ALHs, armed ALHs and additional FRA. The 1st LCA Sqn may be operational in IOC configuration by 2010. IAF also seeks new helicopters to replace the Chetaks and a new heavy-lift heptr. Inter-Government Agreements have been signed for the 5th Generation Fighter and Medium Transport Aircraft with the Russian Govt.

Air defence will be significantly strengthened with modern weapon-systems and sensors, including the AWACS & Aerostats. Integration of civil radars will commence this year, for gap-free surveillance of the entire Indian airspace. Force-multipliers, air dominance fighters and a converged, secure 'Combat Communications Network' – including the IACCS and later the ODL – will fundamentally alter the IAF's Air Defence doctrine. For effective command & control, extended reach and to reduce the sensors-to-shooter loop, we are laying due emphasis on Networks and Space, which are essential 'next steps'.

INDIA'S AIMING MODERNIZATION OF GREAT-POWER STATUS

Indian leaders have pursued power and influence in a variety of ways. Like the heads of most emerging states, Indian officials have sought to build their country's material self-help capabilities via economic and military expansion, albeit in various ways. India has also followed a longstanding strategy of using multilateral institutional venues and weak-state ententes to project a louder political voice than India's capabilities would otherwise permit. Third, Indian officials have often sought to position their state between the existing great powers to seek triangular leverage—i.e., the influence that comes from being closer to two stronger rivals than they are to one another.

India has not followed all of these strategies—building capabilities, using institutional channels for influence, and cultivating triangular leverage—all of the time or with consistent success. The road has been bumpy, India's progress was slow during the decades following independence. Conditions over the past two decades have been more favourable, enabling and encouraging India to revitalize its economy, expand its leadership in selected forums, mend fences with the United States, and establish new leverage as a "swing state."

Guarding Independence Without Might, 1948-1970

In the decades immediately following independence, India pursued great-power status primarily in the three ways. Building material might was one consideration. The relations among states depend heavily on perceptions, but underlying "objective" military and economic might provides much of the basis for those perceptions and the ordered social relations that flow from them. India's first foreign secretary, Gijra Shankar Bajpai, made this point in a 1952 essay, declaring, "armed power supported by industrial power...constitutes the only safeguard against a threat to a country's independence."

India was materially weak, however, and needed to prioritize domestic regime consolidation. Nehru thus sought to compensate through an active and moralistic form of diplomacy, particularly in multilateral forums. Nehru lamented in 1946 that the postwar settlement smacked of "a continuation of power politics on a vaster scale." He thus declared, "there really seems no alternative between world conquest and world association; there is no choice of a middle course." Beneath such poetic pronouncements, however, Indian leaders understood institutions to be both venues for fostering cooperation and crucial arenas for power politics. In practice, that meant charting precisely the "middle course" to which Nehru alluded: steering between the advancement of specific state interests and the development of broader normative frameworks and institutional arrangements within which those interests could be achieved.

India's diplomatic approach was thus a kind of "institutional realpolitik." Without enough guns or butter to qualify as a major power, it used multilateral venues to level the playing field, promote desired norms, and boost its influence in world politics. Indian leaders subscribed to the view that skilful and assertive diplomacy can help a state punch above its weight, that their own rigorously selected civil servants had the skills to do so, and that their experience as anti-colonial vanguards put them in a position to lead the Global South. Officials in New Delhi saw institutions as important spaces for norm incubation but were well aware that the norms that hatched and took flight depended largely on a competitive political process. India thus used—and has continued to use—liberal institutional venues, norms, and rhetoric in the service of a foreign policy rooted largely in national interests.

India also tried to use triangular leverage to guard its independence and improve its standing. Adopting a relatively neutral position among stronger powers was one way that India—like many developing countries—sought to avoid subservience to a superpower patron, maintain relative autonomy, and increase diplomatic and economic leverage by playing off the superpowers. This strategy merged to a considerable extent with India's institutional agenda, as Nehru spearheaded initiatives to advance the political and economic interests of developing countries. These include the Non-Aligned Movement (NAM), which Nehru helped to establish in 1955, and the G-77, founded in 1964 to influence UN policies.

Nehru expected that non-alignment would deliver material benefits to India by helping the country avoid exploitation and by prompting rival great powers to vie for influence on the subcontinent. He also believed that Third World solidarity would help the country enjoy secure relations with neighbours and enable it to devote resources to national development strategies instead of military uses. Indeed, India enjoyed economic support from both Washington and Moscow during the early years, and China and India had something of a honeymoon period in the 1950s. As strategic divides hardened, however, India's refusal to take sides and reap the military rewards of an alliance left it acutely vulnerable. India's policies under Nehru tended to emphasize norms over firepower. They raised India's international profile but did little to address the country's hard power deficit.

The humiliating 1962 defeat in the war against China shattered Nehru's faith inThirdWorld cohesion and encouraged India to refocus attention on military capabilities and increase reliance on the USSR. China's nuclear tests and the 1965 war against Pakistan—a friend of the PRC and a treaty ally of the United States—drew further attention to India's military weakness. The looming threat of another war with Pakistan in 1971 finally pushed India decidedly away from its avowed policy of non-alignment and into an informal alliance with the USSR, a relationship fortified by the clear American "tilt toward Pakistan" during the Indo-Pakistani conflict.

Suffering Sluggish Growth, 1971-1990

As Indo-Soviet ties solidified, officials in New Delhi redoubled their efforts to build military strength through the development of nuclear weapons. For some, the nuclear program was a means to counterbalance the Chinese bomb. Nehru's daughter,"Prime Minister Indira Gandhi, also believed nuclear weapons were the key to achieving great-power status.

The 1974 "Smiling Buddha" test at Pokhran—India's first test explosion of a nuclear device—certainly helped, but it did not catapult India onto the world stage as officials in New Delhi might have hoped. Rather, it resulted in ostracism, as the United States led the establishment of a forty-five member Nuclear Suppliers Group for legitimized nuclear powers and pointedly excluded India.

India's conventional armed forces developed only sluggishly during the period. The breakup of Pakistan (and birth of Bangladesh) in 1971 had left India the dominant military force in South Asia, and Soviet arms helped India sustain its lead over Pakistan and likely helped to deter further Chinese advances. However, India's resources remained limited, and many of the weapons sent by the USSR were outdated. Consequently, India was able to maintain an army that could defeat Pakistan but had little strategic reach and influence beyond its immediate borders, and it would be no match for China.

Although close ties to Moscow helped fortify India's external security, they did little for India's stunted economy, which would likely have been better served by orienting toward the West and plugging more fully into capitalist channels of trade and finance. In that sense, a pro-Soviet tilt frustrated India's great-power aspirations over the medium term. An autarkic economic model and "license raj"—the pejorative label applied to India's heavy-handed bureaucracy—severely constrained the country's growth. The interests of a powerful civil service were partly responsible, but a desire to avoid dependency on Western capitalist powers also helps explain why Indian leaders allowed statist principles and red tape to suffocate the economy. The Indian government began to liberalize and boost growth in the late 1980s, but dire poverty and industrial weakness remained albatrosses to the government's foreign policy aspirations.

Politically, India continued to emphasize anti-imperialism in the NAM and other forums. Severe economic problems in India and other parts of the Third World during the 1970s led to an increasing focus on principles of distributive justice as the "north" raced ahead economically, leaving developing states even further behind. India was a leading member of the G-24—set up in 1971 as an unofficial shadow IMF board for developing countries—and a key driver of the movement for a "New International Economic Order" in the 1970s and 1980s. Naturally, India's anti-imperial push and pro-Soviet tilt had political drawbacks as well, contributing to India's second-class status in Western-led institutions and clubs. In short, India's Cold War experience showed the difficulty of pursuing several strategic goals—autonomy, security, development, and status—in a dangerous and polarized international environment. It also reinforced the difficulty of achieving any of those aims without the benefit of strong raw capabilities.

Repositioning and Revitalizing, 1991-2000

The end of the Cold War brought about a profound shift in Indian domestic and foreign policy. The economic reforms that began under then Finance Minister Manmohan Singh in 1991 were the most decisive turning point in the country's effort to build great-power capabilities. The end of the Cold War brought serious economic and security challenges to India and essentially shocked the country into liberalization. Economically, the 1991 Gulf War led to a spike in oil prices and led India's fragile economy into a balance-of-payments crisis. At the same time, the loss of Soviet military support left India vulnerable from a security standpoint. To secure an IMF rescue package, repair relations with Washington, and plug into a globalizing economy that was leaving it behind, India undertook a series of economic reforms that began to unlock the country's potential. The decision to plug into the global economy indeed helped India begin to mend fences with the United States after decades of relative estrangement. Growth during the 1990s also put India in a position to devote more resources to defense. This was crucial to India's emergence as a great-power candidate, because a great power cannot be built easily on the back of a frail economy.

Regionally, India worked during the 1990s to develop leadership in South Asia. That effort was best encapsulated in the "Gujral Doctrine" developed by Prime Minister Inder Kumar Gujral in the 1990s, which laid out a series of core principles for South Asian regional relations, including accommodative Indian policy toward much smaller states, non-interference in neighbours' political affairs, a respect for territorial integrity, and a commitment to peaceful dispute resolution. Indian leaders also sought with limited success to exercise leadership by promoting trade liberalization and confidence-building measures through the South Asian Association for Regional Cooperation (SAARC), a regional institution founded in 1985.

In multilateral diplomacy, India remained broadly committed to multilateralism and the interests of the Global South. Its leaders continued to work assiduously to develop institutional clout at the United Nations, largely by mobilizing diplomatic coalitions in the General Assembly, often to oppose or counteract Western initiatives and to make up for India's lack of a vote on the Security Council. In fact, even in the decade following the end of *leaders continued to position* the Cold War, India voted against the United States in the General Assembly more often than Cuba. Indian leaders continued to position themselves as chiefs of the "outsiders." Thus, even when India has not had direct interests at stake, it has often sought to mobilize "Third World" coalitions. Its opposition to Western-led interventions in Iraq, Kosovo, East Timor, and elsewhere can be viewed partly through this lens. Despite stronger growth and a thawing relationship with the United States, India's aspirations for recognition as a major power continued to be frustrated. New Delhi's "Pokhran II tests" of nuclear weapons in 1998 were a turning point in the country's effort to gain that recognition. More about demanding attention and respect than meeting any military necessity, they reflected both India's mounting aspirations and a continuing streak of defiant independence in its foreign policy. Foreign Minister Jaswant Singh referred to the tests as an escape from "nuclear apartheid."

The Pokhran II episode quickly resulted in a new wave of sanctions—which temporarily set back India's great-power quest—but ultimately appears to have had the desired effect. As India awoke economically and as Cold War tensions receded into history, New Delhi began to draw more serious attention from major capitals—especially Washington. The relatively even-handed U.S. response to the 1999 Kargil crisis, in which Pakistani forces moved across the Line of Control in Kashmir, was a key pivot in Indo-U.S. relations. President Bill Clinton demanded a Pakistani withdrawal and helped broker an end to the fighting, suggesting to Indian officials that the United States was not irrevocably committed to siding with Islamabad in a crisis.

Becoming a Key "Swing State," 2001-2010

Over the past decade, India has arguably made better progress on its great-power quest than in any previous period and has been better able to advance its core foreign policy objectives. It has done so by continuing to grow its economy, pursuing rapprochement with the United States, and keeping ties open to other major powers, which enables New Delhi to reap the rewards of status as a key swing state.

Enhancing Capabilities

Perhaps the leading driver of India's progress toward great-power status this decade has been its robust economic growth; a general consensus exists across Indian political parties on the centrality of economic growth to the country's great-power aspirations. Former Finance Minister P. Chidambaram said in 2007 that, "India is not respected because it has acquired the capacity to launch rockets or satellites, or because of the size of its population...The world respects India because of its capacity to emerge as an economic powerhouse." Since 2002, India has enjoyed an average annual real GDP growth of roughly 8 percent, one of the highest in the world. The country's dynamic high-tech sector and entrepreneurial successes have also encouraged investment and fed expectations of future growth. The vestiges of India's state-controlled economy were blessings in disguise during the Asian financial crisis in the late 1990s, and although India suffered in the crisis of 2007-2009, it has rebounded well.

After decades of a relatively closed economy, India still lacks global economic impact commensurate with its size. For example, its total external trade still falls well short of Taiwan's—a country with roughly one-fiftieth its population. Infrastructure bottlenecks also threaten to choke off future growth.

As the poverty and inequality remain major problems, challenging the credibility of India's great-power aspirations at home and abroad. India's economy has not arrived at the great-power level yet, though its trajectory is broadly positive.

The same can be said of India's military. The challenges it faces are considerable. Tensions with China and Pakistan continue to simmer on land and at sea. India's efforts to cultivate influence in Kabul to contain Pakistani influence have generated an uptick in tensions between the old adversaries, and the possibility of a U.S. withdrawal from Afghanistan could further complicate India's regional relations.

However, greater aggregate wealth has helped India build its hardpower capabilities, with military expenditures rising by approximately 350 percent in nominal terms between 1999 and 2009 and including purchases of more high-end systems. India has long had one of the world's largest armed forces in terms of personnel; in recent years its quality has also improved.

Economic openness and a stronger military have helped India develop triangular leverage more effectively. During the Cold War, India lacked the independent power capabilities to make a decisive difference in the systemic balance of power at that stage. As growing capabilities put it on the map as a major power, its influence as a potential swing state has risen. Further, financial and trade ties have facilitated rapprochement with the United States and, to a lesser extent, with China. India's two-way trade with the United States has grown from less than USD 15 billion in 2000 to a projected USD 50 billion in 2010, and its trade with China has exploded from a mere USD 2 billion to nearly USD 60 billion over the same period.

Mending Ties with the United States

Rapprochement with the United States has been at the centre of India's recent approach to building capabilities and clout. Shared counterterrorism concerns after September 11 helped solidify the new Indo-U.S. partnership. The United States dropped the post-Pokhran sanctions, and India entered into more substantial defense arrangements with the United States and its Asia-Pacific allies. The expanded annual *Malabar* naval exercises are perhaps the most noteworthy indication. They began bilaterally in 1992 in the western Indian Ocean but now include Australia, Japan, and Singapore, and feature war games in the Bay of Bengal, closer to the crucial Straits of Malacca. They constitute a major way in which India is trying to secure its own naval environs as China develops a blue-water fleet.

Indo-U.S. rapprochement also paved the way toward a series of arms deals and the headline civil-nuclear agreement. U.S. officials came to see India as a key swing state in the international system and hoped that it would become an informal ally vis-à-vis China, a stalwart supporter of the campaign against terrorism, and a possible partner in advancing the spread of democracy. Indian leaders used that perception to their advantage, especially after the start of George W. Bush's second term in 2005. The civil-nuclear deal arguably knocked down one of the most salient impediments to India's accession to great-power status. The deal was not easily sold in India given the country's longstanding commitment to an autonomous foreign policy. After decades of mutual estrangement, Indian parties on both the left and right raised significant domestic political resistance to what Jaswant Singh called "strategic subservience" to the United States. Nevertheless, the deal survived, and India was the primary immediate beneficiary. It helped usher India into the club of legitimate nuclear powers (albeit through the back door), it led to similar pacts with other states to develop civil nuclear technology, and it helped quench some of the Indian economy's growing appetite for energy. India's tilt toward the United States has not revolutionized its raw capabilities, but it has helped at the margins and has increased expectations about India's potential for future economic and military expansion.

The desire for autonomy remains a core Indian priority, however, and New Delhi has by no means pursued ties with the United States alone. Instead, it has returned to the policy Nehru advocated in the early Cold War era of seeking triangular leverage through multidirectional partnerships. Thus, as it became closer to the United States on issues related to defense and counterterrorism, India was also able to strengthen bonds elsewhere. Indo-Russian ties have rebounded since the conclusion of a "strategic partnership" in 2000. Moscow is again India's dominant arms supplier, swapping obsolete Soviet-era hardware for modern equipment, and in recent years the two countries have concluded a number of pacts for military, technical, and economic cooperation. India's trade with China is booming despite residual distrust in thc New Delhi defense establishment. In 2005, India became an observer to the Shanghai Cooperation Organization, a group led by China and Russia that is focused on transnational threats in Central Asia.

India's loose alignment with the United States has not come entirely without constraints on policy autonomy. For example, India's relative restraint in opposing the U.S.-led war in Iraq reflected a degree of accommodation of U.S. interests. India has also taken a more neutral line on Iran's nuclear program. New Delhi originally opposed sanctions, but its cordial ties with Tehran—fostered largely to secure energy resources and reduce reliance on pipelines through Pakistan—have ruffled feathers in Washington. It is unclear whether India will support the U.S. position when it assumes a rotating Security Council seat in January 2011. On other issues, India has shown a clearer willingness to assert its autonomy from Washington. For example, seeing economic opportunities and fearing instability or excessive Chinese influence in neighboring Myanmar, India has resisted U.S. calls for tighter sanctions. India has also refused periodic U.S. requests that it sign the Nuclear Non-Proliferation and Comprehensive Test Ban treaties.

Pursuing Reforms in International Institutions

India's independent streak has been even more manifest in its continued approach to international institutions, and a stronger economy has supported a larger role for India in multilateral talks. India was the leading champion of the poor-country cause in the World Trade Organization (WTO), it spearheaded opposition to wealthy states' agricultural subsidies during the Doha Round, and it has been perhaps the most important state in resisting the Western trade liberalization agenda. Its role has been much maligned in first-world capitals—Commerce Minister Kamal Nath is often accused of sinking the Doha Round—but India was able to cast a large shadow by leading the emerging world opposition. India has also remained a strident critic of the governance of the IMF and multilateral development banks (although it is a major customer of the latter) and a loud proponent of the need for UN Security Council reform.

India's positions are partly attributable to normative convictions but also reflect an effort to maintain credibility as a leader of the NAM and the Global South. By speaking for developing countries, India can enjoy importance vis-à-vis the great powers that it lacks in the context of unequal bilateral relationships. India can become something of an alternative power centre in negotiations. Multilateral groups and institutions also offer a way for India to amass influence even before it achieves bona fide great-power capabilities. India's greatest recent success in building multilateral clout has come through the G-20, which has emerged from its humble 1999 beginnings as the G-7's weaker sibling to play a more central role in the international economic system. Indian leaders have also been invited as guests to some recent G-8 meetings and have risen in the unofficial pecking order that determines the meeting calendars of senior great-power officials on the sidelines of major multilateral gatherings.

India has also had recent success building clout at the Bretton Woods institutions. India has long been underrepresented at the IMF, World Bank, and Asian Development Bank (ADB) in terms of its capital contribution (and thus voting power). Its capital share at the IMF actually dipped from 1.95 percent to 1.91 percent—a share smaller than Belgium's—in the 2006 round of IMF quota reform, which then Finance Minister P. Chidambaram called "hopelessly flawed." However, in October 2010, the G-20 reached agreement on major reforms to the IMF's governance structure. In November, the IMF announced that it will give emerging powers greater weight and make India the Fund's eighth-largest shareholder, with 2.75 percent. This change, which could presage similar reforms in the World Bank and ADB, represents a significant institutional step for India, marking it more clearly as a major power.

Permanent membership on the UN Security Council—which one scholar calls "the holy grail of Indian foreign policy"—remains elusive. It would require amending the UN Charter, which would mean winning a two-thirds vote in the General Assembly and the approval of all five permanent members. India received a much-coveted U.S. endorsement *"the* in November 2010, when President Barack Obama visited the Indian parliament and said: "in the years ahead, I look forward to a reformed United Nations Security Council that includes India as a permanent member." The United Kingdom, France, and Russia have also supported New Delhi. China has been the most wary permanent member, but took a cautious half-step toward supporting India's bid in May 2010 when Chinese Premier Wen Jiabao said that he "supports India's aspiration for a greater role in the UN, particularly the [Security Council]." Foreign Ministry spokesman Hong Lei repeated similar language in response to questions about President Obama's statement of support in November, leaving China's exact position unclear.

Despite recent progress, India faces an uphill climb for a permanent seat. Reform will require difficult deal-making that involves the G-4 candidates (India, Germany, Japan, and Brazil) and aspirants from Africa and elsewhere. Any proposals for change will likely face considerable opposition. Pakistan has already sought to block India's bid, working with large countries such as Italy, South Korea, and Argentina under the rubric of "Uniting for Consensus" to oppose a deal that would empower their respective G-4 neighbours. In addition to concerns about specific candidates and regional representation, at least a few members have expressed fears about lost efficiency and effectiveness if the Council becomes too large. Given these concerns, Indian accession to the permanent members' club seems relatively unlikely in the short term.

At the regional level, India has also made some progress. It is the natural leader of SAARC, but that organization continues to underperform in the context of the ongoing feud between its two largest members (India and Pakistan). India has plugged eagerly into Asian institutions, joining the ASEAN Regional Forum in 1996 and the East Asia Summit in 2006, and has launched a bid to join the Asia-Pacific Economic Cooperation (APEC) forum, thus far without success. As in global institutions, India is encountering some regional headwinds despite its rising capabilities, as existing regional leaders—especially China—remain cautious about welcoming New Delhi into the fold.

In sum, India has pursued its three basic strategies quite effectively over the past ten years. In a period of relative peace among the great powers, it has been able to diversify its defense linkages as well as economic and diplomatic linkages. Doing so has helped India build capabilities and establish itself as a key "swing state" in the eyes of the U.S. government and others. Identification as a pivotal state helped admission to one of the key clubs that defines great-power status: the club of legitimate nuclear powers. At the same time, India has managed to pursue an international agenda that often runs directly counter to U.S. preferences in the WTO, the Bretton Woods institutions, the United Nations, and elsewhere.

Looking Forward

India's recent policy approach has performed well at building capabilities and influence and at advancing the country's core foreign policy goals. For the first period since early in its independent history, India enjoys friendly relations with almost all major powers. By trading on its potential as a swing state, India has obtained significant gains in status and security from the United States without major concessions in autonomy. It has also lifted millions out of poverty and raised its international profile. Nevertheless, India's road to great-power status is not complete. The country's significant challenges have been noted. Growth has not ended the problem of poverty; military modernization has occurred in the context of new security challenges; New Delhi faces new constraints on its policy choices; and India has not been granted full admission to the inner institutional sanctums of the great-power club.

MODERNISATION PLANS OF THE INDIAN ARMY

Despite the army leadership's best efforts, the ongoing Revolution in Military Affairs (RMA) had, till recently, almost completely bypassed the Indian Army. For well over a decade the army's efforts to modernise had been thwarted due to political neglect and lack of adequate budgetary support. The funds made available for modernisation are extremely limited and a large portion of these funds is surrendered year after year. For Financial Year 2006-07, a sum of Rs 3,000 crore was surrendered as unspent. The fact that 155 mm ammunition for the Bofors howitzer had to be imported from South Africa during the Kargil conflict in 1999 tells its own tale of persistent shortages. Had the conflict not been confined to the 150 km frontage of the Kargil sector, T-72 and 130 mm medium gun ammunition too would have run short and it would have been politically embarrassing for the government as well as the army. In the plains the army would have had to fight with obsolete Vijayant tanks and several other vintage equipment that were unsuitable for combat. However, sustained efforts by Army HQ have now borne fruit and the army's modernisation drive is once again well underway.

In the prevailing era of strategic uncertainty, while terrorism has become the primary threat, the external and internal threats and challenges faced by India are such that a large army is still required to be maintained. Also, a high degree of preparation and operational readiness is still necessary as conventional war, though improbable, cannot be categorically ruled out. At the same time, heavy capital investments in modern defence equipment are undoubtedly a drain on a developing economy that is ill-equipped to handle the burgeoning defence expenditure. Several eminent analysts have recommended that qualitative upgradation should be accompanied by quantitative downsizing of personnel strength of the army. However, given its responsibilities for border management and the manpower-intensive low intensity conflict that the army is involved in, this is easier said than done.

Future conventional conflict on the Indian sub-continent will in all probability result from the ongoing low-intensity limited war on the Line of Control (LoC) with Pakistan or the unresolved territorial and boundary dispute with China and will be predominantly a land conflict. The Indian Army seriously lacks a potent firepower punch, especially in the mountain sector. Precision-guided munitions (PGMs) have still to enter service in numbers large enough to make a real difference. The reconnaissance, surveillance and target acquisition (RSTA) assets necessary for the optimum exploitation of even the existing firepower assets are grossly inadequate. Automated command and control and decision support systems have been on the drawing boards for several decades but are yet to mature.

In a future conventional war that will be fought under the nuclear shadow, manoeuvre will be extremely limited. This restriction will lead to much greater emphasis being placed on firepower to achieve the laid down military aim. Hence, it is imperative that artillery modernisation is undertaken with alacrity so as to generate firepower asymmetries on the future battlefield. After a long spell of keeping the powder dry, action on modernisation of the Indian artillery is livening up once again. Since January 2008, the Ministry of Defence (MoD) has issued three global tenders for 155mm guns and howitzers for the mountains, the plains and self-propelled guns for the deserts. Summer and winter trials are expected to be held over the next one year and, red tape permitting, contracts may be awarded as early as in the first half of 2010.

Artillery firepower had paved the way for victory during the Kargil conflict. Despite the lessons learnt in Kargil, modernisation of the artillery had continued to lag behind. The last major acquisition of towed gun-howitzers was that of about 400 pieces of 39-calibre 155mm FH-77B howitzers form Bofors of Sweden in the mid-1980s. This gun had proved its mettle in the Kargil conflict.

Just when a contract for 120 tracked and 180 wheeled self-propelled (SP) 155mm guns was about to be concluded after years of protracted trials, South African arms manufacturer Denel, a leading contender for the contract, was alleged to have been involved in a corruption scam in an earlier deal for anti-material rifles (AMRs). The other two howitzers in contention, from Soltam of Israel and BAE (Bofors) of Sweden did not meet the laid down criteria according to the COAS and Army HQ recommended fresh trials, setting the programme back at least three to four years. Another key issue was that the howitzers that had been offered were technology demonstration models and not guns that were in actual service with the home country armies.

The probability of the next conventional war breaking out in the mountains is far higher than that of a war in the plains. With this in view, the artillery recently conceptualised a requirement for a light-weight towed howitzer of 155mm calibre for employment in the mountains. Neither the present Bofors howitzer nor its replacement will be capable of operations in the mountains. A light-weight 45-calibre 155mm howitzer weighing less than 5,000 kg, with a light but adequately powered prime mover, is ideal for the mountains. The gun-train should be capable of negotiating sharp road bends without the need to unhook the gun from the prime mover. The two British 45-calibre 155mm howitzers that competed for the US contract for a similar howitzer some years ago – the UFH (Ultra-lightweight Field Howitzer) and the LTH (Light-weight Towed Howitzer) – could be considered for licensed production with transfer of technology.

In January 2008, the MoD floated a Request for Proposal (RfP) for 140 pieces of ultra-light 39 calibre 155mm towed howitzers for use by the Indian Army's mountain formations and, presumably, by its rapid reaction divisions – as and when these are raised as it will be easy to transport by air. 140 howitzers will be adequate to equip seven medium artillery regiments and will cost approximately Rs 3,000 crore. The RfP has been reportedly issued to UK's BAE Systems (which now owns Bofors), for the M777 howitzer claimed to be the lightest in the world at under 4,220 kg, and to Singapore Technologies for the Pegasus SLWH.

India has floated a global tender for the purchase of 400 155mm towed artillery guns for the Army, to be followed by indigenous manufacture of another 1,100 howitzers, in a project worth a whopping Rs 8,000 crore. The RFP was issued to eight prospective bidders including BAE, General Dynamics, Nexter (France), Rhinemetall (Germany) and Samsung (South Korea). An RfP has also been issued for 180 wheeled self-propelled guns for around Rs 4,700 crore for employment by mechanised forces in the plains and semi-desert sectors. Since the Bofors 155mm Howitzer was introduced into service, the indigenously designed and manufactured 105 mm Indian Field Gun (IFG) and its (not so) light version, the Light Field Gun (LFG), have joined the 75/24 Indian Mountain Gun, the 100mm Russian field gun and the 122mm Russian howitzer on the obsolescence list. Approximately 180 pieces of 130mm M46 Russian medium guns have been successfully "up-gunned" to 155mm calibre with ordnance supplied by Soltam of Israel. The new barrel length of 45 calibres has enhanced the range of the gun to about 40 km with extended range ammunition.

A contract for the acquisition of two regiments of the 12-tube, 300mm Smerch multi-barrel rocket launcher (MBRL) system with 90 km range was reported to have been signed with Russia's Rosoboronexport in early-2006. This will be a major boost for the long-range firepower capabilities of the army. If this weapon system had been available during the Kargil conflict, Pakistan's brigade HQ and forward airfield at Skardu and other targets deep inside POK could have been hit with impunity. Extended range (ER) rockets are being introduced for the 122 mm Grad MBRL that has been in service for over three decades. The ER rockets will enhance the weapon system's range from 22 to about 40 km. A Rs 5,000 crore contract has also been signed for the serial production of the Pinaka MBRL weapon system, another DRDO project plagued by time delays and completed with help from Larsen and Toubro and the Tatas.

The modernisation plan of tube artillery alone is likely to cost Rs 13,000 crore. The major acquisitions will be of initial lots of 400 towed howitzers of 155mm calibre, with a barrel length of 52 calibres, costing about Rs 4,000 crore, 140 ultra-light weight 155mm towed howitzers, with a barrel length of 45 calibres, costing Rs 3,000 crore and 180 SP 155mm howitzers costing Rs 5,000 crore. The "Shakti" project for a command and control systems for the artillery, called Artillery Combat Command and Control System (ACCCS), has reached the stage of maturity and is now being fielded up to the regimental level.

The BrahMos supersonic cruise missile (Mach 2.8 to 3.0), with a precision strike capability, very high kill energy and range of 290 km, was inducted into the army in July 2007. It is a versatile missile that can be launched from TATRA mobile launchers and silos on land, aircraft and ships and, perhaps in future, also from submarines. Fifty BrahMos missiles are expected to be produced every year. Efforts are underway to further increase its strike range. BrahMos Aerospace has orders worth Rs 3,500 crore from the army and the navy, which has opted for the anti-ship as well as the land attack cruise missile (LACM) versions. These terrain hugging missiles are virtually immune to counter measures due to their high speed and very low radar cross section and are far superior to sub-sonic cruise missiles like Pakistan's Babur. Chile, Kuwait, Malaysia and South Africa have shown interest in acquiring this missile.

The Indian army is extensively engaged in ongoing internal security (IS) and counter-insurgency operations (CI) and simultaneously needs to prepare itself for a future border conflict that may spill over to a larger conventional war in the plains. In keeping with these twin requirements, Army HQ have apparently decided to upgrade the IS and CI capabilities of infantry battalions as well as enhance their Infantry firepower-mobility-EW (electronic warfare) punch for a possible war in the plains against Pakistan or in the mountains against China. The Army Chief's modernisation vision is to "adapt to high-end technology, improve night-fighting capability... (and) information technology, information warfare and network centric warfare."

Despite its large-scale employment on border management and extensive commitments in Internal Security and Counter Insurgency operations, infantry modernisation had been languishing for several decades when the Ministry of Defence (MoD) finally cleared a visionary plan to modernise the army's infantry battalions by according "in principle" approval in the form of Modification 4B to the war establishment (WE) of a standard infantry battalion in 1998. However, no funds were specially sanctioned for this purpose till the BJP-led NDA government approved the expenditure of Rs 3,500 crore in September 2003. Thereafter, approval had to be sought on file for each new weapon system or piece of equipment on a "case-by-case" basis as has become the norm. It is by now well-known how each such case chronicles the saga of an uphill struggle to get approval first from the MoD, then MoD (Finance) and, finally, the Ministry of Finance (MoF). All this is only possible after the DRDO has first certified that the weapon system or equipment in question cannot be developed and manufactured indigenously and such a certificate is hard to come by.

While 250 Kornet-E anti-tank guided missiles (ATGMs) with thermal imaging sights have substantially increased the anti-tank capability of infantry battalions, most efforts to modernise the equipment held by infantry and Rashtriya Rifles (RR) units are aimed at enhancing their capability for surveillance and target acquisition at night and boosting their firepower for precise retaliation against infiltrating columns and terrorists holed up in built-up areas. About 200 hand-held BFSRs with practical ranges up to seven to eight km where clear line of sight is available, 2,000 hand-held thermal imaging devices (HHTIs) with ranges up to 2,000 metres for observation at night and stand-alone infra-red, seismic and acoustic sensors with varying capabilities have enabled infantrymen to dominate the Line of Control so completely that infiltration has come down to almost a trickle.

The newly acquired weapons, which complement these surveillance and observation devices, include: 1,500x84 mm rocket launchers, including some disposable ones; 1,000 AMRs (anti-material rifles); 8,000 UBGLs (under-barrel grenade launchers); 4,000 new generation carbines; 300 bullet proof vehicles; and, several hundred accurate sniper rifles. However, the numbers acquired and the ammunition stocks are still inadequate and need to be made up more rapidly. While the INSAS 5.56 mm assault rifles have now been in service for almost 10 years and proved to be effective, the light machine gun (LNG) version is still facing teething problems and the carbine version for close quarter battle has not found favour with the army. New 5.56 mm assault rifles of bull-pup design with an integrated laser range finder and grenade launcher are under development. Efforts are also being made to provide infantry platoons and sections with integrated GPS-based navigation system, secure light-weight walkie-talkie radio sets and better protective gear with a helmet that incorporates a built-in head-up display.

The mechanised infantry is now equipped with the BMP-2 ICV Sarath of which over 1,000 have been built since 1987. A new variant is the 81 mm Carrier Mortar Tracked Vehicle (CMTV) that is based on the chassis of the Sarath ICV and has been indigenously developed to enhance the integral firepower available to mechanised infantry battalions. Other variants include a command post, an ambulance, armoured dozer and engineer and reconnaissance vehicles. Mechanised reconnaissance and support battalions need better surveillance radars, fire-and-forget ATGMs and effective night fighting capability. However, their capabilities can be upgraded on a lower priority compared with infantry battalions that are engaged in border management and IS/CI operations.

The army's infantry battalions also need their own mini or micro UAVs like Elbit's Skylark or Rafael's Skylite, among others, to partly reduce the extent of patrolling necessary in internal security environment and to improve their surveillance capability in conventional conflict. These UAVs should have a range of about 10 to 15 km, should be light-weight (less than 10 kg), hand-launched, carry a single payload, e.g. a daylight video camera or infra-red camera for night operations, and should be inexpensive enough to be dispensable. A mini ground control station should be authorized at battalion HQ for planning and control. Ideally, these should be indigenously designed and developed and locally manufactured.

A new DRDO project, that is reported to be ongoing, aims to equip future soldiers with lightweight force multipliers. Soldiers of the future will have miniaturised communication and GPS systems, small power packs, weapon platforms and smart vests with fibre-optic sensors. The soldiers will also have better and lighter combat fatigues, boots, belts, ammunition pouches, rucksacks and rations in the form of meals-ready-to-eat. Though somewhat akin to the US Army's Land Warrior programme, the Indian Army programme for modernisation of infantry battalions will result in only incremental changes. However, these would be significant enough to make a difference on the battlefields of the Indian sub-continent. The infantryman's average combat load is approximately 27 kg, including the 3.06 kg 5.56 mm INSAS assault rifle and its "on weapon" ammunition. If this can be reduced by even a few kg, it will enable the soldier to improve his agility in battle and counter-insurgency operations. Ultimately an infantryman has to be prepared to engage in hand-to-hand combat and agility can make a difference between life and death.

For over 350 infantry battalions, plus about 150 Rashtriya Rifles, Assam Rifles and Territorial Army battalions, these major changes will be extremely costly to implement and will spill over at least 10 to 12 years – that is, if the funds can be found. What is certain is that there is no alternative to making the financial commitment that is necessary to enhance the operational capabilities of the army's infantry battalions. Without modernising this cutting edge of its sword, the army will soon begin to resemble the armies of India's lesser neighbours.

The indigenously designed Arjun main battle tank (MBT) has been in the pipeline for over two decades. Though the tank has many good features, it has consistently failed to meet the army's GSQR for an MBT and orders have been placed for only 124 tanks to be manufactured. The lack of progress on the Arjun MBT had slowed down the pace of armour modernisation. India then signed a deal with Russia to acquire 310 T-90S tanks in the year 2000. Subsequently, India began to assemble these tanks at Avadi. It has recently been reported that in addition to these, India has decided to acquire another 347 T-90S tanks and assemble them within the country.

The first Indian assembled T-90S (Bhishma) rolled off the production line on January 8, 2004. While T-90S Russian tanks have provided new teeth to India's strike formations in the plains and corrected the imbalance that had resulted from

Pakistan's acquisition of T-80 UD from Ukraine and the Al Khalid tanks jointly designed with China, a large number of T-72 (Ajeya) tanks are still awaiting modernisation. The lack of a suitable fire control system and night fighting capability are major handicaps. As soon as the obsolescent Vijayanta tanks are phased out of service, it will be time to also discard the old T-55s as well as they can no longer be either upgraded or modernised. Armour modernisation is now proceeding apace and can be classified as a success story.

The air defence (AD) of mechanised forces is another area that is crying for attention. The Kvadrat missile system that has been the backbone of AD for strike formations since the early 1970s are now ageing and need urgent replacement. With the DRDO's indigenous Akash medium-range and Trishul short-range missile projects not making major headway, it is time to start looking at import substitutes. In fact, the assets of Army Air Defence corps of the army are grossly inadequate to provide effective protection against enemy aircraft during war. This young corps requires substantial capital infusion to really come into its own.

Another DRDO project that is way behind schedule is the Nag anti-tank missile system. The antiquated Jonga-mounted SS-11 B1 anti-tank guided missile (ATGM) system has been replaced in missile battalions by MILAN shoulder-fired ATGMs. However, a vehicle-mounted missile system like the Nag is definitely necessary for reconnaissance and attrition tasks. The experimental Plan AREN tactical communications system for strike formations needs early replacement. The ability to carry broadband data needs to be enhanced in particular. Even the more recent static communications network called ASCON lacks ISDN capability for the real-time transmission of maps and streaming video.

While some Stentor long-range BFSRs have been in service for over a decade, medium-range radars are still to be acquired. At least about 30 to 40 weapon locating radars (WLRs) are required for effective counter-bombardment, especially in the plains, and only a few have been procured so far. Israeli

Searcher-I unmanned aerial vehicles (UAVs) have been introduced into service but these are few in number and it will be a long time before these will really make a difference by providing a real-time surveillance capability so that ground forces can initiate action even as a fresh input is received. Only a small number of Searcher – II UAVs, with an upper ceiling that makes them suitable for the mountains, have been acquired.

An automated command and control and decision support system for use by the General Staff is still a far cry and so are supporting systems like the battlefield surveillance system and air space management system. The urgent requirement of real-time satellite reconnaissance systems has still not been accepted despite the nuclear overhang under which the armed forces now operate. Even though the cameras on India's remote sensing and cartographic satellites now have sharply enhanced resolutions, less than one metre, military-grade photographs of still better resolution are needed to be purchased from the open market. These sources may dry up quickly during war.

A "system of systems" approach must be followed so that scarce RSTA and communications resources can be synergistically configured and optimally exploited. The war in Iraq fought in March-April 2003 was based on the concept of "network-centric warfare" in which surveillance sensors, targeting systems and "shooters" are fused together in a seamless "system of systems" that reduced response time between the acquisition of a target and its destruction to 15 to 20 minutes. While such a system may take over a decade to establish, a beginning must be made right away.

PGMs are increasingly gaining currency as weapons of choice in conflict on land, both to accurately destroy critical hard targets quickly as well as to avoid or at least minimise collateral damage. During the Gulf War I in 1991, despite all the CNN-generated hype of smart bombs flying unerringly through ventilators, PGMs formed less than 10 percent of the total high explosive dropped over Iraq and were rather inaccurate. The "collateral" destruction of an air raid shelter harbouring women and children has been too well documented to bear recounting. The coalition forces did not destroy a single Iraqi Scud missile launcher. In Kosovo, PGMs accounted for about 30 per cent of the ordnance dropped and accuracies had improved considerably by 1999. In the post-September 11, 2001 retribution inflicted on the Taliban militia and its al Qaeda supporters in Afghanistan, the share of PGMs had risen to nearly 60 percent. In Gulf War II in Iraq, the ratio of PGMs went up to nearly 70 per cent. The Indian artillery does not have any PGMs worth the name. Only limited quantities of the Russian Krasnopol PGM have been imported for the Bofors 155 mm howitzer. Among others, the Bofors Bonus PGM is a suitable candidate, subject to successful trials in the deserts and the mountains.

Finally, the approach to army modernisation must be more focused; the priorities must be clearly established and then adhered to. The government must give a firm commitment in terms of funds and the Ministry of Defence must streamline its procedures and processes for speedy procurement of high priority weapons and equipment. It is time to institute a rolling, non-lapsable defence modernisation fund of Rs. 25,000 crores as a viable method of ensuring that defence procurement is not subjected to the vagaries of annual budgets. The present situation is disturbing and, if allowed to go on indefinitely, will seriously compromise the army's preparedness to fight the next border war that inimical neighbours like Pakistan can be expected to thrust on India.

FUTURE OPPORTUNITIES

Shape of Things to Come

The most obvious and significant opportunity is already before us. I refer to the modernisation plan. Ideally, modernisation should be evolutionary and continuous. Yet, for a variety of reasons the IAF has in the past modernised in spurts, often as a reaction to circumstances. Today, the IAF is in throes of a most comprehensive modernisation, as I described earlier. We call it transformational, for it will change everything dramatically. Being based on long-term perspective plans, most of it is already crystallised.

Yet, a lot remains to be determined; many new capabilities are still short of the decision stage. At this juncture, if we are able to synchronise these plans with national security objectives, we would really have utilised this opportunity well. From that arises another opportunity that must be seized and that is the formal enunciation of long-term national security objectives, strategies, as well as technology roadmap and indigenisation strategies.

Much also depends upon the way aerospace power will develop in the future. Beyond the MMRCA and FGFA, with their 40 year 'lives', we are at 2060. It is not easy to guess the shape of aerospace power then. Would the accent shift to unmanned flight, to missiles; or would 'air' be more of 'space'. Technological advances are sure to revolutionise military affairs in future too.

Despite the unpredictabilities, it is certain that the need for 'application and transportability' of national power – hard and soft – and thus for aerospace power, with enhanced fundamentals, would remain. Nations that lack it will seek it, as also will non-state agencies. Aerospace power is bound to proliferate.

We also expect aerospace power to permeate the national security apparatus more completely, including for homeland security. IAF foresees greater specialisation; tailored capabilities for each occasion; an increased dependence on unmanned vehicles; greater accent on force enhancers; particularly the intangible ones, such as quality of people and their skills.

Networking and assimilation of space, both interdependent, are already the way forward and can tilt the balance considerably. A quiet 'space race' is the current reality and weaponisation, a distinct possibility.

Perhaps more than any other, it is air power that is most significantly enhanced by the integration of space-enabled capabilities, for there are essential similarities. Evolving into an aerospace force is thus a logical progression. But, it is getting crowded up there and we need to act fast. Certainly, 'space' empowers all, and the IAF supports tri-service initiatives. Yet, any fledgling capability requires residing in an appropriate 'parent capability'. Air Power, or the IAF, are the closest such 'capability', or organisation suitable to host and nurture 'military space'. India's rising status and acceptability are an opportunity for us to push for creating an adequate military space capability.

Since IAF requires a comprehensive capability, its future in the long-term, will largely mirror the future of aerospace power itself. Though this path is invariably influenced by leading nations, India and countries like it, must be selective and seek creative variations, both in terms of hardware and doctrine.

Outward Orientation

We have made mention of India's outward orientation and IAF's part in it. We find that our international interactions are increasing. Leading nations want to engage us and probably seek to include us in their calculations. Smaller nations look up to us for support, assistance and training. UN commitments are also considerable. We could ignore these opportunities, or we could use them to build Indian influence, generate goodwill and reap multiple dividends.

Synergies

We now turn to synergies and jointness, which the IAF is convinced is the way forward. Just as every tool has a place in the toolbox, every discipline too has its own niche. At the edges of our competencies in complex tasks we often confront impossibilities or failure.

If we traverse the boundaries of our discipline into neighbouring or related ones, we can, in concert with them, achieve our aims. In other words, there are other organs of national power and we must learn to use them and interface with them effectively. Such synergy creates desired effects, perhaps at lesser cost and in quicker time. This calls for wisdom, knowledge of other disciplines and lack of parochialism. The future also brings with it the opportunity for creating synergies and national capabilities.

We feel, therefore, that the trick lies in perfecting internal core-competencies, identifying complimentary capabilities in other organisations, developing effective interfaces and training to create and employ a new, enhanced hybrid. We are convinced that such 'jointness' is the way forward and that core competencies of each Service, indeed of all organs of national power, must be synergised to generate the required effect and capability.

A capability-based approach from development to employment will encourage an inter-disciplinary integration and the coming together of all organs of national power. At the end, it is people that make an institution or system work. The best ones can be rendered ineffective for want of skills and commitment and vice-versa. Essentially, we believe jointness and synergy have less to do with new structures and ownership, but depends upon joint thinkers, planning, capability creations, as well as joint training and execution. Perhaps it is better to grow in an evolutionary manner.

Similarly, it is also imperative that military and civil aviation integrate, to take advantage of each others' capacities, for better efficiency, cost-effectiveness and for greater options. We have already made available 19 of our front-line air fields for civil air traffic and also allowed transit through Air Force controlled air space, to save time and fuel. IAF has also proposed the 'flexible use of air space'; and the process for integration of civil and AF radars has begun.

Beyond generating national synergies, aerospace technologies are so expensive, cutting-edge and hard to develop, that I dare say, our quest of these increasingly encourages joint-ventures and sharing of knowledge & resources between nations, and accord opportunity to forge international synergies.

Conclusion

Considerable changes are taking place in the global and regional scenario and in our neighbourhood. Old issues persist, while newer concerns are added. The role of military power has increased, as security concerns spread beyond national boundaries. Aerospace power is futuristic and increasingly utilitarian.

The IAF has come a long way and has demonstrated its professionalism and the world has acknowledged it. A strong and professional IAF can contribute to national options and to peace and stability, not only within the country but also within the region. It is a considered opinion that the IAF, with its current capability and plans has the potential to make a very significant impact on the postures we adopt in the future. IAF must therefore grow in step with nation.

7

Growth and Future of India Air Power Projection

India, along with China, is an emerging world power. For a long time India was more inward-looking and fixed on the conflict with Pakistan about Kashmir. As an emerging world power, India has its vital interests.

The protection of the supply flow of oil and gas from far away regions is one of India's most significant vital interests. Securing this supply is the aim and objective of political, diplomatic, economic and military actions. In the strategic triangle – China, India and the United States – hard power is an important currency in combination with elements of soft power. Concerning soft power India has a comparative advantage – e.g. its status as a democracy – in comparison to China. But India recognizes that it has to improve its hard power capabilities.

India's defence purchases should be seen as an essential part of the overall security environment that hinges on relations with Pakistan, China and America. The country is slated to spend US$100 billion in modernizing its defence forces over the next decade, with air power being a major component. Since 1999, India's military purchases have been worth US$25 billion; the country is likely to spend another $30 billion by 2012, making it one of the biggest military buyers amongst developing countries. In the last couple of years India, as the new US strategic partner in Asia to dilute the growing influence of

China has been sensitive to US urgings. One critical issue has been relations with Iran, with New Delhi taking a stand against Tehran at international forums. Awash with its new stature as "America's friend," New Delhi has been accused of deliberately delaying the US$7.5 billion, 1600 mile-long Iran-Pakistan-India (IPI) gas pipeline to keep Washington happy.

However, in the recent past the Congress Party-led New Delhi government headed by Prime Minister Manmohan Singh has stood up to the US on Iran, making an effort to emphasize an independent foreign policy not influenced by Washington's ideas.

Earlier this year in May, India hosted for a few hours President Mahmoud Ahmadinejad, the first Iranian head of state to visit India in five years. Although Ahmadinejad's Indian stopover was short on time, it was very high in its symbolic content and laid bare some of New Delhi's strategic thinking. While energy issues remained the main focus of the visit, attention was as much on perceptions of Washington, which has a major problem with Iran's independent nuclear program and has been urging nations, including India, not to deal with Tehran.

Indeed, the reasons for India's new approach (standing up to America and appearing neutral in its foreign policy and strategic dealings) are many: Firstly, India desperately needs energy sources, with competitor China equally keen to tap Iran's rich hydrocarbon fields. China has expressed the willingness to join a truncated India-Pakistan-Iran (IPI) pipeline project should India keep away from it. Pakistan has been irked by Washington's pro-India tilt and would be happy to accommodate China. Pakistan's foreign office spokesperson has been quoted to have said that "If there are prospects of China joining the IPI project with or without India, we will welcome it. Pakistan is committed to the pipeline because of its desire to achieve energy security."

Keen to obtain new gas, India has formally joined the Asian Development Bank-sponsored and US-backed Turkmenistan-Afghanistan-Pakistan (TAP) pipeline project that has now been officially renamed as the Turkmenistan-Afghanistan-Pakistan-India (TAPI) gas pipeline.

Secondly, domestic Indian politics play a major role. Political parties will look to label New Delhi as a "US stooge" in the general elections due in the summer next year. There is fear of a backlash from Indian-Muslim voters who constitute a sizable constituency and despise America due to its attack on Iraq and the problems with Iran.

Indications are that whoever wins in the elections next year – be it the Congress Party, the main opposition Bharatiya Janata Party (BJP) or a Third Front formation – they will have to seek outside support from regional parties, many of which rely on Muslim backing. New Delhi's moves can also be seen as an attempt not to completely alienate the anti-US parties of the left, though the two have now fallen out over the Indo-US nuclear deal.

Thirdly, there is also a growing view that New Delhi has to learn how to deal and balance its various national interests in order to sustain a fast-growing Indian economy that is in need of new markets for both export and import. India's gross domestic product (GDP) has been growing at 8-9% per annum over the past few years. A tilt towards the US and an economy heading towards recession will not help matters when business is of concern. Such an approach can have its dividends and result in win-win situations.

AIR POWER

Chicago-based Boeing, Pentagon's number two defence supplier has said that it plans to bid for US$15 billion of military orders in India over the next 10 years. Boeing is negotiating for the $2 billion P-8i long-range maritime reconnaissance aircrafts for the Indian Navy. Meanwhile, competitor Lockheed Martin has broken into the Indian defence market with a billion dollar deal to sell six Super Hercules aircrafts, the biggest ever Indo-US defence contract. Competition and lobbying is also going to be intense for the US$11 billion

126 multi-role combat aircraft (MRCA) deal, with a 50% offset clause that India is likely to sign a couple of years from now, for which both Boeing and Lockheed are bidding, apart from others.

Indeed, given the lethargy with which the Indian bureaucracy moves it is due to the almost obsolete state of India's arsenal and enormous pressure from the armed forces that matters are looking up. The Indian Air force (IAF) has begun replacing its Soviet-era MiGs, used for training pilots, with Hawk trainer jets from BAE Systems. In addition to the 66 Advanced Jet Trainers (US$1.45 billion deal signed in 2004), the IAF has sought 40 more.

New Delhi has invited global tenders for 312 light military helicopters to replace the vintage French and Russian fleet procured in the 1960s. Aviation firms in France, Italy, Russia and the US have been approached about the proposal. The IAF and Army have combined their respective orders, following the cancellation of the French Eurocopter deal. India has issued a request for global bids for a $1.5 billion upgrade for its 30 military airports; India and Russia have managed to clear the upgrade of 67 IAF MiG-29 fighter jets.

THE INDIAN AIR FORCE AND 24 X 7 CAPABILITIES

A nation of the size, power, responsibilities and stature of India cannot ignore global happenings. Indeed we must anticipate and if possible shape them or risk being overtaken by events. It is a decided advantage to be proactive but we have been far from it. This requires the backing of analysis, determination of national interests and long-term policies. A smaller nation could get away without it but not India in the contemporary world.

Apart from having a volatile neighbourhood and the associated threats and influences, India is faced with the full spectrum of threats. The spectrum itself is increasing in complexity and technological sophistication. With the changing spectrum, its unpredictability, and India being looked upon to play a bigger role in global affairs, we have no choice but to ensure that we have full-spectrum dominance. The Armed Forces are an important component of national power and can help generate options for the Govt. The application of Air Power is intrinsic to the gamut of National Power and we will have to focus in the same direction.

If we have to tread the path of full spectrum dominance, it is prudent that we move away from a threatbased assessment to a capabilitybased approach. A capability can always be tailored or applied to meet the emerging challenge. Capability will also allow us to apply the right force in any form of conflict. Transformation for us will be a continued series of fundamental changes each leading to a better capability. Keeping all this in mind, we need to understand what we need for our capability build-up.

Pillars of Capability

Our National zone of interest and influence stretches from the Gulf of Hormuz in the West, to the Malacca Straits in the East and beyond. Just like other capabilities, strong and comprehensive aerospace capability is required in today's scenario to meet our country's aspirations. I envisage that the capability build up of our aerospace power will be based on four pillars.

Very simply put, these are SEE, REACH, HIT and PROTECT. We need to SEE farthest and first. This involves utilisation of space based assets, long range radars, aerostats, AWACS and other ISR sensors. We need to collect and process relevant information in real time. Having SEEN, we need to REACH our area of interest. Trans-oceanic reach by long range combat and transport aircraft, along with air to air refuellers, is the next pillar of our capability. Once we reach, we need to HIT the target. Hit the target with precision; hit it hard. And so, modern weapons are required. While doing all this, we need to PROTECT our assets both in war and peace. This involves all aspects of Air Defence, EW (Electronic Warfare), Cyberspace and Information Warfare.

Effect on IAF and its Preparedness

Aerospace power is going to play a major role in all operations in the future. Technologically, aerospace power will definitely seek to enhance its fundamentals. Reach, Accuracy, Lethality, Situational awareness as well as command and control are going to improve manifold. Aerospace power will find increasing application in homeland security as well as in tackling asymmetric forces with faint footprints.

The path that we have to tread is influenced by emerging technologies and I can state with confidence that aerospace power's applicability will only increase in times ahead. Aerospace power will proliferate and find utility with many agencies.

In addition to the Armed Forces, the Paramilitary and now the Home Ministry want their integral aircraft and Air Wings. This will raise a host of fundamental questions on organisational structures, management and ownership issues. Undoubtedly, aerospace power will be the 'preferred tool' for all conveniences and contingencies, but we need to manage it properly.

In the future, there are many challenges but also opportunities. Some are evolutionary and some are truly revolutionary.

On one end, we have 5th generation fighters like F-35 and F-22, PAK-FA or T-50, while on the other end, increasingly capable RPAs (Remotely Piloted Aircraft) are also stealing limelight. Since these RPAs are offering new horizons for air and space operations, they have started playing critical roles in war and conflict zones. From surveillance to delivering ordnance with precision, RPAs will undoubtedly continue to make revolutionary advances. Similarly, precision munitions are getting smaller, more precise and more autonomous while on the other side, weapons using directed energy are beginning to emerge.

There will be a need for specialisation, greater networking and assimilation of space, for any air force that has a reckonable area of interest. Transportability of national power by airlift will be more essential than ever before.

IAF'S Future Roadmap

If this be the future of air power then, then the vision and long term perspective of IAF is clear. The underlying objective of the Air Force during the coming 10 to 15 years is to build itself into a credible aerospace power. Always keeping in mind that there is a compelling need to keep the technological level of our equipment at such a pitch, that it is viable for precise and effective force application in all possible types of threat scenarios.

IAF envisions itself to be a networkcentric force. The Aim being to have a common operating picture, reduce the sensor to shooter time and enable successful time critical operations. In fact all this will shortly become "bread and butter" stuff. Capabilities like the Integrated Air Command and Control System (IACCS), AWACS and Operational Data Link (ODL) are different aspects of an emerging network-centric environment. Space would be very vital, though largely an invisible component in this mosaic of Network-Centric operations.

Contemporary capabilities like AWACS and some others in the pipeline are already changing and transforming the way we are likely to fly and fight. The demands on the aerospace leadership of the future are also going to change. Leaders will also have to transform themselves. A change of mindset is mandatory to meet the challenges of the future.

Technological advances will continue to revolutionise military affairs in future too. Despite the unpredictabilities, it is certain that the need for application and transportability of national power – hard and soft – and thus for aerospace power, with enhanced fundamentals, would remain. We expect aerospace power to permeate the fabric of national security more completely, including homeland security. IAF foresees greater specialisation; tailored capabilities for each occasion; an increased dependence on Remotely Piloted Vehicles and a greater accent on force enhancers; particularly the intangible ones, such as quality of people and their skills. Hardware is important but it is converted into capabilities by people.

Aerospace power requires highly-skilled and trained personnel. Attracting quality youth, training and retaining them is another of IAF's challenges. Inculcating qualities of leadership and innovativeness will be vital on IAF's agenda.

Networking and assimilation of space, both interdependent, are already the way forward and can tilt the balance considerably. Perhaps more than others, it is air power that is most significantly enhanced by the integration of space-enabled capabilities. Evolving into a potent aerospace force is thus a logical progression in the scheme of things. But then, the vulnerability of satellites to anti-satellite weapons becomes an issue, due to risk of attack from adversaries. Development of ASAT technologies is taking place in our neighbourhood. In order to ensure that our increased dependence on space does not become our vulnerability, defending space based assets would assume vital importance within the 21st Century.

AVIATION SCENE

EADS

According to reliable media reports, New Delhi is seriously looking at offset options due to purchases from Boeing and EADS, the parent of Airbus and Eurocopter.

Government-run air carriers (Air India and Indian airlines that are now merged) have placed orders of around US$8 billion and more purchases are on the horizon. Indian Airlines had placed an order for 43 aircraft from Airbus (a division of EADS) worth US$2 billion, which carries an offset clause.

EADS has thus proposed Indian investments of 2 billion euros over 15 years. Offsets will also arise out of the $11 billion MRCA deal. One way to use up the investment requirement is to set up assembly units for medium-size civil transport aircraft. This could begin with 70-seater ATRs. According to reports, EADS is looking to closely engage with New Delhi and is open to a "mutually beneficial" arrangement that could also reassess a helicopter contract with Eurocopter for the defence forces. The deal was cancelled due to allegations of discrepancies in field trials, though pressure from the US to re-negotiate the contract played a role. A senior government official was recently quoted to have said that: "To begin with, we are looking to set up an assembly unit for turboprop aircraft with a capacity of 25 to 60 seats. Regional air-connectivity will grow to create adequate demand for any plane-maker to set up a unit."

High growth is expected in India's civil aviation sector despite the recent slow down and losses due to high crude oil prices. According to a recent survey by Airports Council International, the Indian civil aviation industry has grown twofold in the past four years and by 2010 the figures will double again.

India's Federal Civil Aviation Minister Praful Patel said that India's air travel industry will need US$50 billion in investment in its infrastructure over the next decade. Patel said the sector, which has seen almost frenzied plane buying and airline launches in the past 4-5 years, would grow by 25-30 % in the near future. Indian aircraft carriers, both private and state owned, are expected to buy nearly 300 new planes by 2010, valued at US$15 billion, and spend another US$15 billion in the following decade.

Boeing

Boeing has said that India's Tata Group will supply parts for its 787 Dreamliner, which has been declared a "turning point" for the Indian aerospace business. A Boeing and Tata joint venture (JV) intends to produce defence-related aerospace components in India, with expected exports of US$500 million initially. In December last year, Boeing and state-owned Hindustan Aeronautics Limited (HAL) signed a deal to transfer more than US$1 billion of aerospace manufacturing work to India. There have also been discussions between the Tata Group and Microbiotics, a US aerospace company, to work out new opportunities in instrumentation and navigation systems. Not to be undone, US defence giant Lockheed has teamed up with top Indian software firm Wipro to produce electronic warfare systems, radars and flight simulators.

Tata Group

Recently, the Tata Group and European aerospace giant EADS agreed to jointly bid for a US$1-billion deal to supply tactical communication systems to the Indian Army. "The teaming arrangement would ensure that the solution proposed is cutting edge and meets all the requirements of the Army," said Tata Group chairman Ratan Tata.

The Tata Group has also signed an agreement with Israel Aerospace Industries for manufacturing a full swathe of defence products, including missiles, unmanned aerial vehicles, radars, electronic warfare and security systems.

Tata is also tying up with US helicopter producer Sikorsky to set up a manufacturing unit in India.

Others

US-based aerospace solutions provider Rockwell Collins (turnover close to US$4.5 billion) is setting up an engineering center at India's technology hub Hyderabad. This is the first such center outside Rockwell's headquarters. Rockwell supplies solutions to private Indian airline carriers, including IndiGo and Jetlite.

India's largest construction firm Larsen & Toubro (L&T) has also signed agreements with Boeing and EADS for joint exploration of businesses in India. Others such as BAE Systems, Bombardier and SAAB are planning forays.

MRCA Deal

Quite a bit of the interest of aviation majors in India has to do with the MRCA deal and the consequent offset norms that will require mandatory investments in India's defence sector of over US$5 billion.

The acquisition of the jet fighters is a crucial cog in India's defence modernization efforts. In April this year, the six contenders for this mega contract submitted their bids to the federal defence ministry, each offering "strategic and unequivocal partnerships" including joint production, government support and advanced jets at the cheapest cost. The request for proposal (RFP) for the deal was issued in August 2007 after delays that span over a decade and a half.

The fighters in the fray are the American Boeing's F/A-18 Super Hornet, Lockheed Martin's F-16 Falcon, Russian MiG-35, Swedish Saab's Gripen, French Dassault Rafale and the Eurofighter Typhoon by the consortium EADS. "We will now seriously examine all the bids and shortlist the companies in due course to two or three, before taking a final decision," a defence ministry spokesperson said. "Even if everything does work out smoothly, we don't expect the first batch of fighters in India before 2011."

Around 20 fighters will be bought off-the-shelf and the remaining ones will be produced in India under a Transfer-of-Technology (ToT) agreement. New Delhi has said in the past that it will ultimately settle for a single fighter jet platform instead of multiple sources. Many defence analysts say that Lockheed and Boeing are front runners to win the jet contract, but the race is far from over, given domestic Indian politics that oppose any US "hegemony" in any sphere, whether actual or apparent, apart from the technical considerations. The delayed Indo-US defence deal is one example.

"The protection of the supply flow of oil and gas from far away regions is one of India's most significant vital interests."

UNDER PROCUREMENT

Fighters

HAL initiated the Light Combat Aircraft (LCA) programme in 1983 to develop a replacement aircraft for IAF's ageing MiG-21. After development during the 80s and 90s the first flight occurred in 2001. The aircraft has since been named HAL Tejas. Finally after Initial Operation Clearance status (IOC) Tejas is officially inducted in IAF for Final Operational Clearance (FOC)on 10 January 2014, after achieving the FOC status IAF is going to order 10 squadrons of the aircraft for its aging fleets of MiG-21s. The IAF is reported to have a requirement for 200 single-seat and 20 two-seat conversion trainers. It has ordered 40 Tejas Mk1 aircraft. The Initial Operation Clearance was granted to the IAF on 10 January 2011 by the Defence Minister Mr.A.K.Antony.

The IAF issued a Request of Intent (RoI) for the procurement of 126 multi-role combat aircraft. Contenders for the $10 Billion Indian MRCA competition were the MiG-35 from Mikoyan of Russia, the Rafale from Dassault Aviation of France, the Eurofighter Typhoon, from EU, JAS 39 Gripen from Saab of Sweden, the F-16IN Super Viper from Lockheed Martin and F/A-18E/F Super Hornet from Boeing.

The order is for 126 aircraft with the option to buy another 64–74 more. While there were reports of the direct order being increased to 200, or split between two vendors, Former Chief of Air Staff of the IAF, Air Marshal S.P. Tyagi stated during Aero India 2007 that the number would remain the same, and would be sourced from a single vendor. The first squadron would be directly supplied by the vendor, while the rest would be manufactured under license in India by HAL. He stated however, that as the bidding progressed, this could change.

On 31 January 2012, it was announced that Dassault Rafale has won the competition. The cost of the deal is revised at USD 20 billion. On 29 February 2012 It was reported that India will phase out MIG-21s from 2014.

Transports

On 15 June 2009, the IAF announced that it was interested in purchasing about 10 C-17 Globemaster III tactical military transport aircraft. The C-17 deal, worth $4.1 billion, has been signed through Pentagon's Foreign Military Sales (FMS) route under which Boeing will deliver the planes to India over the next four years. It is possible that the deal might include an option for 10 more aircraft. India took delivery of the first C-17 in February 2013.

In early 2008, the IAF signed a deal to acquire 6 C-130J Super Hercules, modified for special mission roles, for US$1.06 billion. The aircraft are based at Hindon Air Force

Station in Ghaziabad and Lockheed Martin has delivered all 6 by October 2011. On 16 September 2011, the Government of India sent a Letter of Request to the United States to price out the purchase of an additional 6 C-130J's which will be based in the eastern theatre.

On 24 July 2012, the IAF issued a Request For Information for 56 transport planes at $2.4 billion. These will be the replacement for ageing fleet of 55 Hawker Siddeley HS 748. The first 16 planes under the deal will be directly procured from the vendor. The winning company will have to tie-up with an Indian private or a public sector firm to acquire components for manufacturing the rest 40 planes.

Trainers

The IAF was planning to acquire 181 basic trainer aircraft & had to select an aircraft from six contenders- Grob G-120TP, Embraer EMB 314 Super Tucano, Korean Aerospace Industries KT-1, Hawker Beachcraft t6, Finmeccanica M-311 and Pilatus PC-7MkII after flight trials. In June 2011, IAF selected Switzerland's Pilatus Aircraft to supply 75 PC-7MkII trainer planes for $1 billion

Helicopters

On 26 May 2009, the Indian Ministry of Defence invited bids for 22 combat helicopters and 15 heavy-lift helicopters in a deal worth US$2 billion. Companies which have expressed their interest in the tender include — Russia's Kamov and Mil Moscow Helicopter Plant, Europe's Agusta Westland and Eurocopter and United States' Bell Helicopter andBoeing. Boeing submitted its initial bid on 23 October 2009 offering the AH-64D Apache Longbow attack helicopter and the CH-47F Chinook heavy-lift, twin-rotor helicopters. In 2011, it was reported that the American AH-64D Apache had emerged as the winner ahead of the Russian Mi-28N defence deal for 22 Attack Helicopter. CH-47F has emerged as the "L-1 (lowest bidder)" in comparison to the Mi-26 after both the huge helicopters passed the extensive technical field trials conducted by Indian Air Force. In December 2008, India and Russia inked a deal for the supply of 80 Mi-17V-5 medium lift helicopters at a cost of US$1.2 billion. The two countries had earlier negotiated a price of $650 million, but early in 2008 Russia asked for a revision of the contract price. Russia is expected to deliver the Mi-171 to the IAF in 2010. The deal also envisages a US$405 million "offset" obligation by Russia. The new choppers, which have an 18,000 ft operational ceiling, will replace 50 Mi-8s currently in service with the IAF, some of which are over 35 years old, and boost IAF's capability to support high-altitude posts in Siachen and Ladakh sectors. The helicopter will come with the circuitry and hard points to carry weapons. In September 2010, the IAF placed an order for 59 more MI-17V5 helicopters in addition to the 80 ordered in 2008, this is to replace its ageing fleet of the older MI-17s and MI-8s; the process would be completed by 2014.

The Indian Air Force has signed a 560 million euro contract with Italy's AgustaWestland for 12 AW101 helicopters. The aircraft will be delivered with self-protection equipment capable of warning off missile threats and will serve as VIP transports the Indian President and Prime Minister. IAF will deploy indigenously developed HAL Light Combat Helicopter for its combat operations. HAL Light Observation Helicopters are also expected to join the airforce and army to replace the ageing Chetak and Cheetah helicopters.

Unmanned Aerial Vehicles

The Indian air force has submitted a request for information to international suppliers for an unmanned combat air vehicle (UCAV) with low radar cross-section, high service ceiling, an expected range of 500 nm (925 km) and the capability to carry precision-guided weapons in an internal weapons bay.

Surface to Air Missile Systems

In June 2007, India signed a $250 million to purchase SPYDER (*S*urface-to-air *PY*thon and *DER*by) mobile air defence missiles from Israel. The two countries signed an additional $4 billion deal for the joint-development of a medium range surface-to-air missiles. However, the procurement of

SPYDER missiles was delayed because of an ongoing investigation against Israel Aerospace Industries and RAFAEL by Indian intelligence agencies for its alleged kickbacks in the Barak-I deal with the Indian Navy. In August 2008, a $2.5 billion deal was signed by India and Israel to develop an advanced version of the SPYDER.

Cruise Missiles

DRDO is developing the air-launched version of the BrahMos cruise missile in a joint venture with Russia's NPO Mashinostroeyenia. The air-launched version for the Indian Air Force is ready for testing. The IAF has signed a contract with Russia to upgrade 40 Su-30MKIs to give them the capability of carrying the BrahMos cruise missile by 2012. DRDO is also developing the nuclear capable Nirbhay cruise missile.

UNDER DEVELOPMENT

Fighters

In October 2007, India and Russia signed a pact to develop a Fifth Generation Fighter Aircraft which is a derivative project from the PAK FA. The Indian version will be a two-seater, air superiority fighter.

Another agreement was signed between India's Hindustan Aeronautics and Russia's United Aircraft Corporation (UAC) in December 2008 which detailed the joint development and production the aircraft. Work on the program will start by mid-2009 and the program is expected to be completed by 2017. Indian Air Force will get 200 twin-seated and 50 single seated FGFAs. Sukhoi/HAL FGFA when fully developed is intended to replace the MiG-29 Fulcrum and Mikoyan MiG-27 in the Indian inventory.

HAL has also started design work on an Advanced Medium Combat Aircraft (AMCA), which is a twin-engined 5th generation stealth multirole fighter. It will complement the HAL Tejas, the Sukhoi/HAL FGFA, the Sukhoi Su-30MKI and the Dassault Rafale in the Indian Air Force. The main purpose of this aircraft is to replace the aging SEPECAT Jaguar & Dassault Mirage 2000 fighters. IAF has a requirement of at least 250 AMCAs.

Airborne Early Warning

In 2004, Defence Research and Development Organisation revived the Airavat Project, which was India's first attempt in developing an indigenous AEW aircraft. A $210 million deal signed with Brazil's Embraer in 2008 for the supply of three Embraer EMB-145 regional jets. Embraer Defence and Security, on 16 August 2012, delivered the first EMB 145 Airborne Early Warning and Control (AEW&C) class of aircraft. The delivery followed successful completion of ground and flight tests of the aircraft which met operational targets established by both Embraer and Centre for Airborne Systems (CABS) of Defence Research & Development Organisation (DRDO). Later on, the aircraft will be delivered to the Indian Air Force after integration of missions systems of DRDO by CABS in India. India has sent a request for proposal to six vendors for the supply of Active Array Antenna Unit (AAAU) and various other sub-systems. These vendors include Israel's Elta, the European consortium EADS, France's Thales, Sweden's SAAB Erikson and the United States' Raytheon and Northrop Grumman. The IAF has a requirement for 24 DRDO AEW&CS.

Transports

HAL entered a joint-venture with the United Aircraft Corporation (UAC) of Russia to develop the UAC/HAL Il-214 Multirole Transport Aircraft (MTA) which is a medium-lift military transport aircraft. Both companies will invest US$300 million each in joint venture. The aircraft will be able to perform regular transport duties and also deploy paratroopers. The jet is expected to fly by 2014 and inducted by 2015/16. The Indian Air Force plans to acquire 45 MTAs. The aircraft will have a maximum payload of 18.5 tons, with a range of 2500 km and a speed of 870 km/h.

The IAF has also placed an order for 15 NAL Saras light transport aircraft designed by the National Aerospace

Laboratories (NAL) which is still under development. The manufacturer has stated that the Indian Air Force intends to place an order for up to 45 aircraft.

Trainers

HAL has developed the HAL HJT-36 Sitara intermediate jet trainer aircraft for the IAF which carried out its maiden test flight in 2003. These aircraft are scheduled to replace the aging HJT-16 Kiran mk.I. The Indian Air Force has placed an order for 73 aircraft, of which the first 12 are in production. The order by the Indian Air Force could eventually grow to 250 aircraft. Two prototype aircraft have been built. These aircraft have undergone 280 test flights. The HJT-36 is scheduled to enter service with the Indian Air Force in Dec, 2012 or January 2013. HAL will also develop the HAL HTT-40 which will replace HAL HPT-32 Deepak as basic trainer. HAL has decided to rope in an international partner for the design and development of the much needed ab initio turbo trainer for the Indian Air Force (IAF) and the Navy.

Helicopters

HAL is developing the Light Combat Helicopter (LCH) for the IAF based on the successful HAL Dhruv platform. It is being designed to fit into an anti-infantry and anti-armour role and will be capable to operate from altitudes of 6,500 metres. The first prototype of the LCH has successfully completed its first flight run on 29 March 2010

The Hindustan Aeronautics Limited of India is now developing the HAL Light Observation Helicopter (LOH) to replace the fleet of Cheetah and Chetak helicopters. The project is in preliminary stages and is in the design phase. The project is expected to be completed within next 5–6 years.

The Hindustan Aeronautics Limited of India is now developing the HAL Dhruv Weapon System Integrated (WSI) helicopter named HAL Rudra. It is a variant of Dhruv (ALH) MK-4 to strengthen the fleet of attack helicopters. The project is in under various trials. The project is expected to be completed by the year 2012.

Unmanned Aerial Vehicles

The DRDO of India is developing a Medium Altitude Long Endurance Unmanned Aerial Vehicle (UAV) called the Rustom(English: Warrior) for all three branches of the Indian Armed Forces. The Rustom will replace/supplement the Heron UAVs in service with the Indian armed forces.

DRDO is also developing the AURA (Autonomous Unmanned Research Aircraft) which is an Unmanned Combat Air Vehicle (UCAV) for the Indian Air Force. The design work on the UCAV is carried out by Aeronautical Development Agency (ADE). The AURA UCAV will be a tactical stealth aircraft built largely with composites, and capable of delivering laser-guided strike weapons. It would be a stealthy flying-wing concept aircraft with internal weapons and a turbofan engine.

Surface to Air Missile Systems

India and Israel have agreed to expand their missile development cooperation with a longer-range version of their extended-range Barak ship defence system for the Indian Air Force. DRDO is in talks with MBDA to develop Maitri LLQRM (Low Level Quick Reaction Missile) for all three branches of the armed forces. Sources said that DRDL is preparing feasibility report and is awaiting formal clearance from defence ministry.

CONCLUSIONS AND RECOMMENDATIONS

There is no doubt that India's foreign and external security policy is showing signs of maturity. Balancing business interests between America and Europe and with other important players such as Israel is tricky. While it is not easy to fend off the immense lobbying powers of US companies, New Delhi has realized from past experience that relying on a sole partner/supplier is always fraught with risk. Many countries, including India, have faced the brunt of the sanctions-ridden American foreign policy.

Recommendations

1) New Delhi should look to strike a synthesis between

private, foreign and public industry and smoothen several irritants in Indian defence dealings.

2) India could do well to amend its foreign direct investment (FDI) norms in the defence sector to enable foreign partnerships to be more effective.
3) New Delhi should relax rules on arms imports to ensure a smooth ride for foreign majors and rule out the involvement of middlemen in defence deals. In this, foreign defence majors and Indian private players are pitted against each other, so the going has not been easy.
4) US and European industry should push for FDI limits to be raised to 49% from the existing 26%.
5) Foreign firms could ask for more flexibility in finance, profit repatriation and technology transfers to build India as a manufacturing base. Many companies should look at this as an essential process to meet the 30-50% defence offset norms. The arguments could also center round the need for free competition as opposed to protection and artificial barriers to ensure the best products.
6) On the other hand Indian firms, supported by state-run units could push the government not to raise the 26% FDI limit for fear of being swamped by the superior technology and expertise of foreign players. They could argue that years of efforts to develop indigenous technologies would go to waste as new players piggy-back on foreign firms. Aggressive local campaigners include big players such as L&T and Kirloskars that can lobby the defence ministry.

   Thus, the federal government has relaxed the FDI norms on a case-to-case basis. The process has received support due to the success of Brahmos cruise missiles, an Indo-Russian 50-50 JV.
7) The defence ministry should clear more JVs with Israel and Russia. However, a piecemeal approach cannot be an efficient system as the volume of new defence

contracts with offset requirements gather steam. So far the government has not firmly indicated its stand on the issue which will have to be resolved into a policy framework.

8) In this context, India should also emphasize the transfer of technology in its defence deals so that indigenous firms develop the capability to produce defence wares over a period of time.
9) India has to move away from excessive dependence on imports which is a drain on the country's foreign exchange coffers and makes it vulnerable to various arm-twisting tactics that are not very healthy in a strategic arena such as defence.

MODERNIZATION AND DEVELOPMENT OF INDIAN AIR FORCE

The Indian Air Force is a young service. The oldest of its units is only 60 years old. Its birth in 1932 and its growth to date can be conveniently divided into four 15-year periods: 1932-1947-1962-1977-1992. By a coincidence these dates correspond to the major changes in the structure, composition and the capability of the Air Force.

The origin of the IAF can be traced to the recommendation of the Skeen Committee set up by the British in 1925. This committee looked into the local demand of Indians for a greater say in matters of defence.

The committee, chaired by Sir Andrew Skeen (then Chief of General Staff) was formally constituted as the Indian Sandhurst Committee in 1925. It recommended, among other things, the induction of the Indians into the RAF College at Cramwell and the formation of an Indian Air Arm manned fully by Indians. As a follow-up of this report, 6 Indians were sent to the RAF college for the first time in 1930. When 5 out of the 6 successfully became pilots, the Indian Air Force came into being on 8 October 1932. The first unit of the IAF, No. 1 Squadron, was formed on 1 April 1933 at Drigh Road Airfield, Karachi.

The Beginning, 1932-46

It was a slow start. No. 1 Squadron was formed with only one light of 4 aircraft, 5 pilots and 9 technicians. The rate of training was only two pilots per year. Pilots had to go to the RAF College for training as there was no facility in India. Three years went before the second flight was added, with only one more aircraft Another flight was formed in June 1938, initially with no aircraft at all. The squadron so far had no real existence as a unit. The flights were being moved about as appendages to various RAF units. Then at long last, the three flights came together in Ambal in July 1938. A committee in 1938 recommended the formation of an IAF Volunteer Reserve and 5 Coastal Defence Flights manned by this. An act authorising the formation of the IAFVR was passed, but nothing much else happened. Even though the war cloud had by then started gathering over Europe, the colonial government did not seem interested in letting the Indian Air Force grow.

In the twenties and the thirties, the RAF was engaged in man experiments to find out the best way to utilise air power. One of the expensive operations of the British Imperial Forces in those days was to mount punitive expeditions against rebellious tribes on the fringes of the empire, mainly in Iraq and Afghanistan. The RAF postulated that punitive expeditions could be replaced or at least largely supplemented by aerial strafing and bombing of the rebel strong-holds as a more economical alternative. This proposal was accepted.

RAF set up a number of airfields and secured a presence for itself in India. In 1920, it had 8 squadrons in India. This force was reduced to 6 squadrons in the thirties and again went back to 8 squadrons by the end of the decade. When the formation of the Indian Air Force became inevitable, the RAF wanted to use this token force as its appendage in the rebel-suppression role. 'A' flight of No. 1 Squadron was tried out for six weeks in this role in 1937 The 'C' flight was deployed for a couple of months in 1938. Technical the Indian units performed at par with the RAF units both in air and on the ground. No. 1 Squadron was then re-equipped with a slightly better aircraft, the Hart, and one of its flights was introduce to a new task of maritime air patrol while the other two flights went back to its air suppression role in the NWFP. After Britain entered the war, it stopped training Indian pilot at Cramwell for the IAF. However, it took in a large batch of Indian for training. These pilots were commissioned into the IAFVR an were utilised by the RAF. Those pilots who survived their operational tour in Europe came back to the IAF in 1942.

In 1940 the proposed IAFVR coastal defence flights came into being. Pilots were recruited from British and Indian civilians in the five metropolitan cities of Karachi, Bombay, Madras, Cochin and Calcutta. Available aircraft of the local flying clubs and some small airlines were pressed into service. The RAF squadrons in India were not at full strength. A decision was taken to fill the existing vacancies in these squadrons by training Indians. An RAF squadron at Risalpur was converted to training role. The initial recruits for IAFVR were trained in this squadron and sent to the coastal defence flights o to RAF squadrons in India.

By 1941, it had become clear that the total requirements of air force for the defence of India could not be made available from the RAF. The assessed need was for 21 squadrons and 5 coastal defence flights, whereas the RAF could at the most supply 11 squadrons. Therefore the IAF had to be expanded to a 10-squadron force. Large scale induction into the IAFVR began. To cope with the increase training needs, two Elementary Flying Schools and one Service Flying School were set up at Begumpet, Jodhpur and Ambala. To train technicians and other supporting tradesmen, one airmen's training school was set up at Ambala. This proved to be inadequate. Soon airmen's training was spread over 20 schools all over the country.

Two squadrons were formed in 1941. No. 2 in April, and N 3 in October. In July 1941, No. 1 Squadron changed over from Ha to Lysanders and No. 2 Squadron discarded their Wapitis for Harts handed over by No. 1 Squadron. No. 3 Squadron didn't get their full share of aircraft for some time. In December 1941, Japan entered the Second World War. No.

1 Squadron was sent to Burma in February 1942, but came back in March of the same year when Rangoon fell to the Japanese. After returning from Burma, No. I Squadron converted to Hurricanes. Four more squadrons were formed in 1942: No. 4 in February and Nos. 6, 7 and 8 in December. Throughout 1941 and 1942, IAF squadrons remained on training role in addition to air suppression duties in the NWFP. During the same period, the IAFVR coastal flights were closed down. It was not cost-effective to run these unit with unsuitable aircraft and untrained crew. The task was taken over by better equipped and trained RAF units.

No. 9 Squadron was formed in 1943, but was able to start training only in February 1944. No. 10 Squadron was formed in February 1944. Between 1943 and 1945, some of the units took part in air operations against the Japanese. No. 1 Squadron operated from Kohim from January 1944 to April 1945. No. 2 Squadron from October 19 to May 1945 in Cox's Bazar and various airfields in Burma. N 3 Squadron from January to April 1945 in Burma, No. 4 Squadron from Feni between April 1944 to April 1945, and then in Japan with the Allied Occupation Forces in 1946. No. 6 Squadron from November 1943 to June 1944 from Cox's Bazar, No. 7 Squadron from March to June 1944 from Uderbund near Kumbhigram in support of the Chindits Operation, and again between March and May from various airfields in Burma. No. 8 Squadron operated from Double Moorings near Chittagong between December 1943 and 1944, and again from July 1945 till the end of the war from Mingladon. No. 9 Squadron operated from April 1944 to April 1945 from Kulaura, and again from November 1945 to January 1946 from Hmawbi. For this second operational tour, No. 9 Squadron was accompanied by No. 10 Squadron. In recognition of the work done by the IAF units in the Arakaan the IAF was given a 'Royal' prefix to its name. From then on till the country became a republic in 1950, the Air Force was known as the Royal Indian Air Force or the RIAF.

By 1946, all units had come back to India, and by now the process of "Indianization" had also proceeded quite far. By

1943, the charge of Kohat airfield had been handed over to the Indian Air Force from then on, till August 1947, all Station Commanders were from the RIAF. Those RAF or Commonwealth personnel who had operated with the Indian units during the war went away by 1946.

New Branches

The equipment branch had received its first Indian Officer in 1932. A new branch called Administrative and Special Duties Branch was formed in 1940. Pilots who were unfit for flying duties were transferred to this branch. Fairly large-scale direct recruitment was also made into this branch. Apart from routine administration, this branch took over the duties of air traffic control and codes and cipher duties. The Meteorological Branch took its officers and men from the India Met Department. There was direct recruitment for the Accounts and Education branches. The Medical branch drew its doctors from the Army Medical Corps.

Up to the early forties, the aircraft being flown by the Air Force were simple. The units didn't need an Engineering graduate as an Engineer Officer. Therefore, there was no direct recruitment for the technical branches. By 1942-43, when a need was felt for an engineer in the officer grade due to the increasing complexity of the aircraft and reduced time of the air-crew under the pressures of war to devote to matters technical, a steady stream of senior technicians were commissioned into these branches from the ranks. This solution was adequate for the needs of the unit, but it prevented the growth of a technical staff who would be able to take a broad view of the technical needs at higher staff levels notwithstanding the presence of a few very eminent personalities who thus rose through the ranks. The weakness was rectified after independence, but the later entrants have often had to struggle to get out of the grooves made by the pioneers.

Organisation in the Early Days

The Air Force was a tiny force for the first 10 years of its existence. No separate Headquarters existed For it. It was controlled as a part of the British Air Forces in India under the AOC India, who in turn was controlled by the Commander-in-Chief in India and the GHQ. The HQ of the AOC India was called AHQ(I) and it consisted of a single branch with a Senior Air Staff Officer (SASO) as its head, and about 20 officers. The AOC held the rank of an Air Marshal. With the expansion of air activity in India, this organisation expanded and a second branch, Administration, was added under a Senior Officer Administration or SOA.

By 1942, the rank of the AOC India had risen to that of an Air Chief Marshal and his designation had become AOC-in-C India. Up to 1943, there was no room for IAF officers in the AHQ(I). But as the organisation grew further, certain number of RIAF officers were inducted into it at an Assistant Director level. By 1945, certain RLKF officers had reached the level of Deputy Directors. In 1946, an RIAF officer took over the directorate of training, and he was the first RIAF officer to enter the Air HQ at that level. It might be interesting to note however, that in 1943, AHQ(I) was divested of most of its functions including that of recruitment and training. With the formation of the office of the Supreme Allied Commander South East Asia (SACSEA), two new air headquarters were formed. Air Command South East Asia (ACSEA) controlled all the operations against Japan, while Base Air Forces South East Asia (BAFSEA) did the house-keeping chores for all the Air Forces operating in India including the RIAF. The AHQ(I) was left to perform only the 'Watch and Ward' duties in the NWFP which were carried out mainly by (and at times only by) the RIAF. This situation continued until the war-time headquarters were dissolved.

The Air Force upto 1945 was purely a tactical air force. It had no transport capability until No. 12 Squadron was formed in 1946. It had no long-range bombers. Apart from the few months of 1938 when a flight of No. 1 Squadron carried out Coastal Patrol duties, and the interregnum of the coastal defence flights between 1940 and 1942, it had not developed any maritime expertise. However, during the War, its equipment was progressively upgraded. Whereas in 1939 it had only one under-staffed and under-equipped unit operating obsolete aircraft, in 1946 it had nine fighter and one transport squadron using equipment that were current if not state-of-the-art, and a reasonably balanced infrastructure. In retrospect, it is quite interesting to observe this metamorphosis.

The IAF was not meant to grow quickly Both pilot and technician training schemes were of small intakes and long durations. There was no attempt to induct Indians into non-flying branches of the commissioned rank, notwithstanding the commissioning of one officer in the equipment branch from the first batch of pilot trainees. Selection of pilots was from the metropolitan cities with previous flying experience. This automatically restricted the choice to the westernised and affluent.

By 1940, immediately after the rate of recruitment was expanded, the then traditional source proved to be inadequate. Rich city boys were not really interested in joining the shooting war. In the initial days of the war, no one really knew how long it would last and how it would end. The Air Force therefore attracted the venturesome from the public schools who had no previous flying experience. This lot was also from a reasonably affluent background. But even this source was not large enough to fill the needs.

Recruitment was then expanded to include the young ones from the middle classes. Here, the recruitment drive came face to face with lack of air mindedness then prevalent. This problem was battled by formation of display flights which toured the country to fire the imagination of the youth from the smaller towns and induce them to join the Air Force.

A sustained effort was also launched to induct university students through an Air Training Corps. Despite all these efforts, however, it was not possible to fill all the vacancies in the nine existing squadrons with Indian pilots, Right up to 1946, the units had some RAF and other Commonwealth pilots on their strength, albeit in a progressively reduced number.

The response to recruitment in the non-flying cadre was more prompt. Indeed, it became necessary to restrict the entries into the non-flying branches to only those who were medically or otherwise not found fit to become air crew. To increase the number of volunteers for air crew duties, army officers were permitted to join the Air Force temporarily. Some of them liked the Air Force enough to stay back permanently while some others returned to their parent cadre and still others went back to civilian life at the end of the war.

Not all air crew recruited were to become pilots. In the earlier types of aircraft, there was room for an additional air crew called the OBSERVER. In the first decade of the existence of the IM, two pilots used to crew each other in the Wapiti. However, under the pressures of war, when training institutions were formed, training of a separate Observer's stream within the general duties branch commenced. After a few courses, direct recruitment of this stream was discontinued, the vacancies being filled by pilot rejects.

At that stage, some of the earlier Observers opted to re-train as pilots and did so successfully. With the phasing out of the two-seat fighters from the service, some of the Observers were transferred to the newly formed A&SD Branch while some others were employed in various ground duties retaining their General Duty status. Later, with the induction of the Dakota, the Observers were utilised in the Navigator's role. For the first decade, No. 1 Squadron did not move about much. From April 1933 to April 1936, 'A' Flight of No. I Squadron stayed put at Karachi. With the formation of the 'B' Flight, it moved to Peshawar, Multan, and Sialkot for training exercises. After the 'B' Flight had stabilised, it moved to Bangalore for exercises and then moved into Ambala as its permanent base. In 1938, the 'C' Flight joined the 'B' Flight at Ambala. From then on, the three flights took turns to operate from Miranshah and Fort Sandaman, two of the most used forward airfields, in the air suppression role; and did short army-air cooperation exercises all over the country while maintaining Ambala as the home base.

When the rush of formation of new squadrons came, the RAF spread its wings to many new bases in the country. The IAF units moved at random to these stations. The most frequently used were Kanpur, Allahabad, Calcutta, Ranchi, Begumpet and Amarda Road. With the formation of SACSEA, the peninsular airfields become active. The IAF used Trichinopally, Tambaram, Sulur, Yellahanka, Kolar and Arakonam. More airfields became active in the North and East. Delhi, Bhopal, Chharra, Pune, Vizag, Kumbhigram, Chittagong, Cox's Bazar, Kohima, Feni and a whole host of small and big airfields in Burma and Thailand were used. The Air Force got to know India from one corner to the other. This habit of treating the whole country as one unit, along with its recruitment base being devoid of any caste, creed, region or faith, gave the Air Force a stamp of secularity that has withstood the test of time.

Changes in Equipment

Like its change in size, the change of equipment came to the IAF in an explosive jolt. From 1933 to 1938, the IAF flew the Wapiti which was obsolete even in 1933. No wonder that the aircraft acquired the nickname of What-a-Pity! This was followed in 1938 by the Audax and the Hart which were by no means modern. These were the products of the transitional period where propellers were made of wood and had a fixed pitch, unable to match the engine speed with variable airspeed. The designers were not sure of making aircraft fully out of metals. Wood and fabric were still considered as major construction material for aircraft. The Audax and Hart were followed by the Vengeance and Lysander which were both slow limbering army co-operation aircraft with poor armament capability. The IAF had to fight a war with these planes where its task was often in the offensive role. The IAF displayed a great deal of innovation in usage and maintenance of these aircraft. Two famous examples were the fitment of a bomb rack on the Lysander and the fitment of a wooden tail wheel on the Vengeance when regulation metal ones were out of stock!

Aircraft design in the UK was revolutionised with the arrival of the Hawker Hurricane and Supermarine Spitfire. Both these aircraft entered the RAF just before the war, but reached the RIAF only by 1943-45. Anyway, they were still modern when they came. By the time the War ended, all Air Force units were equipped with various marks of these aircraft in the Western world. The aircraft factories were still producing modem aircraft that were no more required by the RAF. India had a very healthy balance-of-payment situation with the British Government. Independence was also on the horizon. The Air Force therefore found itself discarding its semi new Hurricanes and Spitfire Mark VH aircraft for Spitfire MV which again gave way to Tempest IIa and Spitfire XVIII within the short span of 1946-47. There was no British transport aircraft in the market at that moment. The new Transport Squadron was therefore formed with war-surplus Douglas DC3 Dakota aircraft. The Indian Army had formed a parachute brigade. A Paratroop Training School was therefore established at Walton with the Dakota as its mount.

For training purpose, no specific aircraft was initially provided for. After basic and advanced training with the RAF, the pilots flew the aircraft allotted to their units. The Wapiti, Audax and Hart had the second cockpit fitted with flying controls.

The Squadron Commander or the Flight Commander could therefore use the operational aircraft to test or train the unit's aircrew. When the Flying Training Schools came about they used the DH Tigermoth and the North American Harvard. These two aircraft proved to be very hardy, and continued in their respective roles even beyond 1947. With the re-equipment of the fighter unit with single seat aircraft, a couple of Harvards were added to the unit establishment for dual checks and instrument flying practice.

The IAFVR flew a large variety of aircraft during its short life span. The more exotic varieties like the Atlanta and the Blenhim did not find a place in the regular units when the coastal defence flight were closed down.

When the EFTSs and the SFTS were formed, they were manned fully by RAF personnel. As the war progressed, a sprinkling of India flying instructors, trained at the RAF's Central Flying School Little Risington, took their place in these units. By 1946, Indians formed the majority of instructors, though the units were still commanded by RAF personnel. A number of fighter pilots were also trained in UK as Pilot Attack Instructors. Indian pilots, by and large performed very well at these courses.

By 1946 therefore, the Air Force had digested its explosive growth in size and technology fairly well and had become a fairly stable Service. It was also unfortunately realised by then that the impend independence would bring with itself a partition of the country and a partition of the Air Force. For an organisation that was cosmopolitan and secular by design and upbringing, a partition on religious lines was not an easy concept to digest. Many non-Muslim men and officers hailed from areas that were to constitute Pakistan, just as there were many Muslim men and officers who had their roots in what to continue as India. Each and every such person had to decide for himself which side of the fence he wished to be on. Many such decisions were invariably influenced by the communal holocaust had engulfed the country or by the uncertainties that prevailed about the future of the two new nations. When the dust settled, however we found that although almost all non-Muslim men and officers had opted to stay back in India irrespective of their place of birth a large segment of Muslim personnel with their roots in India had done the same and remained with the country of their birth.

The nitty-gritty of division of assets was amicably sorted in four months precending 15 August 1947. The assets of 1, 6 and 9 Squadrons were handed over to Pakistan and these units were number-plated. Similarly the depots and other assets were partitioned and re-located. Personnel were suitably relocated and moved safely with close mutual protection. On 15 August 1947, the first phase of the Air Force came to an end and a new phase began.

MEETING THE CHALLENGES: IAF 2020

Modernisation of the IAF involves acquisition of expensive capital equipment that has a life span of three to four decades. Acquisition of equipment for the IAF in the past has generally been characterised by slow decision making and complex procurement procedures leading to delays in the operational integration of the equipment with the organisation. The process is a long drawn and in the best case may take seven to ten years to fructify. As such, plans drawn up today must remain valid in the decade of the twenties by which time changes in the operating environment might render decisions of today irrelevant. Modernisation plans must therefore take in to account the challenges of the evolving scenario in the geo-political, geo-strategic, technological and operational environment in the region and the world as these would impact on the role and responsibility of the IAF. It is therefore necessary to trace the historical perspective of regional equations and visualise the scenario that is likely to prevail in the twenties before undertaking plans for modernisation of the IAF.

CONFLICT AND THE DEVELOPING WORLD

In the first half of the 20th century, the world went through the convulsions of two major wars that apart from the widespread death and destruction, divided the world in to two distinct camps hostile to each other and ushered in an era of cold war and global peace, essentially on account of a balance of power arising out of superpower rivalry. While the two superpowers continued to maintain a balance of terror, conventional proxy wars continued to rage and were confined largely to the developing world. These wars served the political and economic interests of the superpowers as they helped perpetuate strategic relationships and turn the wheels of the military industrial complex of the developed world.

Sino-Indian Relations

Emerging as a dismembered but independent nation in the middle of the 20th century, India inherited several thousand kilometres of land borders that had a potential for conflict whose origins lay in the flawed policies of the British Government. The border between India and Tibet had been defined unilaterally by the British Government during their reign in India without any formal agreement with China who constantly maintained that in the first place, there was no need for a redefinition of borders as the traditional boundaries were well known and that there was no need to indulge in the exercise at all. At no stage did the Chinese endorse or accept the British action with regard to the delineation of the border with Tibet. The alignment of the traditional boundaries claimed by China were also not universally known except perhaps to the Chinese themselves.

The unresolved legacy inherited from the past left an unwary nation traumatised in 1962. More than four decades later, efforts are now on to resolve the fundamental dispute and notwithstanding the inspiring rhetoric emanating from the political establishment of both India and China and the somewhat regimented bonhomie at the military outpost at Nathu La beamed on the visual media occasionally, the ground situation has not changed in favour of India. In fact, in some ways it has indeed worsened as in the intervening years, the Chinese have only consolidated their gains of 1962 in Ladakh and are continuing to develop regions bordering Arunachal on a scale that cannot be justified for economic reasons alone. It would be imprudent to believe that it is possible only through dialogue to alter the age old position held by China regarding the alignment of international borders between India and Tibet. But in the absence of any other option, the dialogue must continue. However, we need to ensure that the unfavourable situation on the ground is not aggravated by inadequacy in military capability. We ought not to ignore the fact that it is more important for us to come to an amicable settlement of the border dispute than it is for China. As per a renowned Chinese leader, it may be desirable to shelve the problem for now and leave it to the future generations who may be wiser to find a solution. A politically weak position combined with a visibly weak military posture on our part therefore could seriously undermine the process of the ongoing dialogue as also the fragile relationship that we seem to have succeeded in building in the recent past.

Apart from the ongoing border dispute, the economic rivalry that is building up slowly but surely between the two of the fastest growing economies in the region, has the potential for conflict arising out of clash of vital interests. While India aspires to emerge as a regional power, China's sights are set on superpower status. China acquired nuclear power status several years ahead of India to achieve a credible deterrent against a perceived threat from a superpower. And now China has successfully completed her second space mission. China is clearly ahead in the race with India.

Indo-Pak Confrontation

On the western front, the status of Jammu and Kashmir, truly the only cause of conflict, also owes its origin to the legacy of the colonial past. In the wake of super-power rivalry, Britain was replaced in the region by the USA, and while Pakistan was drawn quite readily in to the American camp, India adopted a philosophy of non alignment opting for a diverse inventory of military equipment ie British and French. However for strategic, economic and political reasons India had to subsequently lean heavily on the Soviet Union to meet with the demands of national security.

Even though formally not allied with the USSR, India was seen by the USA as being squarely in the Soviet camp and was treated with extreme suspicion and unconcealed disdain. Nearly six decades and four major conflicts later, there appears to have been some qualitative change in the equation between India and Pakistan. People to people contact, exchange programmes in a variety of fields, restoration of rail and road transport, liberalisation of visa regimes, trade both official and unofficial and cooperation in the wake of the disastrous earthquake in the recent past have rekindled hopes for peace between the two adversaries. The media has also by and large played a very constructive role in exposing the reality of India to the several brainwashed and misled generations of Pakistanis. All these developments have served to weaken the anti-each-other platforms that the political establishment on both sides have so far thrived upon.

However, the situation with regard to the status of Kashmir has not changed, and like a persistent virus, resurfaces with irritating regularity, seemingly frustrating efforts at forward movement. In spite of all noble intentions, it appears difficult if not impossible for the Pakistani establishment to retreat from or significantly alter their long held position vis-à-vis Kashmir as it would amount to political suicide for the leadership whether military or civilian.

As for the Indian view, it is only for Pakistan to demonstrate flexibility which the leadership is not prepared to do. And then there is the unfinished business of POK. In view of the inflexible position on both sides, Kashmir will continue to be a major impediment in any effort at securing the western borders from the possibility of conflict. Nothing short of reunification of India and Pakistan can help resolve the dispute over Kashmir. Solution to the Kashmir problem will however remain as much of a fantasy in the foreseeable future as the suggestion for the reunification of the two nations.

Apart from the Kashmir issue, the growing economic inequality between India and Pakistan could aggravate the sense of insecurity that a small nation perceives from a bigger and more prosperous and powerful neighbour with whom there are deep ideological differences and a long history of turbulent relationship. The sense of insecurity may be further aggravated if our western neighbour finds her position vis-à-vis Kashmir weakening. Under such circumstances for Pakistan, a conflict may appear to be an inevitable and desperate option. Under the shadow of the nuclear threat, in all likelihood, Pakistan may prefer to sustain low intensity conflict in the valley and undermine our interests through covert support to insurgency in other parts of the country bordering Nepal and Bangladesh. This certainly would be a more convenient and cost effective option for Pakistan.

Prospects of Peace

It should be clear from the preceding that India cannot rest on its oars and take permanent peace in the subcontinent for granted. Perhaps peace can only be ensured if one is well prepared to meet with any conceivable threat to national security by all the means at its disposal, be it political, economic, diplomatic, or military. Encouraging progress in efforts at settlement of disputes with both China and Pakistan ought not to be assumed as good enough reason for scaling down military capability. Besides, in future conflicts with either or both the neighbours, India needs to be prepared to fight and survive in a nuclear environment.

INDIA: AIRPORT PROJECTS IN INDIA: THE PRIVATISATION PROCESS

India is at the threshold of emerging as an economic power. However, it is recognised that infrastructure holds the key to this transformation. The infrastructure gap in India is obvious to all. Of late the Government has dedicated itself to address this on a war footing. The task is huge. It involves not only harnessing financial resources but also technology and know-how. Around the world more and more airports are moving towards privatization. This is the trend in Asia, Europe and Latin America. In India too private participation is felt necessary and therefore the Government has opened up this sector to the Public Private Participation (PPP) route.

At first blush, it may seem that Government's efforts are too little too late but it may be worthwhile to bear in mind that air traffic in India has witnessed a 35 percent average growth, year upon year, for the past about 6 years, as against the global growth of only 9 percent per annum. In this chapter we explore the path adopted by the Government so far in airport privatisation. Essentially we look at three segments:

First, we examine the basic approach in the Concession Agreements (Agreements), comparing both the Greenfield and Brownfield sectors.

Second, we draw attention to the need to have an independent Regulator in place and

Third, we examine the dispute resolution mechanism put in place in the Agreements.

Basic approach in the Concession Agreements:

So far the Government has signed off four Concession Agreements - two in the Greenfield sector (Bangalore and Hyderabad) and two in the Brownfield sector (Delhi and Mumbai).

For the purposes of this chapter we take up the Agreements for Bangalore and New Delhi as our model (i.e. one in the Greenfield and the other in the Brownfield sector).

Notwithstanding the privatization route, the Government has retained in these airports 26 percent shareholding (either through the Airport Authority of India or through the State Government). This crucial 26 percent shareholding ensures that the Government is able to veto certain "fundamental resolutions", which as per the Companies Act requires a minimum of 75 percent shareholders vote (for instance, issuance of new shares; change of directors; change of auditors etc). Hence the Government does continue to retain some level of control over the private entity.

The commercial backbone of the project is the large chunk of land the private entity is "gifted" i.e. allowed to develop along with the airport for any commercial purpose it may please (subject to local laws). Here it may set up not only hotels or malls - it can even go for Special Economic Zones, manufacturing factories, country clubs, golf courses, power plant etc. At Bangalore the concessionaire got about 300 acres of land and at New Delhi 250 acres for free commercial development.

Nature of the concession

Basically the concession is for construction, development, operation and maintenance of the airport over a period of 30 years (concession period) extendable at the sole option of the concessionaire by another 30 years - (i.e. total 60 years). The land is leased out to the concessionaire by the State Government at a nominal rent.

The Government has extended its full commitment and support for the project; for instance, the Bangalore concession Agreement states, "GOI acknowledges and supports the implementation of project". It further states that the Government of India will not take any steps or action in contradiction with the concession Agreement which results in or would result in its shareholders or the lenders being deprived or substantially deprived of their investment or economic interest in the project. Further all statutory and non-statutory bodies under the control of the central Government will act in compliance with the concession agreement as if they are a party thereto and the Government of India shall ensure that all statutory compliances as may be required are granted promptly. The State Governments have similarly entered into State Support Agreements. This is a unique feature in airport privatization Agreements. The Port sector or Road sector do not have similar obligations on the Government.

Types of construction

Here we find a departure between the approach taken in the Greenfield sector and the Brownfield sector While the Greenfield projects, pretty much leave it to the concessionaire to plan the construction, as per the approved Master Plan, the Brownfield agreements are far more specific. The agreement for New Delhi for instance stipulates development of a Master Plan within six months of the agreement. This is to be updated and reviewed every 10 years. Any delay in submission of the Master-Plan would entail liquidated damages at the rate of US$ 65000 per day. The concession Agreement sets out certain type of works called the "Mandatory Capital Projects" (which are set forth in a Schedule). For instance, for New Delhi airport, a parallel runway is listed as one such work, which is required to be completed within 24 months of the signing of the agreement and if it is not, liquidated damages would follow. Then, there is a category of works which fall under the heading of "Major

Development Plan". These comprise of projects expected to have a capital cost in excess of US $ 25 million.

All the above are subject to review and approval by the Government. While strict time lines are stipulated for submissions of the Plans for approval, the AAI or the Government concerned is not obliged to revert with their approval/ suggestions within any time stipulation. This can lead to a situation where work is commenced (as it has to in order to meet the time deadline) and belatedly the same is not approved, or some modification is required by the Government.

Adherence to standards

Here again we find that the approach of the Government in the Greenfield versus Brownfield sector is not consistent. In the Brownfield sector (Delhi and Mumbai) the concessionaire is required to:

i. adhere to Good Industry Practices;

ii. adhere to Development Standards and Requirements - these are specified in a Schedule. For instance, it is stated that the airport must conform to the ICAO Aerodrome Design Manual (DOC 9157); the Airport Services Manual (DOC 9137); the National Building Code of India etc;

iii. adhere to Operations and Maintenance Standards and Requirements. These again are set forth in a Schedule. For instance, it is stated that the relevant standards prescribed by the ICAO (Chicago Convention) are to be followed.

However in the Greenfield sector the approach is far more hands off. The specifications are very broad and vague.

Monitoring of the project

The inconsistent approach of the Government between the Greenfield and Brownfield sector comes out most dramatically when it comes to monitoring of the project and imposition of damages for default. In the Brownfield sector the agreement has in place an aggressive manifold monitoring mechanism. To begin with "objective" and "subjective" service quality requirements are set forth in separate Schedules. To illustrate one "objective" service requirement states that the maximum queue - in time for check in should be 5 minutes for business class and 20 minutes for economy passengers. The waiting time for security checking should be less than 10 minutes for 95% of the passengers. "Subjective" requirement are based on passenger feedback survey as per IATA SCIA / AETRA guidelines. If a certain specific rating is not achieved within a stipulated period then liquidated damages follow. Further the concessionaire is required to achieve ISO 9001-2000 Certification. This is to be done within 2 years of the Agreement coming into force and if the same is not achieved, liquidated damages are to follow.

In contrast, in the Greenfield sector (Bangalore and Hyderabad) monitoring is only through passenger survey. Further (unlike the Brownfield sector), liquidated damages do not necessarily follow but if the rating through passenger surveys is consistently below the stipulated norms (over a period of years) and if the targets for rectification are not met, it may become an "event of default" leading to termination.

While examining the inconsistent approach between Greenfield and Brownfield sectors we may lastly take a look at the liquidated damages provision. In the Greenfield sector, even where there is delay in opening of the airport (something which ought to be a matter of serious concern), the concessionaire is allowed 6 months extension of time if it can show that the delay was allegedly on account of failure by the Government in the performance of its obligations (a provision which is easily capable of abuse and likely to lead to disputes).

After this, liquidated damages follow at the rate of only US$ 2500 per day upto the next six months of delay - surely a very nominal amount considering the consequences of delay (even one aeroplane hovering for landing permission can incur costs of more than the LD stipulated). In contrast, in the Brownfield sector, the concessionaire faces a prospect of liquidated damages of about US$ 65000 per day merely on account of delay in submission of the Master Plan beyond the stipulated period of 6 months even though prior to the agreement it had already submitted an Initial Master Plan (on the basis of which its bid was selected).

In fact Brownfield operators run the risk of paying liquidated damages (ultimately leading to termination of the contract) on at least 20 different counts - many of which are beyond their control e.g. security delay, check-in-delay etc., which can all result in liquidated damages and finally cancellation of the contract, (even though these are matters arguably beyond the control of the concessionaire). Airport security is a matter within the control of the Government and check-in formalities and efficiency is within the domain of the airline concerned. It seems unreasonable to penalize the concessionaire for shortfalls in targets here.

A Greenfield operator pays liquidated damages on only one count i.e. delay in opening of the airport. Here delay for six months mount up to less than half a million US$. Contrast this with the 10 million US$ a Brownfield operator may have to end up paying for a delay of 6 months for mere delay on account of submission of the Master Plan.

Absence of Regulator

In infrastructure projects concerning the public, an independent regulatory authority has become necessary. Accordingly the Agreements stipulate that an Independent Regulatory Authority would be set up to regulate all aspects of the airport. Vast powers are envisaged to be cast upon the Regulator. The Regulator would lay down and regulate standards, approve charges, impose penalties etc. Further the Regulator would be empowered not only to settle disputes between the public and the Government but also contractual disputes between the Government and the Concessionaire, as it is stipulated that once the Regulator is in place, the arbitration agreement as per the Agreements shall stand overridden. Firstly, the Regulator is not yet in place and considering that the Bangalore airport agreement was signed as far back as July

2004 the delay is unexplainable. Further the Regulator would work only if there is a mechanism to ensure that people of highest caliber, independent of Government control occupy the position. Once the Regulator is appointed the Regulatory philosophy has to evolve and there has to be transparency. All this will take time. We are years away from any of this as the Government is still discussing and deliberating preliminary issues. Even a Bill has not yet been placed before Parliament.

Secondly pure contractual disputes between the Government and the Concessionaire need not be referred to the Regulator. These, (in the event of dispute) need to go to the arbitrator. To override the arbitration agreement is bound to discourage foreign players. Resolution of disputes through the Regulator would cause serious problems of lack of confidence (amongst foreign parties) and also result in delay. The Regulator would naturally be subject to the hierarchy of the Indian legal system. Any decision of the Regulator would be appealable to the appellate authority. One is actually looking at three or four stages in dispute resolution - first, a decision by the Regulator followed by that of the appellate authority, followed by a Writ to the High Court, followed by an appeal to the Supreme Court. Given the delays under the Indian legal system, dispute resolution would become inefficient and expensive. Perhaps the Government should have segregated pure contractual disputes between the concessionaire and the Government and reserved these for international arbitration (which would have been as per the expectations of the international investing community also). The Regulator should step in only where public interest is involved.

Dispute Resolution

Planners (and contract writers) apparently tire out by the time they reach the dispute resolution clause (tucked away at the end of the Contract). Most dispute resolution provisions do not get the attention they deserve. Here too, we find the Agreements very unimaginative in their approach. Briefly, the concession Agreements stipulate that dispute resolution shall be through adhoc arbitration through a panel of 3 arbitrators, with the venue of arbitration as India. To understand what is wrong with this clause we need to step back and see the nature of the project. These are no ordinary construction or management contracts. These are mammoth and diverse projects involving public interest as well. What is most significant is that we are looking at a project which is to have a longevity of 60 years. Considering that the history of independent India is just about 60 years it can well be imagined what a long period of time 60 years can be in the history of a nation! The technological, political and social changes which may happen in the contractual period of 60 years cannot be visualized and therefore captured within the four corners of any contract (no matter how thoughtfully written). Therefore the dispute resolution clause must be flexible and geared to handle contingencies which may arise in the working of the contract. One possibility is that in matters of this type the arbitrators must be empowered to even modify or alter the contract if subsequent developments so warrant. This is no doubt a revolutionary concept but one which may well meet the demands of a situation where parties enter into such long term commitments and then events overtake them. The dispute resolution mechanism must not be found to be wanting in such situation. Indeed there is no mechanism for mediation or conciliation or Dispute Review Boards in the Agreements, all of which could have worked towards a just, fair and expeditious resolution to disputes.

Conclusion

The Indian Government has done well to embark upon the privatization process but it would seem that we need to pause and debate the approach so far. The Government's ambitious plans in this sector need to be accompanied in equal measure with a bold and fair approach. At the end of the day there needs to be a fair bargain for all parties.

8

Air Defence and Offensive Air Force Operations

Air defence was the primary function of the IAF until offensive air operations were also accorded the same priority. It remains an important component of the air power doctrine and the IAF has invested heavily in upgrading it. The air defence set up has three components – namely-armed interceptors, surface to air missiles and an extensive sensor network.

The backbone of the IAF's air defence fleet comprises of MiG-21s. Almost 16 operational squadrons fly in the air defence role. The oldest MiG-21 sub-types are being progressively retired, but both the MiG-21M and MiG-21bis continue to carry the IAF's primary air defence mantle. They continue to pull all the routine alerts along the border and form an important component of the air force's tactical reconnaissance force. The Gulf War and conflicts since have highlighted the need for aircraft with sensors that are more advanced and the ability to engage targets at increasing ranges. The baseline MiG-21M and MiG-21bis, given the vintage of their designs, are sorely lacking in these capabilities. However, the sheer size of the IAF's MiG-21 fleet has meant that any modernization plans would have to include these aircraft. While the MiG-21FL/Ms are now over 25 years old, the oldest MiG-21bis airframe is only 18 years old and the latter type is eminently upgradable. In the 1980s, the IAF did carry out a limited upgrade to configure the MiG-21Ms and MiG-21bis to carry the Matra Magic II air-air missile (AAM), and later for the R-60 AAM. A number of MiG-21bis were also fitted with head-up displays (HUD), but the aircraft remained sorely lacking in sensor ability.

Until the mid-1990s, a comprehensive upgrade of the MiG-21 had to be repeatedly postponed for either a lack of funds, or a dearth of suitable upgrade packages. However, a comprehensive upgrade of 125 "new" MiG-21bis is now underway. The program is almost two years behind schedule. The delay has been caused primarily due to re-design problems. The replacement of the MiG-21's original avionics by newer generation lightweight systems had altered the aircraft's center-of-gravity. These have now been overcome and the first 36 upgrade kits arrived in India during the last quarter of 1999. Under this program, the MiG-21 will be fitted with new avionics, the lightweight Super Kopyo multi-mode radar, IRST, and a comprehensive self-defence suite. While endurance and payload restrictions will remain, the MiG-21s will now be able to deploy almost as wide a range of air-air and air-surface ordnance as the most modern aircraft – including the R-77 AAM (AA-12 "Amraamski") and the Kh-31 ASM. One can expect to see this potent point defence fighter remain in service well into the second decade of the 21st century. Indeed the MiG-21s proposed replacement – the LCA – is not expected to begin entering service until 2010.

The move to make the MiG-21 fleet BVR capable, underscores the importance that the IAF accords staying on the cutting edge. The benefits of a BVR capable air defence force was much appreciated during operations over Kargil, where offensive air operations went unchallenged by the Pakistan Air Force. By all accounts, R-77 and R-27 armed MiG-29s on escort duty and CAP, ensured that PAF fighters stayed well over 40 km away from the border.

Even more modern types are undergoing comprehensive upgrades as well. The MiG-23MF, however, is an exception, with the sole remaining unit, filling an important role as a BVR training unit. Both the IAF's second-generation BVR types –

the MiG-29 and Mirage 2000 – are also being upgraded with sensors that are more modern. In case of the former, it is expected that all aircraft will have their N-109 radar replaced by an electronically scanned Phazatron system. The older "A" versions are also being upgraded to fire the R-77s, like the newer "SE" variant. While the latter has more capable radar (NO-19M), it too will be the subject of an avionics upgrade. The MiG-29 is also being equipped for air-air refueling to increase endurance. A major component of upgrade programs for air-superiority fighters across the board will eventually see them equipped with the HMS/R-73 combination. Both squadrons of Mirage 2000s will undergo an avionics upgrade, although the exact nature of the upgrades remains unclear. The Mirage 2000 was India's first second-generation BVR capable aircraft and its multi-role capabilities came in very handy during PGM strikes over Kargil in 1999. The aircraft has consistently maintained the highest serviceability of any type in IAF service (>90%) and has a superb safety record. The flexibility offered by the type has led the IAF to consider "topping up" existing units with a purchase of ten additional Mirage 2000Hs. Also under consideration is the purchase of the up to two squadrons of Mirage 2000Ds. Whether the latter deal comes through will depend as much on finances as on a successful completion of the Su-30MKI development program. Russia is currently filling an order for 50 Su-30MKIs. Eighteen Su-30MKs are already in service with No.24 squadron and a second squadron (No.20) has been earmarked for conversion.

In an effort to simplify logistics, the IAF has successfully integrated western missiles with its Soviet designed aircraft and vice versa. Under the first such program, MiG-21s were retrofitted with a capability to launch the Magic II AAM. More recently, MiG-29s have been adapted to carry the Super-530D. Integrating Soviet missiles with the Mirage 2000s proved more of a challenge, but was overcome by the mid-1990s. Indeed Mirage 2000s on missions over Kargil in the summer of 1999 were carrying R-73 AAM. The Mirage 2000 is also capable of deploying the R-27 AAM. It is more than likely that once the

R-77 enters service in quantity, it will be integrated with the Mirage 2000.

The IAF's APD now puts offensive air operations on par with air defence. Allied air campaigns since the Gulf War have been very closely studied by the Indian Air Force. A series of studies from the College of Air Warfare (CAW) have acknowledged that the quickest way to bring a military campaign to a successful conclusion is to destroy the enemy's war making potential. Not surprisingly, the IAF's attack fleet is increasingly being equipped with enhanced standoff attack capabilities. Since the early 1990s, the IAF has made a determined effort to build up stocks of PGMs.

There has been an increase in the number of armed helicopters within both the IAF and the Army Aviation Corps (AAC). This has allowed the IAF to reorient its attack away from the role of "flying artillery" that has been demanded of it in the past.

Indeed as the air campaign over Kargil demonstrated, the IAF achieved the best results only when it was able to persuade the Indian Army that it's fighters were better utilized in closing enemy supply lines and taking out C3I nodes, rather than providing support to company and battalion sized operations. It should be recognized that the situation in Kargil was unique, and that close air support still has some applicability in the plains. Joint exercises since Kargil have convincingly demonstrated the merits of the IAF's re-orientation of its air support doctrine.

Kargil provided the air force with unique environment to hone its attack skills. The IAF launched PGMs in anger for the first time. Mirage 2000s, MiG-27s, and MiG-23BNs carried out devastating attacks against enemy command nodes and logistics in the area. In what became a much-celebrated event, Litening equipped Mirage 2000s took out the Pakistani battalion HQ atop Tiger Hill with pinpoint accuracy. 1000 lb. bombs fitted with IR seekers were used extensively against vital C3I facilities. The Mirages tracked ground targets from 15 km out and then released their weapons at about 6km and holding the lasers onto target at the closest of about 3-4 km. This allowed them to remain well outside the envelope of enemy air defences. As mentioned earlier, the conflict also exposed some of the limitations of the attack fleet and tactics. In particular, battlefield interdiction was found to be of greater utility than close air support in the mountains.

It also alerted the air force to the ever present dangers of operating in a MANPADS (and indeed SAM) rich environment. The IAF lost two fighters, one MiG-27 and one MiG-21M, and an attack helicopter over Kargil.

While the MiG-27 was lost because of an engine flameout due to ingestion of smoke and debris, the MiG-21 was lost to a SAM while searching for the downed MiG-27. It is now appreciated that a lack comprehensive of countermeasures (chaff/flare dispensers) across the MiG-21 fleet contributed significantly to the tragedy. Until Kargil, only the MiG-23BN, few Jaguars, and a handful of MiG-27s were fitted with automated countermeasures (in addition to the air defence types). Upgrading the self-defence and jamming capabilities of the rest of the attack fleet has now assumed a sense of urgency and base repair depots have taken on the task of upgrading chaff/flare dispensers.

The bulk of the IAF's attack fleet is relatively young, most of the aircraft having been procured since the 1980s. The MiG-27 forms the backbone of the IAF's tactical strike aircraft, equipping some eight squadrons and one training establishment. Three squadrons of MiG-23BNs support these. Their sophisticated electronic warfare capability has caused them to be called "most modern" of IAF strike aircraft.

Five squadrons of Jaguars form the IAF's deep penetration strike fleet. The IAF expects all of these types to remain viable for the near future. Both the MiG-27 and Jaguar are expected to remain in service until 2020. To this end, a comprehensive sensor and electronic warfare upgrade program has been initiated. The IAF's commitment to keeping the Jaguar in service for many years to come has been re-affirmed by its decision to order two more batches of the type. A 1999 order for 17 two-seaters is currently under production. An additional 20 single-seaters have been ordered this year. Extremely versatile Mirage 2000s and Su-30s complement the dedicated strike fleet.

In addition to fulfilling overland strike duties, the IAF is tasked with the providing tactical air support to the navy. One Jaguar squadron has been specifically earmarked for this role on the western coast and is equipped with a mix of Sea Eagle armed Jaguar IS and IMs. Additionally, the IAF is in the process converting a MiG-27 squadron to cover the eastern coast. These aircraft operate in conjunction with the Navy's own air assets – including Sea Harriers and Tu-142s.

The 1990s have seen the IAF's strike fleet take on the additional task of delivering nuclear weapons. The Jaguar was the first aircraft evaluated for the role and was found too sluggish with the first generation gravity bombs. Consequently, Antilope equipped Mirage 2000s have taken on the task of providing India with a viable nuclear deterrent. It is now believed that the compactness of the second generation of nuclear warhead has allowed the nuclear delivery role to be taken on a by a larger number of aircraft – namely MiG-27s and Jaguars. It can reasonably be expected that in the future the Su-30 is likely to provide the backbone of India's manned deterrent force. It is also believed that the IAF is entrusted with the operation of India's emerging nuclear missile force. Unspecified numbers of Prithvi SRBMs and Agni IRBMs form the basis of this force. It should be noted that as the size and sophistication of the missile arsenal grows manned delivery platforms will loose a great deal of their importance. As things stand today, the IAF offers adequate deterrence vis-à-vis Pakistan, however the situation vis-à-vis China is less clear. Unfortunately, until the Indian missile arsenal reaches maturity, India's ability to inflict unacceptable damage on China remain restricted. While the IAF is likely to remain the sole strategic service for some time, it is likely to be joined by the navy when the latter deploys cruise missiles and if its lease/purchase of Tu-22Ms materializes.

NEW 'SPECIAL MISSION' AIRCRAFT FOR THE INDIAN AIR FORCE

In recent years the Indian Air force (IAF) as part of its 'transformation' has been progressively augmenting its fleet of special mission aircraft beyond the usual fighter and transport squadrons. After having brought in refuellers and airborne early warning aircraft, the IAF is now quite keen to augment its electronic warfare (EW) capabilities with more specialised aircraft in such roles. In late April last year, the Defence Acquisition Council put its stamp of approval on the IAF's proposal to procure nine 'special mission' aircraft for 1100 crore rupees or more. The status of the request for proposal (RFP) that the IAF was supposed to issue subsequently is unclear. But it is still worthwhile to look at this program more closely.

The IAF's RFI for the nine aircraft issued way back in 2012 specifies that two of the nine aircraft should be certified to perform the signals intelligence (SIGINT) role, given that the mission package for SIGINT commonly requires permanent modifications to the airframe. The remaining seven aircraft according to the RFI are to be configured by the prime contractor for the multi-mission role, 'supporting aerial survey, target towing, communications jamming (COMJAM) and flaring'. The RFI further specified that these missions i.e. for the seven COMJAM aircraft will be flown in addition to their original passenger and cargo roles.

Now what the IAF is essentially looking for has emerged as a classic combination over the last two decades. The special mission aircraft sought by the IAF are essentially militarized business jets that give a very good mix of deployability and endurance. The RFI issued last year spells this out by explicitly wanting 'aircraft powered by twin turbofan engines with low noise and vibration levels, with hot-and-high capability in all roles, certified for deployments at air bases up to 3,300 meters (10,000 ft.) above mean sea level.' The certification according to the RFI must be done by the airframe supplier. Reportedly the IAF may be looking for a biz jet platform with a cruise speed of Mach 0.75-0.80 and a minimum range capability of 4500 kms.

While all nine are to be based on a single platform the requirement for only two of them to be specialized for SIGINT probably follows from the fact that the IAF already operates two Learjet 29A and three Gulfstream III SRA platforms in that role for the Aviation Research Centre (ARC). The seven COMJAM units will therefore be filling the shoes of the IAF's retired Canberras and Avros.

The RFI however does suggest that the IAF wants the best that is out there when it says that '[sigint] system must be a futuristic, state-of-the-art system using cutting edge technologies, algorithms and software.' Furthermore the IAF wants that the set up should be up to the task of 'rapid system acquisitions and data processing with a high degree of automation', besides being 'capable of transmitting data to the ground through data links'. Interestingly the IAF also seems to be looking to move to systems that merge cyber and EW techniques. According to the RFI apart from the usual profiles, 'electronic countermeasure (ECM) systems on board the COMJAM specialized units need to be able to deceive adversaries by introducing false information into the enemy's communications' network and degrading enemy communications'. This kind of capability is akin to what the United States is looking for in its next generation jammer (NGJ) initiative wherein mutating algorithms are sought to be 'fired' through the aperture of enemy radar antennae to take over as 'system administrator' or at least 'infect' the enemy's network. Of course technologies of this kind are being developed by the US under the aegis of a program known as Senior Suter.

On the other hand the IAF wants the electronic support measures (ESM) used by the SIGINT aircraft to have the ability 'to intercept, identify, fingerprint and locate the source of electromagnetic emissions from radars, ECMs, Identification Friend or Foe/Successor interrogators (1030 mhz), transponders (1090 mhz), Tactical air navigation/Distance Measuring Equipment interrogators signals (1025-1150 mhz) and communication signals.' Making these acquisitions a full blown intelligence surveillance reconnaissance (ISR) buy is the fact that seven of the aircraft for their 'aerial survey' role will have to be outfitted with 'microprocessor-based high-performance aerial survey camera systems with camera magazines, gyro-stabilized mounts, cockpit displays and automatic GPS-controlled photo flight systems. '

For COMJAM missions the IAF requires that the aircraft have enough space to accommodate up to five operator workstations and other related equipment with the overall ability to carry up to 10 passengers.

This requirement to carry up to 10 passengers represents an enlargement of mission requirements compared to what was laid out in a previous RFP issued in 2009 for this same procurement category which had seen Embraer and Israel Aerospace Industries (IAI) shortlisted with both vendors offering ELTA's EL/I-3001 Airborne Integrated Signal Intelligence System (AISIS) mission system. That time over the Ministry of Defence (MoD) cancelled the RFP since vendors escalated prices based on an apparent lack of clarity in India's offset policy at the time.

This time over both Embraer and IAI are likely to bid again offering ELTA's AISIS which clearly has found favour with the IAF once before. In the words of its manufacturer 'AISIS is an aircraft mounted suite designed to perform long-range, high-endurance missions thus providing tactical and strategic intelligence. The system comprises ELINT (Electronic Intelligence) and COMINT (Communications Intelligence) sensors to search, intercept, measure, locate, analyze, classify and monitor communication and radar transmissions. The Electronic Order of Battle (OEB) picture generated by the EL/I-3001 suite is transmitted in real-time to ground stations for its exploitation via secure line-of-sight data-links, satellite communications and/or HF/VHF/UHF radio sets.' Elta also claims that the system is 'optimized' to effectively deal with low probability of intercept transmission sources and is of course in use with the Israeli defence forces.

Now the last time over Embraer offered a derivative of the EMB-145 with the pull of commonality of platform between these proposed special mission aircraft and the DRDO developed AEW&C currently in the process of being inducted by the IAF. On the other hand IAI had chipped in with the Gulfstream G200 which it manufactures under license in Israel. This time over IAI may offer the new super mid-size it is building- the Gulfstream G280. Indeed G280 based EW platforms are being touted by IAI as an affordable way forward in procuring special mission aircraft.

Affordability will certainly be a key factor in determining success in this tender, given that it has already been shot down by the MoD once before on those grounds. More than the mission systems the basic cost of the airframe and integration both of which are to be done by the airframe provider are likely to carry the day. Thus vendors who have cobbled up such offerings before with decent maintenance support will have a good chance at winning this tender. Of course, given the requirement for a larger aircraft as compared to the previous tender and current prices it remains to be seen how much more than the ball park 1100 crores would the Indian government be willing to expend on this proposal. Naturally something like a Gulfstream G550 based offering is ruled out because that would inflate costs rather considerably. On the other hand G280 sized jets are likely to be in the sweet spot for this tender. Apart from Embraer and IAI, Saab too is likely to bid again even though it was not down-selected the last time over.

From the US, offerings are likely to be made by Hawker Beechcraft in partnership with Raytheon, L-3 communications, Lockheed Martin or Boeing who will provide the mission package. Hawker Beechcraft's Hawker 800 after all already serves in a similar role with the South Koreans with eight specially-equipped aircraft delivered back in 2000. Of course the mission systems providers could also team up with other super mid-size manufacturers such as Bombardier or Cessna. L-3 communications Mission Integration Division (MID) in Greenville, Texas has racked up successes in the special mission space in recent times by integrating ISR capabilities on to business aircraft and is executing a contract for the Saudis along with Hawker Beechcraft at the moment besides on going work with the US Air force on 'Project Liberty'. Incidentally ARC's first SIGINT platform, a Boeing 707 SIGINT, was originally modified for the role by then-US contractor E-Systems which has since then been subsumed by Raytheon.

But participation from US manufacturers, one suspects, may also depend on how much the Indians are willing to pay in the final analysis. For India, familiarity with a manufacturer and technology sharing are likely to be very important considerations for this tender. In that sense Embraer and IAI are probably ahead. In any case successfully completing this tender within a decent timeframe will certainly go a long way in dealing with the constant needling that India's neighbours are resorting to on both fronts.

INDIAN BALLISTIC MISSILE DEFENCE PROGRAMME

The Indian Ballistic Missile Defence Programme is an initiative to develop and deploy a multi-layered ballistic missile defence system to protect India from ballistic missile attacks.

Introduced in light of the ballistic missile threat from Pakistan, it is a double-tiered system consisting of two interceptor missiles, namely the Prithvi Air Defence (PAD) missile for high altitude interception, and the Advanced Air Defence (AAD) Missile for lower altitude interception. The two-tiered shield should be able to intercept any incoming missile launched 5,000 kilometers away.

PAD was tested in November 2006, followed by AAD in December 2007. With the test of the PAD missile, India became the fourth country to have successfully developed an Anti-ballistic missile system, after United States, Russia, Israel. On March 6, 2009, India again successfully tested its missile defence shield, during which an incoming "enemy" missile was intercepted at an altitude of 75 km.

Background

Since the early 90s, India has faced the threat of ballistic missile attacks from Pakistan against which it has fought multiple wars in the past and also from China.

With the heightening of tensions in the region, and in response to Pakistan's deployment of M-11 missiles bought from China, in August 1995, the Indian Government procured six batteries of Russian S-300 Surface-to-air missiles to protectNew Delhi and other cities.

In May 1998, India for the second time (since its first test in 1974) tested nuclear weapons (*see Pokhran-II*), followed by Pakistan with its first ever nuclear test. With Pakistan's testing of nuclear weapons and missile delivery systems, this threat intensified. India has also developed and tested missile delivery systems.

In 1999, the Kargil War between India and Pakistan became the first direct conflict between two declared nuclear powers. As the war progressed, the first hint of the possible use of a nuclear weapon was on May 31, when Pakistani foreign secretary Shamshad Ahmadmade a statement warning that an escalation of the limited conflict could lead Pakistan to use "any weapon" in its arsenal.

This was immediately interpreted as an obvious threat of a nuclear retaliation by Pakistan in the event of an extended war.

The leader of Pakistan's senate noted that "the purpose of developing weapons becomes meaningless if they are not used when they are needed." Some experts believe that following nuclear tests in 1998, Pakistani military was emboldened by its nuclear deterrent cover to markedly increase coercion against India.

Development of an anti-ballistic missile system began in late 1999, suggesting that India initiated the program in light of Pakistan's eschewing of a nuclear No first use policy and heightened tensions during the Kargil war including a possibility of full scale nuclear war.

DEVELOPMENT

Phase 1

Development of the anti-ballistic missile system began in 1999. Around 40 public and private companies were involved in the development of the systems. They include Bharat Electronics Ltd and Bharat Dynamics Ltd, Astra Microwave, ASL, Larsen & Toubro, Vem Technologies Private Limited and KelTech. Development of the LRTR and MFCR (Multi-function Fire Control Radar) was led by Electronics and Radar Development Establishment (LRDE).

Defence Research and Development Laboratory (DRDL) developed the mission control software for the AAD missile. Research Centre, Imarat (RCI) developed navigation, electromechanical actuation systems and the active radar seeker. Advanced System Laboratory (ASL) provided the motors, jet vanes and structures for the AAD and PAD. High Energy Materials Research Laboratory (HEMRL) supplied the propellants for the missile.

Description

The two-tiered BMD System consists of the PAD, which will intercept missiles at exo-atmospheric altitudes of 50–80 km (31–50 mi) and the AAD missile for interception at endoatmospheric altitudes of up to 30 km (19 mi). The deployed system would consist of many launch vehicles, radars, Launch Control Centres (LCC) and the Mission Control Centre (MCC). All these are geographically distributed and connected by a secure communication network.

The MCC is the software intensive system of the ballistic missile defence system. It receives information from various sources such as radars and satellites which is then processed by ten computers which run simultaneously. The MCC is connected to all other elements of the defence through a WAN. MCC performs target classification, target assignment and kill assessment. It also acts as a decision support system for the commander. It can also decide the number of interceptors required for the target for an assured kill probability. After performing all these functions, the MCC assigns the target to the LCC of a launch battery. The LCC starts computing the time to launch the interceptor based upon information received from a radar based on the speed, altitude and flight path of the target. LCC prepares the missile for launch in real time and carries out ground guidance computation. After the interceptor is launched, it is provided target information from the radar through a datalink. When the interceptors close onto the target missile, it activates the radar seeker to search for the target missile and guides itself to intercept the target. Multiple PAD and AAD interceptors can be launched against a target for high kill probability.

Prithvi Air Defence (PAD) / Pradyumna Ballistic Missile Interceptor

The Prithvi Air Defence (PAD) is an anti-ballistic missile developed to intercept incoming ballistic missiles outside of the atmosphere (exo-atmospheric). Based on the Prithvi missile, PAD is a two stage missile with a maximum interception altitude of 80 km (50 mi). The first stage is a Solid fuelled motor while the second stage is Liquid fuelled. It has maneuver thrusters which can generate a lateral acceleration of more than 5 *g*s at 50 km (31 mi) altitude. Guidance is provided by an intertial navigation system with mid-course updates from LRTR and active radar homing in the terminal phase. PAD has capability to engage the 300 to 2,000 km (190 to 1,240 mi) class of ballistic missiles at a speed of Mach 5. LRTR is the target acquisition and fire control radar for the PAD missile. It is an active phased array radar having capability to track 200 targets at a range of 600 km (370 mi). The PAD missile has also been called *Pradyumna*.

Further development led to the improvement of the interception range to the 80 to 50 km (50 to 31 mi) range. The improved missile will utilize a gimbaled directional warhead, a technology that until now has only been used by the US and Russia. This technology allows for a smaller warhead to destroy the target missile.

Prithvi Air Defence Exercise

The PADE (Prithvi Air Defence Exercise) was conducted on November 2006 in which a PAD missile successfully intercepted a modified Prithvi-II Missile at an altitude of 50 km (31 mi). The Prithvi-II ballistic missile was modified successfully to mimic the trajectory of M-11 missiles.

DRDO plans to test the anti-ballistic shield against missiles with a range of 1,500 km (930 mi). The test will be conducted with a modified Prithvi missile launched from a naval ship and the anti-ballistic missile launched from Wheeler Island. The interception of the target missile will take place at approximately 80 km (50 mi) altitude.

On March 6, 2009 DRDO carried out a second successful test of the PAD interceptor missile. The target used was ship launched Dhanush missile which followed the trajectory of a missile with range of a 1,500 km (930 mi). The target was tracked by Swordfish (LRTR) radar and destroyed by the PAD at 75 km (47 mi) altitude.

On March 6, 2011 DRDO successfully test-fired interceptor missile from Advanced Air Defence(AAD) which destroyed a 'hostile' target ballistic missile, a modified Prithvi, at an altitude of 16 km over the Bay of Bengal. Advanced Air Defence (AAD) missile positioned at Wheeler Island, about 70 km across sea from Chandipur, received signals from tracking radars installed along the coastline and travelled through the sky at a speed of 4.5 Mach to destroy it.

Advanced Air Defence (AAD)/Ashwin Ballistic Missile Interceptor

Advanced Air Defence (AAD) is an anti-ballistic missile designed to intercept incoming ballistic missiles in the endo-atmosphere at an altitude of 30 km (19 mi). AAD is single stage, solid fuelled missile. Guidance is similar to that of PAD: it has an inertial navigation system, midcourse updates from ground based radar and active radar homing in the terminal phase. It is 7.5 m (25 ft) tall, weighs around 1.2 t (1.2 long tons; 1.3 short tons) and a diameter of less than 0.5 m (1 ft 8 in).

On 6 December 2007, AAD successfully intercepted a modified Prithvi-II missile acting as an incoming ballistic missile enemy target. The endo-atmospheric interception was carried out at an altitude of 15 km (9.3 mi). The interceptor and all the elements performed in a copy book fashion validating the endo-atmospheric layer of the defence system. The launch was also shown through a video link at a control room of DRDO at Bhawan, Delhi.

The sequence of events of the test was as follows. At 11 a.m. the Prithvi missile lifted off from Launch Complex III at the Integrated Test Range (ITR) at Chandipur Orissa. Radars at Konark, Paradip detected the missile and were continuously tracking it. The target information was sent to MCC for further processing. MCC classified the target, calculated the trajectory of the missile and assigned the target to a AAD battery located on Wheeler Island, 70 km (43 mi) across the sea from Chandipur. The AAD was launched when the Prithvi reached an apogee of 110 km (68 mi). The AAD with the help of midcourse updates and its terminal seeker manoeuvres itself towards the target. AAD makes a direct hit at an altitude of 15 km (9.3 mi) and at a speed of Mach 4. Radars detected formation of a large number of tracks, signifying that the target had broken into multiple pieces. The thermal cameras located on Wheeler Island also picked up the direct hit through thermal images.

Due to two successful interceptor missile tests carried out by India, the scientists have said that the AAD missile could be modified into a new extended range (up to 150 km (93 mi)) surface-to-air missile that could be possibly named as 'Ashvin'.

On 15 March 2010, AAD interceptor missile test from the Orissa coast on Monday was aborted, as the target missile deviated from its path and plunged into the sea. The AAD missile was to intercept the target at an altitude of 15 to 20 km over the sea. The target, a Prithvi missile, fired at 10:02 am from a mobile launcher from the Integrated Test Range Complex-3 at Chandipur-on-Sea, 15 km from here, deviated from its trajectory after traveling about 11 km and fell into the sea.

On 26 July 2010, AAD was successfully test-fired from the Integrated Test Range (ITR) at Wheeler Island off the Orissa's east coast.

On 6 March 2011, India launched its indigenously developed interceptor missile from the Orissa coast. India successfully test-fired its interceptor missile which destroyed a 'hostile' target ballistic missile, a modified Prithvi, at an altitude of 16 km over the Bay of Bengal. the interceptor, Advanced Air Defence (AAD) missile positioned at Wheeler Island, about 70 km across sea from Chandipur, received signals from tracking radars installed along the coastline and travelled through the sky at a speed of 4.5 Mach to destroy it. As the trial was aimed at achieving the desired result with precision, the interceptor missile had its own mobile launcher, secure data link for interception, independent tracking and homing capabilities and sophisticated radars. "It was a fantastic launch. The trial, conducted from two launch sites of ITR off Orissa coast for developing a full fledged multi-layer Ballistic Missile Defence (BMD) system, was fully successful," he said.

On 10 February 2012, AAD was again successfully test-fired from Wheeler Island off the state coast near Dhamra in Bhadrak district, about 170 km from Bhubaneswar.

On 23 November 2012, India again successfully testfired its home-made supersonic Advanced Air Defence (AAD) interceptor missile from a defence base off the coast of the eastern state of Orissa. "The testfiring was part of India's efforts to create a missile defence shield against incoming enemy missiles. The AAD interceptor missile, which was fired from the Wheeler Island off the Orissan coast, successfully destroyed mid-air an incoming ballistic missile launched from the Integrated Test Range in Chandipur, about 70 km from the Wheeler Island."

Swordfish RADAR

Swordfish is the target acquisition and fire control radar for the BMD system. The LRTR currently has a range of 600 km (370 mi) to 800 km (500 mi) and can spot objects as small as a cricket ball. The DRDO plans to upgrade the capacity of Swordfish to 1,500 km by 2011.

Phase 2

Two new anti ballistic missiles that can intercept IRBMs are being developed. These high speed missiles (AD-1 and AD-2) are being developed to intercept ballistic missiles with a range of around 5,000 km (3,100 mi). The test trials of these two systems are expected to take place in 2011. The new missile will be similar to the THAAD missile deployed by the U.S.A. These missiles will travel at hypersonic speeds and will require radars with scan capability of over 1,500 km (930 mi) to successfully intercept the target. On 6 May 2012, Dr. V. K. Saraswat while confirming the completion of Phase-I added that Phase-II would be completed by 2016 to protect against missiles having range up to 5000 km.

India is also planning to develop a laser based weapon system as part of its defence to intercept and destroy missiles soon after they are launched towards the country. DRDO's Air Defence Programme Director V. K. Saraswat says its ideal to destroy a ballistic missile carrying nuclear or conventional warheads in its boost phase. Saraswat further added that it will take another 10–15 years for the premier defence research institute to make it usable on the ground.

PDV

In 2009, reports emerged of a new missile named the PDV. The DRDO is developing a new Prithvi interceptor missile codenamed PDV. It will be a two-stage missile and both the stages will be powered by solid propellants. It will have an innovative system for controlling the vehicle at an altitude of more than 150 km The PDV is intended to replace the existing PAD in the PAD/AAD combination. It will have anIIR seeker for its kill vehicle as well. The PDV will replace the PAD with a far more capable missile and will complete the Phase 1 of the BMD system, allowing it to be operational by 2013. Whereupon Phase 2 development will take over for protection against missiles of the 5,000 km (3,100 mi) range class. The first test flight of the missile was expected in 2010. The PDV is designed to take out the target missile at altitudes above 150 km (93 mi).

Cooperation offered by United States

According to US Deputy Defence Secretary Ashton Carter, there is a potential for cooperation with India to develop a Ballistic Missile Defence (BMD) shield. "That is an important potential area for our future cooperation," Carter said while on his visit to India in July 2012.

Deployment

According to scientist V. K. Saraswat of DRDO the missiles will work in tandem to ensure a hit probability of 99.8 percent. On 6 May 2012, Dr. V. K. Saraswat confirmed that Phase-I is complete and can be deployed to protect two Indian cities at a short notice. He also added that Phase-I is comparable to PAC-3 system. New Delhi, the national capital, and Mumbai, have been selected for the ballistic missile defence shield. After successful implementation in Delhi and Mumbai, the system will be used to cover other major cities in the country. This shield can destroy incoming ballistic missiles launched from as far as 2,500 km away. When the Phase II is completed and PDV is developed, the two anti-ballistic missiles can intercept targets up to 5,000 km both at exo and endo-atmospheric (inside the atmosphere) regions. The missiles will work in tandem to ensure a hit probability of 99.8 per cent.

Criticisms

"India's BMD could indeed be destabilising, as this would substantially reduce the value of Pakistan's nuclear and missile arsenal, tempting it to increase the same." —Air Vice-Marshal (retd) Kapil Kak

Kapil Kak states that it is indeed "surprising" to see the IAF not closely involved with the project.

Non-proliferation experts are appalled at the lack of any visible "political guidance" to the BMD. The obvious response of an adversary to a missile shield is to field greater numbers of missiles with nuclear weapons; that seems to be the track Pakistan is following.

MIT scholar Christopher Clary, "Indian policymakers must be willing to make the calculation that whatever safety comes from missile defences of dubious effectiveness outweighs the risks that come from a Pakistani nuclear arsenal that is larger than it would be without Indian missile defences."

INDIAN MISSILE DEFENCE PROGRAM ADVANCES

India also has tested the sea-launched version of the hypersonic Brahmos cruise missile, jointly developed with Russia. In addition, air- and submarine-launched versions of the Brahmos missile are in development.

Indian media reports suggest that a test of a new high-altitude anti-missile interceptor will occur in January and that India may soon test a submarine-launched ballistic missile (SLBM) for the first time, bringing the country closer to possessing a triad of nuclear weapons delivery systems.

India's nuclear-armed neighbours, China and Pakistan, have significant cruise and ballistic missile capabilities. China has taken steps to acquire missile defence capabilities although Pakistan apparently has not attempted to do so. In the past, Pakistan has justified its pursuit of cruise missiles by citing their supposed invulnerability to Indian ballistic missile defences. China possesses SLBMs, and China and Pakistan are able to deliver nuclear weapons by airplane.

The Chinese and Pakistani reaction to Indian missile defence developments is not yet clear, said Rajeswari Pillai Rajagopalan, a senior fellow at the New Delhi-based Observer Research Foundation. "The new capabilities and counter-capabilities add to the already vexed issue of arms race[s] in Asia," Rajagopalan, a former assistant director of India's National Security Council Secretariat, said in a Dec. 19 e-mail to *Arms Control Today*.

In a Dec. 19 analysis for the Institute for Defence Studies and Analyses, where he is a senior fellow, Vivek Kapur, a group captain in the Indian air force, said that "ballistic missile proliferation in India's neighbourhood requires the development of a more capable" missile defence system.

In the Nov. 23 press release, the Defence Research and Development Organisation (DRDO), the Indian government entity responsible for developing offensive and defensive missile and other systems, said the Advanced Air Defence (AAD) interceptor destroyed a target missile, a modified Prithvi ballistic missile, at an altitude of 15 kilometers.

The interceptor and target missile were launched from sites in Orissa, a state in the eastern part of the country. In the press release, the DRDO said it had demonstrated an ability to track and destroy multiple incoming ballistic missiles.

Rajagopalan said India's efforts are "primarily driven by the threat of short-range missiles in Pakistan"; Chinese missile threats "did not figure prominently in the Indian calculation for a missile defence shield," she said.

The Pakistani government has not issued an official reaction to the AAD interceptor test. Pakistan, however, successfully tested a nuclear-capable Hatf-5, a 1,300-kilometer-range ballistic missile, on Nov. 28. A Pakistani statement following the test of the Hatf-5, also known as the Ghauri, did not mention India specifically, but said the test "strengthens and consolidates Pakistan's deterrence capability." According to the DRDO, the Nov. 23 AAD test demonstrated a capability to intercept ballistic missiles with a range of 1,500 kilometers.

Two-Tiered Defence

India is pursuing a two-tiered missile defence shield, which would give it multiple opportunities to intercept incoming missiles. The AAD interceptor comprises the lower tier, and the higher-altitude, two-stage Prithvi Air Defence (PAD) interceptor currently comprises the upper tier. Like the U.S. Patriot system, both of these Indian systems intercept ballistic missiles in the so-called terminal phase, in which the incoming missiles are descending toward their target.

India first tested the AAD interceptor in December 2007 and, according to the Indian government, has conducted several subsequent tests. India first tested the higher-altitude Prithvi interceptor in November 2006 and again in March 2009. The test reportedly planned for January is of the Prithvi Defence Vehicle, which would be capable of interceptions at a much higher altitude than the PAD interceptor, and may eventually replace that interceptor as the upper tier of the Indian system.

The Indian government has not announced the area that the missile defence system is designed to protect. Media reports have indicated that New Delhi and Mumbai will be the first sites, with the system expanded to protect additional cities later in the decade.

According to the DRDO press release, the AAD interceptor used an explosive warhead to destroy the target missile as the interceptor approached it. In contrast, most U.S. missile defence systems, including the Ground-Based Midcourse Defence and sea-based Aegis systems, rely on "hit-to-kill" interceptors that destroy a target solely through impact.

Eyeing Iron Dome

In addition to developing an anti-ballistic missile capability, India has expressed an interest in purchasing and perhaps producing a domestic variant of the Israeli Iron Dome anti-rocket system, according to the U.S.-based *Defence News*. The Israel Defence Forces claim Iron Dome successfully intercepted 84 percent of rockets fired at Israeli population centres last November during Operation Pillar of Defence, which was intended to halt rocket attacks from groups in Gaza.

In the past, India has expressed interest in purchasing the Israeli Arrow-2 ballistic missile defence system. New Delhi bought two Israeli Green Pine missile defence radars, used for tracking incoming ballistic missiles, in 2002 and 2005. The Swordfish Long Range Tracking Radar, which was used in the AAD test, is based in part on the Green Pine radar.

India and the United States pursued missile defence cooperation during the administration of U.S. President George W. Bush, but such efforts have been less prominent under the Obama administration. Last July, U.S. Deputy Secretary of

Defence Ashton Carter said India and the United States intend to discuss missile defence cooperation, calling it "an important future area for our cooperation." India and the United States should discuss the issue "strategically before they discuss it technically," he said.

WAR-FIGHTING DOCTRINES

The first decade of the century was an unusual period for the IA. There were lessons to be learnt from operations Vijay and Parakram, even as five force headquarters (about 75,000 troops) remained committed on counter insurgency (CI) in J&K. Repeated incursions by the PLA across the LAC demanded attention. The IA was most affected by these transgressions; it needed to worry about its own defunct infrastructure vis-à-vis PLA's excellent border management, capability and capacity-building and likely intentions. Then there were cogent reports of increasing PLA footprints in Pakistan Occupied Kashmir.

The biggest challenge for IA has been to develop its doctrines against Pakistan and China without assistance from the two desired quarters: government and other two services. Considering that military threat from Pakistan has been traditional, the IA continues with its military posture of 'strategic defence and operational level offence(s)', with two changes. Called the pro-active or Cold Start war-fighting strategy, the changes aspire to reduce mobilisation time of offensive forces vis-à-vis Pakistan's strike forces, and have sought to guestimate Pakistan's nuclear weapons red lines in each theatre of likely operations (FORCE December 2011 issue). In truth, the wrought changes are unrealistic. Senior army commanders accede in private that mobilisation time of strike formations as witnessed during Operation Parakram can best be reduced from 22 days to 14 days. Lesser mobilisation period requires building cantonment infrastructure close to the border which is unlikely to happen soon if at all. Even this cannot match Pakistan's advantage of elongated geography; it can mobilise its holding and strike formations in 96 hours simultaneously. On nuclear weapons' red lines, this will eventually be decided by the political and not the army leadership. Past experience of both Operation Parakram and 26/11 attacks suggests that unless pushed to the wall as in the case of Operation Vijay, the political leadership does not have the stomach to fight nuclear Pakistan.

In contrast, the Pakistan Army (PA) has changed its war-fighting strategy drastically after the arrival of nuclear weapons. Anyone who has followed the pattern of warfare between India and Pakistan understood the three distinct stages of war over Kashmir: political subversion, an attack by infiltration, leading to a limited, high intensity conventional war (third generation warfare) where both armies matched one another at the operational level of war for a limited conflict. A mix of each phase in varying proportions is discernible in the 1948 and 1965 wars over Kashmir. Irrespective of the territorial gains made by either side, a compromise was always struck under pressure from outside powers and gains made on the battlefield were lost on the negotiating table in the aftermath of the war. This led to the realisation in Pakistan that a limited war, if taken to the third phase, becomes counter-productive. With the coming of nuclear weapons, the PA adopted the fourth generation warfare, where regular and irregular forces retain flexibility. The irregular (terrorists) forces under the Inter-Services-Intelligence (ISI) could act independently, as well as become the vanguard for conventional forces. The 1999 Kargil war (called Operation Badr by PA) was the litmus test for this doctrine. In PA's assessment, the new doctrine worked well. While keeping the two forces separate, the need was for the top commander to understand their sequential employment. This explains why General Ashfaq Kayani is the first army chief to have had tenures as DG, ISI and DG, Military Operations. With the arrival of ballistic missiles and nuclear weapons, possibility of conventional war has been further curtailed as certainty of achieving worthwhile political objectives has diminished. The biggest benefit of the new doctrine for the PA is that, unlike India, it has little reason to go to war. Its war by irregular forces continues, and should India decide to retaliate, it would be labelled as the aggressor. How has the IA coped with PA's fourth generation doctrine? While continuing to prepare fitfully for the last war, it has built a fence around it and is diligently combating terrorism within J&K.

The PLA threat is new and has been read differently by the three services. The Indian Navy is concerned about the growing PLAN (People Liberation Army's Navy) influence in the Indian Ocean, the IAF is focussed on PLAAF (Peoples Liberation Army's Air Force) capabilities, and the IA has been left to itself to safeguard the sanctity of the disputed border. So divergent is PLA threat to the three services' headquarters that the COSC till date does not have a combined assessment on Chinese military threat. In a largely single-service driven assessment, the army headquarters finally persuaded the defence minister, A.K. Antony to issue his five-yearly directive due in February 2009 differently. Without many details, the directive has asked the defence services to prepare capabilities for a two-front threat: Pakistan and China. Unlike the 1980 interaction between Prime Minister Indira Gandhi and her army chief, this time around it was a bottom-up approval primarily meant as government stamp for financial clearance of defence services' procurements.

According to IA's assessment, India desires a non-confrontationist posture against China, which is considered a powerful neighbour. This means that the IA will patrol well short of its perceived territory, and it hopes that the PLA will not transgress its territorial sovereignty. Should the PLA continue to violate India's borders, beyond a point, it is feared, this may snowball into conflict. Thus, as in the past, disputed border would be the likely reason for crisis turning into conflict. To avoid this from happening, the IA has adopted the military posture of 'Strategic defence and tactical offence.' The government seems to share the IA's independent assessment that border violations may lead to confrontation. To ensure this does not happen, New Delhi hopes to sign an agreement on joint boundary mechanism at the 15th round of bilateral special representatives' talks expected in beginning 2012. The mechanism aims to establish direct contact between New Delhi and Beijing to curb needless escalation over LAC misperceptions.

This will reinforce existing communication channels between local commanders.

India's anxiety that this agreement be signed soonest stems from the assessment that in case of a conflict with China, Pakistan would most certainly open its front against India, leading to the nightmarish scenario of a two-front war. The reverse, India believes, is unlikely. In a war with Pakistan, China is expected to support its ally diplomatically and with military wherewithal only. China, it is reasoned is unlikely to take advantage of an India-Pakistan war. So confident is the IA about this scenario that it has dovetailed employment of four dual-use division-sized formations in a war with Pakistan. According to IA top sources, once the recently-sanctioned four mountain divisions against China are fully raised, it will be possible to move equal numbers of mountain divisions from China to Kashmir. These dual-use divisions would not require re-equipment and conversion training as they would already be on mountain division war establishment tables, and would be adept at fighting in mountains.

As in case of Pakistan, the IA appears to be preparing for the last war, the 1962 war and the 1987 Sumdorong Chu crisis, with China. Its war-fighting strategy of 'Strategic defence and tactical level offence', is meant to defend areas of vital interest with limited offensive capability. One such is Tawang (to be defended at all costs), held by a division, with its 190 mountain brigade holding defences ahead of Tawang round the year at heights between 10,000 to 15,000 feet. The Chinese troops (border guards, equivalent of India's paramilitary forces) facing Tawang has at least 10 tactical advantages.

One, unlike Indian troops that require three-stage acclimatisation (minimum 14 days) each time they come to occupy forward defences, the Chinese on the Tibetan plateau at 16,000 feet and above are already acclimatised.

Two, the Chinese rely on technology much more than the Indian side. They use fully networked tactical surveillance means which are monitored regularly.

Three, the fact that border guards and not regular PLA soldiers are sparsely manning forward posts puts Indian troops under psychological pressure.

Four, between forward defences and PLA regiment headquarters, located way behind, Chinese have huge barren flat ground suggesting reliance on Rapid Reaction Divisions (RRDs).

Five, in the absence of roads and tracks, Indian troops walk from a few hours to two days from Tawang road-head to reach their posts carrying essentials.

Six, Chinese have excellent road communications to all forward posts. The PLA has capability to bring three to four RRDs on the Tawang sector in short time.

Seven, the Indian side lacks essential artillery, both for the contact battle and for interdiction in depth.

Eight, while there is a shortage of forward ammunition dumps, airlifting in case of a crisis poses myriad challenges. Given that land communication are similar to what existed during the 1987 Sumdorong Chu crisis, ammunition worth crores of rupees was lost then as retrieving it after the crisis was not found cost-effective.

Nine, extreme cold, broken terrain and fast changing weather plays havoc with electronic equipment, artillery firing and ISR capabilities. Unlike China, India does not have space-based ISR assets.

And lastly, the build-up of follow-on forces would be a formidable exercise.

Notwithstanding shortcomings, field commanders told FORCE that in the event of a border war, they were confident of a stalemate over Tawang. The battle for Tawang will certainly not be a cakewalk for PLA. With the Dalai Lama ensconced in Dharamshala, what good is Tawang for China? Moreover, Beijing, which is pitted against the United States for supremacy in Asia-Pacific, would lose its enigma if it fought a border war with India. China does not desire to conquer or dominate. What it seeks is deference; that nations in Asia-Pacific have respect for China's core concerns of Tibet, Taiwan and South China Sea, and they consult Beijing while formulating their policies. The United States' strategist, Zbigniew Brzezinski in his book, The Grand Chessboard, writes that: "The Chinese word for China — Chung-kuo, or the Middle Kingdom — both conveys the notion of China's centrality in world affairs and reaffirms the importance of national unity. That perspective also implies a hierarchical radiation of influence from the centre to the peripheries, and thus China as the centre expects deference from others."

Consistent with Chinese thinking and diplomacy (FORCE, December 2011 issue), the PLA has embarked on the fifth generation warfare — a rough equivalent of US' smart power, a mixture of hard and soft power — whose singular war-fighting rule is that there are no rules. The fifth generation warfare combines economic, diplomatic, electronic, cyber, space, proxy, military and propaganda tools to exhaust an adversary and weaken his political will so much that he turns deferential towards Beijing. The fifth generation warfare is about conducting successful coercive diplomacy. As Joseph S. Nye warns in his brilliant book, The Future of Power, "If a threat is not credible, it may fail to produce acceptance and it may lead to costs to the reputation of the coercing state", the Chinese believe in multi-prong pressure on an adversary to ensure that the sum-total outcome is the desired one. Once this is understood, it becomes easier to comprehend Beijing's approach towards India. While maintaining relentless pressure on the disputed border, China had adopted a four-pronged approach to coerce India: showcase military might for a border war, entangle India in a disadvantageous economic relationship, support Pakistan fully short of a bilateral defence accord, and permit no political and diplomatic concessions to India.

Regarding a border war in the Himalayas, the PLA has four distinctive operational advantages over the Indian military. The biggest is unity of command. The TAR is a single unit military district which faces IA's four army commands; northern, western, central and eastern. Moreover in India, command of air and land forces needed for successful air-land battle have different operational boundaries. TAR, on the other hand, will have the benefit of getting resources from two neighbouring military regions, Chengdu and Lanzhou each of which maintains RRDs for quick deployment. All air regiments of PLAAF located in Chengdu and Lanzhou are under the command of the overall commander of the military region. This is not all. Learning lessons on 'jointness' from the successful US 1991 Iraq war, the PLA has evolved improved Group Armies (GA) for its military regions; all GA's have combat, combat support and combat service support or organic logistics under a single commander. Thus, a single PLA commander commands all land forces and air forces in his theatre.

The second operational advantage is that the PLA has concentrated on force multipliers: electronic support measures, defensive and offensive electronic warfare equipment, battlefield command and control systems, increased surveillance capabilities on the battlefield, precision guided munitions, and innovative fire application means to name a few. The third advantage concerns operational logistics. Considering that local resources of food, oils and lubricants are scare on the TAR, the PLA has found an interesting solution. They have emplaced a number of logistics brigades in TAR, which will hold fast-expending commodities including fuel and ammunition stocked and dumped overtime. This brilliant logistics plan will help overcome the organisational weakness of PLA divisions whose manpower is combat heavy with a limited logistics component. The last but not the least, PLA's advantage is preponderance of conventional ballistic missiles. The conventional missile forces (CMF) are consistent with PLA's high-tech warfare where an important requirement is massive firepower. Such thinking has obliged the PLA to have greater terminal accuracy of missiles, and to integrate them into theatre (regional army) united campaign programmes. The CMFs will be employed in conjunction with the PLAAF to allow the latter to retain sorties for achieving air superiority.

The strategic advantages of PLA as an important component of government, and its strategic sustenance system for timely procurements are well known and require little elaboration. What needs emphasis is that in a Himalayan border war, outside powers will be reluctant to intervene and India will have to handle things all by itself. There is thus an urgency to demystify Chinese soldier, especially for Indian political leadership which has not got over the 1962 debacle trauma. More to the point they do not want to resurrect the politico-military debate, a subject they know little about and care even less to learn. This explains why India does not have official military history after the first war of 1948 with Pakistan. Writing account of the 1962 war would require the government to make public the Henderson Brooks' committee report. The two-member committee comprising Lt Gen. T.B. Henderson Brooks as chairman and Maj. Gen (later Lt. General) P.S. Bhagat as member was constituted by defence minister Y.B. Chavan after the war with strict terms of reference. It was to go into the military aspects of the operations only and not concern itself with individual responsibility for the defeat. However, the report submitted to the defence minister in August 1963 would surely have insinuated the political leadership, and indicated how not to conduct politico-military relations. Only a government with courage to reform national security will have the audacity to declassify the report. This is a must for genuine military preparedness against China, the starting point of which could be inclusion of the three service chiefs as regular invitees to the CCS headed by the Prime Minister.

Against this backdrop, it appears that the IA is preparing against Pakistan and China on incongruous turfs. Its capability to cope with fourth and fifth generation warfare necessitates formal political involvement. Once done, this will have the desired consequences: at strategic level, integration of defence services headquarters with the defence ministry, and at operational level, jointness will replace coordination. In the absence of this, the IA has played the safe bet: Transformation, something that the other two services are doing as well.

The thinking at army headquarters is that a war with Pakistan is unlikely; all that is required is expertise in counterterrorism. However, there is the need the keep the powder dry, whatever that means. On China, the view is that as a border war cannot be ruled out, the IA needs to be prepared for three levels of threat. The low level threat would involve five to six divisions, the medium level would comprise 10 to 12 divisions, and the high level threat which is improbable as it would lead to an all-out no-holds bar conflict could involve 18 to 20 PLA divisions. In IA's assessment, the terrain on TAR allows PLA the frontal deployment of maximum 10 to 12 divisions.

Preparing for the PLA border threat has three aspects: IA is raising new divisions. The infrastructure building comprising roads, tracks, defences and storage facilities are under the defence secretary over which the IA has little control. And procurement of equipment is an excruciatingly slow process involving formulation of General Staff Qualitative Requirement, scaling, categorisation, request for proposal, trials and transfer of technology. All this is done under the rubric of IA's long term planning which does not have defined financial underpinning, and annual defence budgets where personalities (relationship of service chiefs with defence ministry mandarins) come into play, and services attempt to get whatever is possible. The biggest casualties of this procedure are the intangibles like stores and ammunition, which requires banishment of the perennial attitude to not lock capital in spares and items that disallow the War Wastage Reserves (WWR) to be maintained optimally. For example, despite claims by ordnance services of fully computerised inventories, it was found after the 1999 Kargil conflict that exact availability of logistics stores and even ammunition was not known. Considering there would be an immediate international clampdown on sales of equipment, stores and ammunition, the IA would need to keep better inventory management.

The other issue that should take precedence are procurements of critical operational gaps. For example, the air defence and artillery are in extremely bad state, the armour and mechanised infantry leaves much to be desired, ISR capabilities including variety of UAVs are nascent, and network centric warfare under the tactical command, control, communication and information system (Tac C3I) is nowhere close to stabilisation. While the latter's sub-systems comprising CIDSS (command information decision support system), ACCCS (artillery command, control and communication system), BSS (battlefield surveillance system), AD&RC (air defence & reporting system), and BMS (battle management system) are in various stages of development and implementation, turf wars are impeding work. Unless the twin issue of WWR and operational gaps are not attended to, the IA will continue to lack credibility for conventional war. The third issue that is intricately related to conventional war is mind-set. The earlier the IA, which prides itself over expertise in counter-insurgency operations, abandons this and goes back to its primary task of fighting external threats, the better.

The IA sees no contradiction in adopting the capability-based approach even when there are threat-based unresolved issues. The IA is not new to the capability-based approach which was first adopted in the Eighties under General K. Sundarji when India had embarked on military activism in the region. Then, 54 division was earmarked to be converted into air assault division; the actual implementation, it seems, will be done now. Given the unique position of IA chief of staff, as senior-most operational commander and procurements manager, it is prudent for him to decide what approach the service should adopt. Should the IA go for transformation (capability-based approach) when the army chief has little interaction with political leadership, there is no jointness between the services, and his authority does not amount to much in procurements matters?

REDUCTION OF FORCE LEVELS AND INCREASED TECHNOLOGY

The IAF has accepted for sometime that the increased costs of maintaining a modern and effective air force in the future would necessitate the need for a reduction in force levels. Consequently, procurement and upgrade programs since the late 1980s have emphasized the need to extract the maximum out of every aircraft. This means two things in practice. First, it means that all existing aircraft will be the subject of upgrades that make them more lethal and enhance survivability. The installation of new radar, avionics, weapons aiming system, electronic warfare suites are all consistent with the IAF's prevailing philosophy. Second, the IAF has decided that all new types of fighters added to inventory will be multi-role-the Su-30MKI and LCA are both designed to meet this requirement.

Where possible, existing platforms are being adapted to multi-role use. Indeed the extensive upgrade package for the MiG-21bis gives it a true multi-role capability. Similarly, trials are in progress to provide upgraded MiG-27s with a secondary air-air capability. The integration of the pod mounted Komar radar will allow the MiG-27 the ability to operate BVR AAMs such as the R-27 and R-77. With the imminent withdrawal of all three of Eastern Air Command's MiG-21FL squadrons, the MiG-27s will have to don the air defence mantle in the east, in the absence of any permanently based air defence units in the region. The quest for additional Mirage 2000s also fits this pattern. It is yet unclear whether the Mig-29 upgrades will bestow the type with multi-role capability.

The IAF's 1990s projection of a leaner meaner force for the beginning of the 21st century is likely to be quite accurate. The force will be meaner and more capable. It is also likely to be smaller. The last remaining MiG-21FL/M squadrons are likely to give up their aircraft in the near future, as is the solitary MiG-23MF squadron. Although the relative age of the latter unit's airframes and the training role that they fill, will likely allow them to outlive the older MiG-21s. If IAF decides to restrict the number of MiG-21bis upgrades to 125 airframes, we could expect to see a more substantial drop in number of operational squadrons. Hypothetically speaking, if procurement and modernization programs remain at present levels, by 2005 we could expect to see total numbers for fighter squadrons decline from the current peak of 39 to 32. The capabilities of newer aircraft ensure that the older MiG-21s need not be replaced one on one (even if cost permitted). For example, a single Su-30 can deliver as much ordnance as a squadron of MiG-21FLs and at greater ranges, and with greater accuracy.

The desire to reduce the multiplicity of combat aircraft types in IAF service is unlikely to produce any significant results for the next decade or so. The retirement of MiG-21 and MiG-23 variants will reduce the number of types in service from 10 to 7. Indeed, as is underscored by the extensive modernization programs, most of these aircraft remain too useful to discard. MiG-21/MiG-23/27/29, Mirage 2000, Jaguars, and Su-30 are likely to fly side by side well into the next decade. And while the multiplicity of types has not adversely affected the IAF's combat performance, it does make logistics more complicated. However, increased commonality between avionics and other sub systems across the fleet is expected to make maintenance and logistics easier than they have ever been. Not only will this fleet be capable of delivering larger amounts ordnance more accurately over greater distances, but can also expect a greater level of survivability thanks to the increasing availability of force multipliers.

Emphasis on Force Multipliers

The IAF has been slow to induct force multipliers. While quick to deploy sizeable numbers of EW, ECM, and Reconnaissance assets, the IAF lacked an in-flight refueling capability and AWACS for years. Until the arrival of the Su-30s, only two aircraft types came with plumbing for in-flight refueling – Jaguars and Mirage 2000s. However, the IAF had the refueling probes of these aircraft removed in service. Until the early 1990s, the IAF remained a largely tactical force in its outlook. The prevailing view was that in case of a war with Pakistan, all major targets could be reached without the need for in-flight refueling. It was envisioned that any conflict with China would remain largely localized, again putting all targets within easy range of its aircraft. However, nuclearization and an expansion in the size of the IAF supporting aircraft forced a reconsideration of this view. The need to deploy specialized aircraft for duties such as Suppression of Enemy Air Defences

(SEAD) and the lengths of time that such aircraft would have to kept airborne created a pressing need for an in-flight fueling capability. The first in-flight refueling trials were conducted between IAF Jaguars and a RAF VC-10 tanker on loan as recently as 1996. Since then, the IAF has placed orders for a number of IL-78 tankers. It is expected that eventually eight such aircraft will be acquired. In the interim, the IAF has inducted UPAZ buddy refueling system for its Su-30s, Mirages, and Jaguars. The MiG fleet too is being equipped with in-flight refueling capability as part of their upgrades. In the context of nuclearization, the introduction of in-flight refueling provides the IAF with a rudimentary, if somewhat less than secure, deterrent capability against China.

The deployment of MiG-21s as airborne radar pickets in 1971, provided the IAF with an early introduction to the benefits of Airborne Early Warning (AEW). Unfortunately, an initial paucity of funds and an eventual inability to find a suitable platform set the IAF's efforts to acquire an AEW/AWACS back by many years. The IAF evaluated the Soviet A-50 in 1988 and rejected it for being incompatible with the existing air defence grid. Recent efforts to build a such a system indigenously has been hampered by the inadequacy of the trials platform (a Hs.748) and the loss of one prototype (of three) along with the R&D team. The need for an AWACS was sorely felt during the Kargil war in 1999. Consequently, the IAF has resumed its search with much vigour. A pair of A-50s with the new Shmel-2 radar was leased from the Russian AF in May of this year to help familiarize the service with operation of such systems. The IAF is reluctant to purchase the A-50 "as is" because, as in 1988, it would be a challenge to integrate the system with the Indian air defence set up. The IAF is also unhappy that some of the information processing for the A-50 has to be done via ground stations. The IAF would like to customize the system with Indian and non-Russian electronic subsystems so that it can be integrated with the Indian air-defence grid with less difficulty. For this reason, it will still be sometime before the IAF fields a viable AWACS/AEW force. The service has a requirement for up to six such aircraft.

There are two further dimensions to the IAF's quest for force multipliers – namely, EW and Reconnaissance. The IAF has rather extensive ELINT gathering and reconnaissance assets available. The bulk of the ELINT aircraft (B707, An-32, and B737) are operated under the auspices of the Aviation Research Center (ARC) and photographic reconnaissance assets are operated by directly by the IAF. Scores of MiG-21MRs and MiG-23BNs form the backbone of the tactical reconnaissance force. For strategic reconnaissance the IAF deploys squadron each of Canberra PR 57/67 and MiG-25Rs, complemented by a few Gulfstream III SRA-1s fitted with oblique cameras, which can look deep into enemy territory. Additionally several types of combat aircraft can be fitted with reconnaissance pods. It is expected that the MiG-21MRs are will be withdrawn in the near future. However, the IAF is looking at potential upgrade packages for the Canberras (both P 67s and B (I) 58 versions) in order to keep these forty-year old aircraft in service until 2010. Most recently, the IAF has acquired the Viten Vicon reconnaissance pods for use in strike squadrons, in order to give then an autonomous reconnaissance capability. The recent introduction of high altitude unmanned aerial vehicles (UAVs) gave the IAF its first significant experience with real-time reconnaissance capability. It is expected that in the next 5-7 years the defence forces will deploy dedicated satellites to enhance their intelligence gathering capabilities.

The IAF accepts the fact that losses in men and materials are to be expected during the course of combat operations. However, the IAF has invested quite heavily in trying to make sure that such losses are kept to a minimum. Budgetary constraints notwithstanding, the IAF has attempted, with some success, to create a comprehensive countermeasures force. Specialized aircraft have been acquired to support strike packages with ECM and ECCM cover. Stocks of anti-radiation systems – both missiles (ARMAT, Kh-25MP, Kh-59) and drones (Harpy) – have been diligently built up for this purpose. A number of MiG-23 airframes have been modified for SEAD duties with ARMs. It is also understood that the both of two-seat Jaguars currently under production will augment existing

SEAD capabilities. The Jaguars greater endurance may have contributed to its selection as the primary EW support aircraft for the future.

IMPROVEMENTS IN C4I AND LAND-BASED AIR DEFENCE

Nuclearization of the Indian subcontinent has important implications for the future of both C4I and land-based air defence. Cognizant of this, the IAF has been working continuously since the early 1990s to shield and harden its communication network/nodes against nuclear attack. This is critical because of the second strike doctrine adopted by India. As the principal operator of India's nuclear weapons, the IAF's C4I network must be able to survive a first strike. In addition to the radiation hardening, it is understood that several levels of redundancy have been built into the network. The IAF has also undertaken the task of incrementally upgrading the strike fleet with EMP shielding.

The IAF already fields a formidable (in a regional context) ground based air defence system. India's air defence network is essentially divided into two parts-the Air Defence Ground Environment System (ADGES) and the Base Air Defence Zones (BADZ). These two components are closely linked and share information relating to air defence tasks. The ADGES and BADZ along with their associated sensor network and SAM units provide India with an extremely potent defence against both Pakistani and Chinese manned aircraft. Additionally, SAMs and fighters of the Navy also defend sensitive nuclear installations along India's western coasts. The ADGES is currently being upgraded with the new Indian and Israeli radar. The Pechora SAMs which form the backbone of the IAF's SAM units are also undergoing upgrades which will see them fitted with more sensitive seeker heads. The IAF is also looking at the Akash to provide it with the next generation SAM. The emerging challenge to the air defence network is defence against ballistic missile attack. Over the last two years, the Indian press has been awash with reports that the government has sanctioned the building of an ATBM defences. The IAF feels that the limited ability of the current sensor network to detect and track missile launches needs to be substantially upgraded. Furthermore, the Russian S-300 SAM is being considered to provide the backbone of ATBM defences. While the system has undergone several trials in India (and may even be deployed in limited numbers), the IAF and the government are wary of relying excessively on the baseline system which has been compromised. Negotiations are underway for Indian to acquire a transfer of technology for the indigenous production of an S-300 derivative with Indian developed electronics and subsystems. It is likely that technology developed for the Akash SAM will be incorporated into any Indian manufactured S-300 derivative. Indeed, it is believed that the Akash SAM and the associated Rajendra phase array radar have some ATBM capability. The creation of an effective ATBM screen is high priority for the IAF but it will be many years before such a screen is operational.

Transports and Helicopters

The IAF has a sizable fixed and rotary winged transport fleet. While not as glamorous as their counterparts in the fighter stream, the IAF transport and helicopter formations contribute more than half of the IAF's annual flying hours. Operating out of some of the world most dangerous and inhospitable airstrips, the IAF's transport and helicopter formations play a crucial role in keeping the Indian Army and Air Force supplied. During last the Kargil operations last year, transport pilots were the unsung heroes of the war-flying day in and day out to maintain an uninterrupted air-bridge to the world's highest battle zone. Indeed post-Kargil the transport squadrons are logging almost 30% more hours than their counterparts in the fighter stream. India's airlift capabilities are significant. The ability to airlift the equivalent of a brigade plus their equipment at a time easily gives the IAF the largest military lift capability in Asia.

Two squadrons of IL-76 provide the IAF with its heavy lift capability, some 1,080,000 kg in all. These aircraft regularly operate out airfields in Ladakh situated at over 10,000 ft above sea level. The IAF is considering replacing the engines of these aircraft with western engines with a view to increasing operating efficiency. Increased logistical commitments in the aftermath of Kargil have caused the IAF to revive plans to add to its IL-76 fleet.

The An-32 from the backbone of the IAF's medium lift capabilities. Originally equipping six operational squadrons and a training unit, several of the type has now been put into storage. The An-32s were hit hard by the chaos in the ex-USSR as spares became harder to obtain.

In response to these problems, the IAF successfully fitted several An-32s with An-12 power plants upon the retirement of the latter, and put a number airframes into storage. Although the spares problem is no longer as acute as in the early 1990s, the IAF has seen fit to keep the type flying with four operational squadrons and prevent wear & tear on the rest. The IAF still maintains one and a half squadrons of Hs.748 military freighters. The retirement of these aircraft in the near future is bound to affect the IAF airlift capabilities. It is not yet clear what aircraft the IAF considering as replacements for the type, although a fleeting interest has been shown in the ATR-42. The An-32s will also need replacements by the end of the decade as spares become harder to come by and airframe life will rapidly expire. The IAF Do-228 light transports are relatively new and the type is still in production in-country and one can expect the type to stick around well into the future.

The IAF helicopter fleet has come a long way from its humble beginnings. The IAF currently operates dozens of helicopter units, including three dedicated attack helicopter units. The "Hip" family is the workhorse of the IAF helicopter fleet. Hundreds of Mi-8/17s fly everything from liaison to assault missions. The Mi-17 fleet was quite active over Kargil and one of the type was lost in action. The recent deal to add 40 new Mi-17-1B helicopters to the IAF, is consistent with the IAF policy to replacing the older Mi-8s with its more modern and powerful stable-mate. A number of Mi-17s are also to be upgraded with sensors such as Forward Looking Infra Red (FLIR) in order to help augment the attack helicopter fleet. The IAF's attack helicopter fleet comprises of between two and three Mi-25/35 units. The Mi-35 recently underwent a comprehensive upgrade in Israel. It is also understood that there is solitary Chetak unit for anti-armour operations. Additionally, the "Hip" family can be fitted with a range of guided and unguided weapons. The IAF flies several Cheetahs and Chetaks in the liaison, SAR, and training roles.

These types will eventually be replaced by Advanced Light Helicopter from Hindustan Aeronautical Limited, that has recently entered production. The IAF also operates a solitary unit of Mi-26 heavy-lift helicopters. The prohibitive cost of operating the type means that they are usually employed on special duties that are beyond the capabilities of other aircraft in the force. There is an ongoing tussle between the Army and IAF, over control of the attack & assault helicopter fleet. The former argues that the optimal deployment of these aircraft is only possible when ownership rests with the service that is expected to benefit from them.

Training

The IAF offers a very rigorous flying training schedule for its pilots. Before being assigned to operational squadrons, pilots are expected to log over 300 hours of flying at the basic, intermediate and advanced levels. However, maintaining the very high standards of training will pose a challenge for the air force in the new century. The problem is particularly acute at the advanced fighter training level. The problem arises form the age and unsuitability of the MiG Operational Flying Training Unit's (MOFTU) aircraft. As of now fighter pilots are expected to log 125 hours on the unit's MiG-21FL and UM before being assigned to squadrons. The some of these aircraft are now over 30 years old and in very poor state of repair. The MiG-21FLs were phased out of Indian production in the mid-1970s hence spares for the type are very difficult to come by. Whatever spares are available are second-hand. Furthermore the early generations of MiG-21s are unforgiving aircraft and pushing over a certain AoA at over 600 knots, sends the aircraft into an uncontrollable spin. Old airframes together with the fact that many IAF pilots go straight from basic training to MiG-21FL/UM explains the high accident rates for the type. In addition to the human cost, this has an unfavorable impact on morale for younger pilots. The IAF has been trying for years to purchase suitable Advanced Jet Trainers (AJT) to ease the transition to high performance aircraft. Both the Hawk and Alpha Jet were evaluated in the 1980s, but funding problems & dithering on the part of the government kept IAF from placing orders. More recently, the IAF has revised its interest in purchasing the Hawk (the Alpha Jet being long out of production). However, Britain's inability (and reluctance) to refurbish Indian Navy Sea Harriers in the face of a US arms embargo have thrown into doubt the UK's ability to provide support for any Hawks that may be purchased. With the acquisition of AJT hanging in the air, the IAF's training problems are likely to get more acute. It is unfortunate that neither the IAF nor the Ministry of Defence has shown any interest in turning the HJT-36 intermediate trainer, now in development, into an AJT.

After a bad patch in the early 1990s, the IAF has been able to restore training in operational squadrons to their normal levels. Increased use of simulators have made a substantial difference to IAF training programs in recent years by making enhancing safety and preserving airframe life. Advanced fighter training has received a boost with the acquisition of Air Combat Maneuvering Instrumentation (ACMI) systems for the Tactics & Air Combat Development Establishment (TACDE) at Jamnagar. TACDE now offers courses in EW and helicopter combat. It also provides Dissimilar Air Combat Training (DACT) facilities to the Sea Harriers of the Navy.

Bibliography

Arend, A.: *International Law and the Use of Force,* London, Routledge, 1993.

Ashton, S.R.: *British Policy Towards the Indian States, 1905-1939,* London, Curzon, 1982.

Bando, Mark A.: *101st Airborne: The Screaming Eagles at Normandy.* Motorbooks International, 2001

Bellamy, C.: *Knights in White Armour: The New Art of War and Peace,* London, Random House, 1997.

Bhaskara Rao: *Military Conversion : Impact on Science and Technology,* Discovery, Delhi, 2003.

Chakravarty, B C Dr.: *Indian Armed Forces - Official History of the 1965 Indo-Pak War.* Ministry of Defence.

Darwin: *A Study of the Aerospace Industry,* North Carolina, Amalie, 1964.

Dixit, Prabla: *Aviation: A Struggle for Power,* New Delhi, Orient Longman, 1981.

Douhet, Giulio: *The Command of the Air.* New York: Coward - McCann, 1942.

Friedman, G.: *The Future of War: Power, Technology and American World Dominance in the 21st Century,* N.Y., Random House, 1996.

Gray, Colin Spencer. *Understanding Airpower,* AFRI: Maxwell, March 2009.

Gupta, SC: *History of the Indian Air Force 1933-45,* Pubications Division, Ministry of Defence, Delhi, 1961.

Halberstadt, Hans: *Army Aviation.* Novato, CA: Presidio Press, 1990.

Holsti, K.: *The State, War, and the State of War,* Cambridge, Cambridge Univ. Press, 1996.

Janowitz, M.: *The Professional Soldier: A Social and Political Portrait,* N.Y., The Free Press, 1960.

Jordan, David: *Air and Space Warfare*, in: Jordan, David et al.: *Understanding Modern Warfare*, Cambridge: Cambridge University Press 2009, p.219

Kapila, AVM Viney: *The Indian Air Force : a balanced strategic and tactical application,* Ocean Books, Delhi, 2002.

Lovering, J.: *Labour and the Defence Industry: An Alliance for Globalisation.* Capital and Class, Delhi, 1998.

Mary, W.: *Asian Power and Politics: the Cultural Dimensions of Authority*, Cambridge, Belknap Press, 1985.

Nair, A. M.: *An Indian Freedom Fighter in Japan*, Bombay, Orient Longman, 1983.

Posen, B.R.: *The Sources of Modernization Military*, Ithaca, 1984, Cornell Univ. Press.

Pushpindar Singh: *Aircraft of the Indian Air Force, 1933-73*, English Book Store, Delhi, 1974.

Rosen, P.: *Societies and Military Power: India and its Armies*, Ithaca, Cornell University Press, 1996.

Rudolph, Heimanson: *Aviation Power*, N.Y.: Oceana Publications, 1967.

Seth, Vijay: *The Flying Machines - Indian Air Force 1933-99.* Seth Communications, Delhi, 2000.

Simon, D. : *Public Administration and Policy of Indian Military*, New York, Knopf, 1950.

Stear, L. : *Design of a Curriculum for Destination Studies*, Annals of Tourism Research, 1981.

Sutton, J., *Technology and Defence Market Structure*, MIT Press, Delhi, 1998.

Tanham, George K.: *The Indian Air Force: Trends & prospects.* Rand, Santa Monica, Delhi, 1995.

Tufail, Kaiser: *Great Air Battles of the PAF.* Ferozesons, Karachi 2004.

Venter, AL J.: *The Chopper Boys: Helicopter Warfare in Africa.* Gibraltar: Ashanti Publishing, 1994.

Vijaya Lakshmi Sharma : *Technology Tools and Aviation Industryy*, Shilpi Publications, Allahabad, 1997

William A.: *An Introduction to the International Criminal Court.* Cambridge: Cambridge University Press, 2007.

Index

D

E

F

H

I

K

M

N

O

P

R

S

T

U

W

❑❑❑